Moodle 2.0 for Business
Beginner's Guide

Implement Moodle in your business to streamline your interview, training, and internal communication processes

Jason Cole

Jeanne Cole

Gavin Henrick

[PACKT] open source*
PUBLISHING   community experience distilled

BIRMINGHAM - MUMBAI

Moodle 2.0 for Business
Beginner's Guide

Copyright © 2011 Packt Publishing

First published: April 2011

Production Reference: 1190411

Published by Packt Publishing Ltd.
32 Lincoln Road
Olton
Birmingham, B27 6PA, UK.

ISBN 978-1-849514-20-0

www.packtpub.com

Cover Image by Asher Wishkerman (a.wishkerman@mpic.de)

Credits

About the Authors

Jason Cole, Ph.D is the Chief Operating Officer for Remote-Learner, US, an official Moodle partner providing hosting, support, and instructional design services. Jason oversees Remote-Learner's daily operations, providing technical services to over 1,100 clients, from small non-profit organizations to Fortune 500 companies.

Jason started using Moodle at San Francisco State University in 2003 when he led the transition from Blackboard to Moodle. Later, he led the implementation of Moodle at the Open University in the UK, currently one of the top three largest Moodle deployments in the world. Over the ensuing two years he successfully architected a system that currently supports over 225,000 student users with multiple enrollments.

Jason is the co-author of Using Moodle (c2006 & 2007) published by O'Reilly Community Press, and has been the organizer of several successful Moodle Conferences in the US and UK.

> I would like to thank my wife, Jeanne, for taking the leap and writing this book with me. Her dedication was an inspiration and her support made the book possible.

Jeanne Cole is a Senior Project Manager for Remote-Learner US. She is an experienced Moodle course developer and project manager who has migrated hundreds of courses from other learning management systems to Moodle, as well as created courses from client materials. She also has experience managing projects applying multiple open source products to meet a wide variety of client needs.

Prior to her Moodle career, Jeanne worked as a project engineer/manager for contractors in the US and UK.

> I would like to thank both of my very experienced and knowledgeable co-authors for giving me the opportunity to work with them on this book. A special thanks to my husband, Jason, for his never-ending patience and support.

Gavin Henrick has worked with technology in business, learning, and development for over ten years. He has been consulting on using Moodle, Mahara, and other open-source applications for the last four years. He has run several websites and runs his own blog (`www.somerandomthoughts.com`). He is a regular speaker at a number of Moodlemoots and conferences on the use of Moodle in the corporate space focusing on practical examples of usage.

Gavin recently joined the Moodle Partner Remote-Learner and is based out of Canada working with a range of organizations in Canada and Europe.

Through working on this book he has learned so much on the diverse and innovative ways of using Moodle to support learning, training, and development.

Firstly I would like to thank Enovation Solutions and Remote-Learner for the opportunity to work with and learn from some fantastic people over the last few years.

I would also like to thank all of the participating organizations for their generosity in contributing the case studies. The case studies in the book will provide inspiration to others as they consider rolling out Moodle.

I would like to thank the Packt editorial team and the book reviewers who provided excellent feedback and direction throughout the editing of the book. You have certainly helped make this a better book.

I would like to thank my co-authors who have taught me so much about writing and about new approaches to using Moodle.

A special thanks to Martin Dougiamas for his vision and dedication to learning and Moodle.

About the Reviewers

Chad Outten has worked as an educator and technologist for more than a dozen years in diverse roles and settings in Australia. He is the Company Director at My Learning Space (www.mylearningspace.com.au), an Australian e-learning solutions provider specializing in expert Consultancy, Hosting, Training, and Support services for learning management systems. They work with numerous organizations in the corporate, education, government, and not-for-profit sectors. Their clients include eBay, Shell, Rip Curl, Queensland Health, and Department of Human Services NSW.

Chad is an active member of the Moodle Community. This includes involvement in the Particularly Helpful Moodlers, and Quality Assurance Testers groups. He was involved as a Moodle certified teacher, mentor, and assessor as part of the internationally recognized Moodle Teacher Certification program. He also organized the Australian Moodle Moot in 2008.

Jordi Piguillem is a Computer Software Engineer by Universitat Politecnica de Catalunya. During the last five years, he has been collaborating on several Moodle projects as a programmer and as a software designer. During Summer '08, he had been working in Google Summer of Code initiative, where he had been developing an IMS LTI compliant client for Moodle. Nowadays, he is working on his PhD about integration of information systems. Due to this research job, he has co-authored several papers about software and service engineering, ubiquitous learning, among other things and collaborated in some books about Moodle and Google App Engine.

I would like to thank the project coordinator for having trusted me to review this book and to my PhD advisors for their assistance.

Mary Cooch (known online as @moodlefairy) is a teacher and VLE trainer based in the UK. She is the author of Moodle 1.9 for Teaching 7-14 Year Olds and Moodle 2.0 First Look also published by Packt. She blogs at www.moodleblog.org and can be contacted for consultation on mco@olchs.lancs.sch.uk. Mary will go anywhere to help you Moodle!

I would like to thank my family for their support and Our Lady's Preston Assistant Headteacher Mark Greenwood, and my Moodle manager, for his tolerance!

www.PacktPub.com

Support files, eBooks, discount offers and more

You might want to visit www.PacktPub.com for support files and downloads related to your book.

Did you know that Packt offers eBook versions of every book published, with PDF and ePub files available? You can upgrade to the eBook version at www.PacktPub.com and as a print book customer, you are entitled to a discount on the eBook copy. Get in touch with us at service@packtpub.com for more details.

At www.PacktPub.com, you can also read a collection of free technical articles, sign up for a range of free newsletters and receive exclusive discounts and offers on Packt books and eBooks.

http://PacktLib.PacktPub.com

Do you need instant solutions to your IT questions? PacktLib is Packt's online digital book library. Here, you can access, read and search across Packt's entire library of books.

Why Subscribe?

- ◆ Fully searchable across every book published by Packt
- ◆ Copy and paste, print and bookmark content
- ◆ On demand and accessible via web browser

Free Access for Packt account holders

If you have an account with Packt at www.PacktPub.com, you can use this to access PacktLib today and view nine entirely free books. Simply use your login credentials for immediate access.

Table of Contents

Preface

Moodle 2.0 for Business will show you how to set up Moodle in your corporation. Think of all the time you could save by putting your existing training material online. Think of the printing costs that you could reduce by putting HR documents on your staff site, and think of the team spirit that could be created by setting up staff forums.

What this book covers

Chapter 1, Getting Started With Moodle introduces you to the background of Moodle. It covers the benefits of using open-source software in business, and how to take your first steps in experimenting with Moodle.

Chapter 2, Moodle in Hiring and Interviewing discusses how to use Moodle to facilitate the hiring and interviewing process. This chapter demonstrates how to use Moodle to accept resumes and job applications, and how to create interviewer resources to support the hiring process.

Chapter 3, Rollout Products and Services with Moodle shows you how to set up a course to cater for product knowledge training. Learn how to set up a glossary and to organize a real-time roleplay using Moodle Chat.

Chapter 4, Moodle for Managing Compliance Training discusses how to deliver compliance training with Moodle. This chapter looks at the Moodle Lesson and how to configure completion tracking for full course completion reporting.

Chapter 5, CPD and Competency Tracking with Moodle explains competencies and how they are used in Moodle. The chapter will shed light on how to use competencies in assessments and how to view them in the gradebook.

Chapter 6, Communities of Practice in Moodle takes a look at building communities with Moodle. You will learn how to set up a wiki, glossary, and database for collaborative projects. You will also learn about how to use roles for specific tasks.

Chapter 7, Web Conferencing with Moodle examines some of the main web conferencing software in use with Moodle and what features and options are available. The chapter covers how to set up and configure two systems with Moodle, BigBlueButton, and Adobe Connect Pro.

Chapter 8, Integrating Moodle with Other Systems introduces a range of systems which can integrate with Moodle including Alfresco, a document management system, Mahara—an e-portfolio platform, and GoogleDocs.

Chapter 9, Integrating Moodle into the Enterprise identifies the authentication options in Moodle. It introduces how enrollment works and how to do basic customizations to the look and feel of your Moodle site.

Who this book is for

If you are responsible for training, recruitment, or maintaining any guidelines within your company, then this book is for you. No previous experience with Moodle is necessary as the examples are easy to follow, although it is assumed that Moodle will be set up and ready to go within your company.

Conventions

In this book, you will find several headings appearing frequently.

To give clear instructions of how to complete a procedure or task, we use:

Time for action – heading

1. Open up your web browser and go to the web page `http://www.moodle.org`.
2. In the top **Menu** you have an option called **Downloads**. Click on this option and select the **Modules and Plugins** option. This brings up the database of modules, and shows the most recent entries in the database.
3. Click on the **Search** Tab.

Instructions often need some extra explanation so that they make sense, so they are followed with:

What just happened?

This heading explains the working of tasks or instructions that you have just completed.

You will also find some other learning aids in the book, including:

Time for reflection

This heading asks the reader to deliberate on the things learned in the previous sections from the point of view of their practical application.

Have a go hero – heading

These set practical challenges and give you ideas for experimenting with what you have learned.

You will also find a number of styles of text that distinguish between different kinds of information. Here are some examples of these styles, and an explanation of their meaning.

Code words in text are shown as follows: "We can include other contexts through the use of the include directive."

A block of code is set as follows:

```
outcome_name;outcome_shortname;outcome_description;scale_name;
scale_items
Mahara Benefits;"Mahara Benefits";"knowledge proficiency";basic,
proficient,advanced
Mahara Description;"Mahara Description";"knowledge proficiency";basic,
proficient,advanced
Mahara Pricing;"Mahara Pricing";"knowledge proficiency";basic,
proficient,advanced
Mahara USP;"Mahara USP";"knowledge proficiency";basic,proficient,
advanced
```

Any command-line input or output is written as follows:

```
# cp /usr/src/asterisk-addons/configs/cdr_mysql.conf.sample
    /etc/asterisk/cdr_mysql.conf
```

New terms and **important words** are shown in bold. Words that you see on the screen, in menus or dialog boxes for example, appear in the text like this: "The **Maximum number of attachments** determines how many attachments a user can add to a forum post."

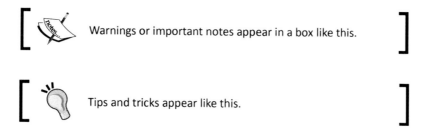

Warnings or important notes appear in a box like this.

Tips and tricks appear like this.

Reader feedback

Feedback from our readers is always welcome. Let us know what you think about this book—what you liked or may have disliked. Reader feedback is important for us to develop titles that you really get the most out of.

To send us general feedback, simply send an e-mail to `feedback@packtpub.com`, and mention the book title via the subject of your message.

If there is a book that you need and would like to see us publish, please send us a note in the **SUGGEST A TITLE** form on `www.packtpub.com` or e-mail `suggest@packtpub.com`.

If there is a topic that you have expertise in and you are interested in either writing or contributing to a book, see our author guide on `www.packtpub.com/authors`.

Customer support

Now that you are the proud owner of a Packt book, we have a number of things to help you to get the most from your purchase.

Errata

Although we have taken every care to ensure the accuracy of our content, mistakes do happen. If you find a mistake in one of our books—maybe a mistake in the text or the code—we would be grateful if you would report this to us. By doing so, you can save other readers from frustration and help us improve subsequent versions of this book. If you find any errata, please report them by visiting `http://www.packtpub.com/support`, selecting your book, clicking on the **errata submission form** link, and entering the details of your errata. Once your errata are verified, your submission will be accepted and the errata will be uploaded on our website, or added to any list of existing errata, under the Errata section of that title. Any existing errata can be viewed by selecting your title from `http://www.packtpub.com/support`.

Piracy

Piracy of copyright material on the Internet is an ongoing problem across all media. At Packt, we take the protection of our copyright and licenses very seriously. If you come across any illegal copies of our works, in any form, on the Internet, please provide us with the location address or website name immediately so that we can pursue a remedy.

Please contact us at copyright@packtpub.com with a link to the suspected pirated material.

We appreciate your help in protecting our authors, and our ability to bring you valuable content.

Questions

You can contact us at questions@packtpub.com if you are having a problem with any aspect of the book, and we will do our best to address it.

1

Getting Started with Moodle

Moodle is the world's leading open source learning management system to improve business performance. Moodle is a great tool for developing learning activities for a wide variety of audiences. But it also has the capability to be used as a community and collaboration tool to meet a wide variety of business needs.

In this first chapter, we will discuss the benefits of open source software as it applies to Moodle, explore how to install Moodle and get a basic course up and running. In further chapters, we will explore how to apply Moodle to specific business processes to enhance collaboration, communication, learning, and performance.

In this chapter, we shall:

- ◆ Discuss Moodle in the context of its use in non-education organizations
- ◆ Install Moodle for experimenting and learning
- ◆ Set up a class and add some resources and a forum
- ◆ Discuss a simple heuristic framework for managing a Moodle implementation

So let's get on with it...

Why Moodle?

Moodle is an open source **Learning Management System (LMS)** used by universities, K-12 schools, and both small and large businesses to deliver training over the Web. The Moodle project was created by Martin Dougiamas, a computer scientist and educator, who started as an LMS administrator at a university in Perth, Australia. He grew frustrated with the system's limitations as well as the closed nature of the software which made it difficult to extend.

Martin started Moodle with the idea of building the LMS based on learning theory, not software design. Moodle is based on five learning ideas:

- All of us are potential teachers as well as learners—in a true collaborative environment we are both
- We learn particularly well from the act of creating or expressing something for others to see
- We learn a lot by just observing the activity of our peers
- By understanding the contexts of others, we can teach in a more transformational way
- A learning environment needs to be flexible and adaptable, so that it can quickly respond to the needs of the participants within it

With these five points as reference, the Moodle developer community has developed an LMS with the flexibility to address a wider range of business issues than most closed source systems. Throughout this book we will explore new ways to use the social features of Moodle to create a learning platform to deliver real business value.

Moodle has seen explosive growth over the past five years. In 2005, as Moodle began to gain traction in higher education, there were under 3,000 Moodle sites around the world. As of this writing in July, 2010, there were 51,000 Moodle sites registered with Moodle.org. These sites hosted 36 million users in 214 countries. The latest statistics on Moodle use are always available at the Moodle.org site (http://moodle.org/stats).

As Moodle has matured as a learning platform, many corporations have found they can save money and provide critical training services with Moodle. According to the eLearning Guild 2008 Learning Management System survey, Moodle's initial cost to acquire, install, and customize was $16.77 per learner. The initial cost per learner for SAP was $274.36, while Saba was $79.20, and Blackboard $39.06. Moodle's open source licensing provides a considerable cost advantage against traditional closed source learning management systems. For the learning function, these savings can be translated into increased course development, more training opportunities, or other innovation. Or it can be passed back to the organization's bottom line. As Jim Whitehurst, CEO of RedHat, states: "What's sold to customers better than saying 'We can save you money' is to show them how we can give you more functionality within your budget." With training budgets among the first to be cut during a downturn, using Moodle can enable your organization to move costs from software licensing to training development, support, and performance management; activities that impact the bottom line.

Moodle's open source licensing also makes customization and integration easier and cheaper than proprietary systems. Moodle has built-in tools for integrating with backend authentication tools, such as Active Directory or OpenLDAP, enrollment plugins to take a data feed from your HR system to enroll people in courses, and a web services library to integrate with your organization's other systems. Some organizations choose to go further, customizing individual modules to meet their unique needs. Others have added components for unique tracking and reporting, including development of a full data warehouse.

Moodle's low cost and flexibility have encouraged widespread adoption in the corporate sectors. According to the eLearning Guild LMS survey, Moodle went from a 6.8 % corporate LMS market share in 2007 to a 19.8 % market share in 2008. While many of these adopters are smaller companies, a number of very large organizations, including AA Ireland, OpenText, and other Fortune 500 companies use Moodle in a variety of ways. According to the survey, the industries with the greatest adoption of Moodle include aerospace and defense companies, consulting companies, E-learning tool and service providers, and the hospitality industry.

Why open source?

Moodle is freely available under the General Public License (GPL). Anyone can go to Moodle. org and download Moodle, run it on any server for as many users as they want, and never pay a penny in licensing costs. The GPL also ensures that you will be able to get the source code for Moodle with every download, and have the right to share that code with others. This is the heart of the open source value proposition. When you adopt a GPL product, you have the right to use that product in any way you see fit, and have the right to redistribute that product as long as you let others do the same.

Moodle's open source license has other benefits beyond simply cost. Forrester recently conducted a survey of 132 senior business and IT executives from large companies using open source software. Of the respondents, 92 % said open source software met or exceeded their quality expectations, while meeting or exceeding their expectations for lower costs.

Many organizations go through a period of adjustment when making a conscious decision to adopt an open source product. Most organizations start using open source solutions for simple applications, or deep in their network infrastructure. Common open source applications in the data center include file serving, e-mail, and web servers. Once the organization develops a level of comfort with open source, they begin to move open source into mission critical and customer-facing applications. Many organizations use an open source content management system like Drupal or Alfresco to manage their web presence. Open source databases and middleware, like MySQL and JBoss, are common in application development and have proven themselves reliable and robust solutions.

Companies adopt open source software for many reasons. The Forrester survey suggests open standards, no usage restrictions, lack of vendor lock-in and the ability to use the software without a license fee as the most important reason many organizations adopt open source software.

On the other side of the coin, many CTO's worry about commercial support for their software. Fortunately, there is an emerging ecosystem of vendors who support a wide variety of open source products and provide critical services.

There seem to be as many models of open source business as there are open source projects. A number of different support models have sprung up in the last few years. Moodle is supported by the Moodle Partners, a group of 50 companies around the world who provide a range of Moodle services. Services offered range from hosting and support to training, instructional design, and custom code development. Each of the partners provides a portion of its Moodle revenue back to the Moodle project to ensure the continued development of the shared platform. In the same way, Linux is developed by a range of commercial companies, including RedHat and IBM who both share some development and compete with each other for business.

While many of the larger packages, like Linux and JBoss have large companies behind them, there are a range of products without clear avenues for support. However, the lack of licensing fees makes them easy to pilot. As we will explore in a moment, you can have a full Moodle server up and running on your laptop in under 20 minutes. You can use this to pilot your solutions, develop your content, and even host a small number of users. Once you are done with the pilot, you can move the same Moodle setup to its own server and roll it out to the whole organization.

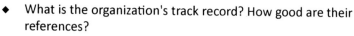

If you decide to find a vendor to support your Moodle implementation, there are a few key questions to ask:

- How long have they been in business?
- How experienced is the staff with the products they are supporting?
- Are they an official Moodle partner?
- What is the organization's track record? How good are their references?
- What is their business model for generating revenue? What are their long-term prospects?
- Do they provide a wide range of services, including application development, integration, consulting, and software life-cycle management?

Installing Moodle for experimentation

As Kenneth Grahame's character the Water Rat said in *The Wind in the Willows*, "Believe me, my young friend, there is nothing—absolutely nothing—half so much worth doing as simply messing about in boats." One of the best tools to have to learn about Moodle is an installation where you can "mess about" without worrying about the impact on other people. Learning theory tells us we need to spend many hours practicing in a safe environment to become proficient. The authors of this book have collectively spent more than 5,000 hours experimenting, building, and messing about with Moodle.

There is much to be said for having the ability to play around with Moodle without worrying about other people seeing what you are doing, even after you go live with your Moodle solution. When dealing with some of the more advanced features, like permissions and conditional activities, you will need to be able to log in with multiple roles to ensure you have the options configured properly. If you make a mistake on a production server, you could create a support headache. Having your own sandbox provides that safe place.

So we are going to start your Moodle exploration by installing Moodle on your personal computer. If your corporate policy prohibits you from installing software on your machine, discuss getting a small area on a server set up for Moodle. The installation instructions below will work on either your laptop, personal computer, or a server.

Time for action – download and run the Moodle installer

If you have Windows or a Mac, you can download a full Moodle installer, including the web server, database, and PHP. All of these components are needed to run Moodle and installing them individually on your computer can be tedious. Fortunately, the Moodle community has created full installers based on the XAMPP package. A single double-click on the install package will install everything you need.

To install Moodle on Windows:

1. Point your browser to http://download.moodle.org/windows and download the package to your desktop. Make sure you download the latest stable version of Moodle 2, to take advantage of the features we discuss in this book.

2. Unpack the archive by double clicking on the ZIP file. It may take a few minutes to finish unpacking the archive.

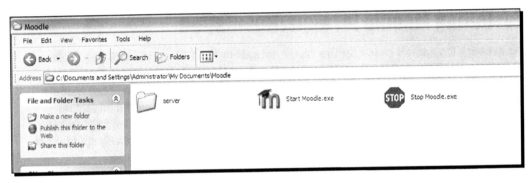

3. Double click the **Start Moodle.exe** file to start up the server manager.

4. Open your web browser and go to http://localhost.

5. You will then need to configure Moodle on your system. Follow the prompts for the next three steps.

6. After successfully configuring Moodle, you will have a fully functioning Moodle site on your machine. Use the stop and start applications to control when Moodle runs on your site.

To install Moodle on Mac:

1. Point your browser to http://download.moodle.org/macosx and find the packages for the latest version of Moodle 2. You have two choices of installers. XAMPP is a smaller download, but the control interface is not as refined as MAMP.

Download either package to your computer (the directions here are for the MAMP package).

2. Open the `.dmg` file and drag the Moodle application to your `Applications` folder.

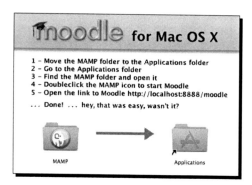

3. Open the `MAMP` application folder in your `Applications` folder. Double click the MAMP application to start the web server and database server.

4. Once MAMP is up and running, double click the **Link To Moodle** icon in the MAMP folder.

5. You now have a fully functioning Moodle site on your machine. To shut down the site, quit the MAMP application. To run your Moodle site in the future, open the MAMP application and point your browser to `http://localhost:8888/moodle`:

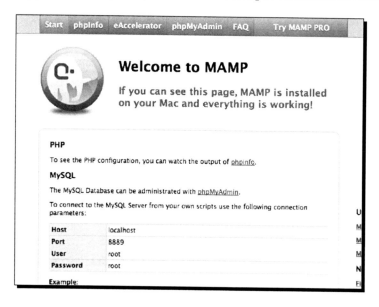

Once you have downloaded and installed Moodle, for both systems, follow these steps:

1. Once you have the base system configured, you will need to set up your administrator account. The Moodle admin account has permissions to do anything on the site, and you will need this account to get started.

2. Enter a username, password, and fill in the other required information to create an account:

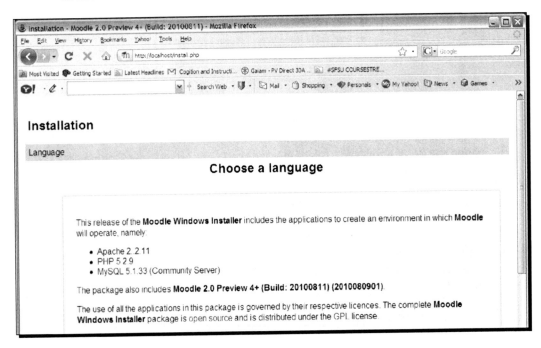

3. A XAMMP installation on Mac or Windows also requires you to set up the site's front page.

4. Give your site a name and hit **Save changes**. You can come back later and finish configuring the site.

What just happened?

You now have a functioning Moodle site on your laptop for experimentation. To start your Moodle server, double click on the `StartMoodle.exe` and point your browser at `http://localhost`.

Now we can look at a Moodle course and begin to look at Moodle functionality. Don't worry about how we will use this functionality now, just spend some time getting to know the system.

Reflection

You have just installed Moodle on a server or a personal computer, for free. You can use Moodle with as many people as you want for whatever purpose you choose without licensing fees.

Some points for reflection:

- What collaboration / learning challenges do you have in your organization?
- How can you use the money you save on licensing fees to innovate to meet those challenges?
- Are there other ways you can use Moodle to help your organization meet its goals which would not have been cost effective if you had to pay a license fee for the software?

Creating a course

A course is the basic organizing structure in Moodle. Throughout the book we will be using courses as the primary place to collect resources and activities. You do not need to use Moodle courses just for the delivery of traditional instructions. Over the next few chapters we will use courses to control access to sensitive information and encourage collaboration, as well as deliver traditional instructions.

Time for action – creating your first course

Courses are essentially containers for resources and activities. You can limit access to courses or open them up to the world. We'll start creating a basic course shell, and then we'll look at how to add some resources and a simple forum.

1. Log into your Moodle site as the administrator.

2. In the **Settings** menu on the main page, select **Site administration | Courses**. This will reveal the course administration sub-menu.

3. Select **Add/edit** courses.

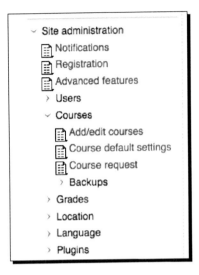

4. You will then see the **Course categories** area. Course categories help keep courses organized and can help your users navigate courses more effectively. You may want to create course categories for various skill groups to help your users find courses that would be valuable to them. Select the **Add a new course** button:

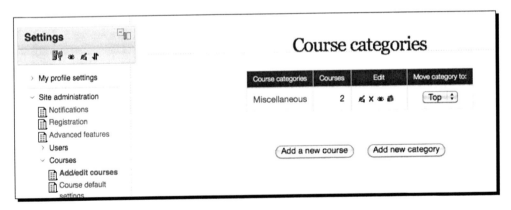

5. You will then be taken to the **Edit course settings** page. Here you will need to enter some basic information about your new course. Don't worry too much about these settings now, you can always change them later.

     ❑ **Course full name**: The full name of the course. The user will see this displayed across the top of the course main page.

- **Course short name**: The course short name appears in the navigation breadcrumbs across the top of the Moodle screen.

- **Course ID number**: The ID number is used to map the course back to an external data source, like an HR system or an ecommerce cart. The ID number is used to automate enrollments as we will discuss in *Chapter 9, Integrating Moodle into the Enterprise* For now, leave this blank.

- **Course summary**: The course summary is a short synopsis of the course that appears in the course catalog.

- **Format**: The course format determines the primary organizing structure of the course. The **Weekly** format organizes the course chronologically. The **Topics** format organizes the course by topic. The **Social** format creates a course with one main forum that appears as the course main page. The users can still access all the activities provided by Moodle. The **SCORM** format uses the course to play a single SCORM object. For now, leave the setting on Weekly.

- **Number of weeks / topics**: The number of weeks or topics the course has.

- **Course start date**: The course start date determines the date the weekly course format should use to start creating sections.

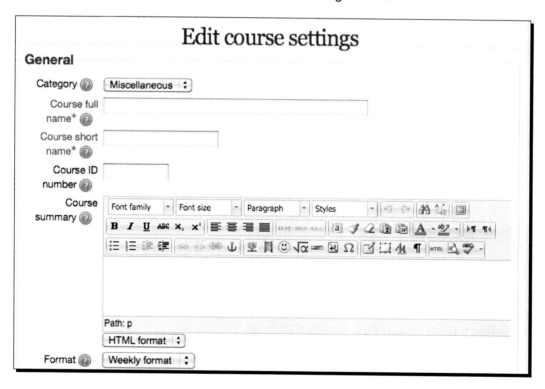

6. For now, leave the other settings at the defaults. We will explore some of these settings in later chapters. If you are curious about what the settings mean, click the question mark next to the setting label to bring up the Moodle help system.

7. Click **Save changes**. You will then be taken to the **Enrolled users** screen where you can add other user accounts to your course. If you are setting up the course on a fresh installation of Moodle, there aren't any other users to enroll. As the admin, you can always get access to the course.

8. Click the short name of your course in the breadcrumbs at the top of the screen:

Home →→ My courses →→ Experiment

9. You will then see the editing screen for your course:

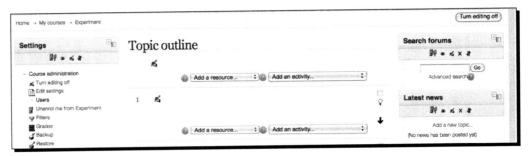

What just happened?

You have now added a blank course to your Moodle site. Courses are containers for resources and tools with controlled access for users on the system. We will be using courses as community sites and resume collection sites, as well as internal and external training sites.

Basic Moodle tools

Now that you have a course on your Moodle site, it's time to start looking at the editing interface. The later chapters will be easier to follow if you have a basic understanding of how to add resources and create simple activities in Moodle. We won't cover all the options or every tool; there are other books and documentation on Moodle.org for the areas we miss (as well as training courses from Moodle partners).

If you have experience developing Moodle courses, you can skip to the next section. But if you haven't built a course in Moodle, you should probably try the activities below. The Moodle editing interface can be a little daunting at first. Once you understand a little of the structure, it is actually quite simple.

Time for action – adding a resource

The most basic use of Moodle is to share files with other people. While there are many ways to distribute files to other people (file servers, e-mail, websites), Moodle does have some advantages over those methods. Moodle has fine grained control over who can access your content, and it's easy for people to get the latest copy of the document.

To add a file to a course:

1. Go to your course and click on the **Turn editing on** button at the top-right corner of the course.

2. In the section where you want to add your file, select the **Add a resource** menu, and then select **File** from the drop-down list.

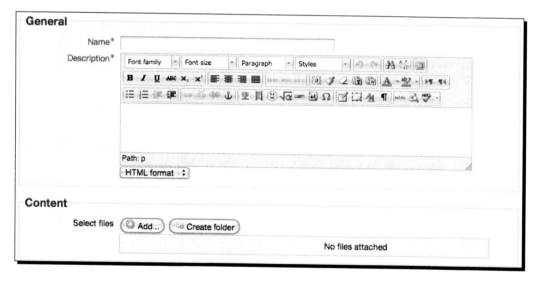

3. Enter the name of your resource. This will be the link your users will click on to access the file.

4. Add a description of the file in the **Description** box. The description should briefly indicate the purpose of the file.

5. Click the **Add** button to bring up the file selection dialog:

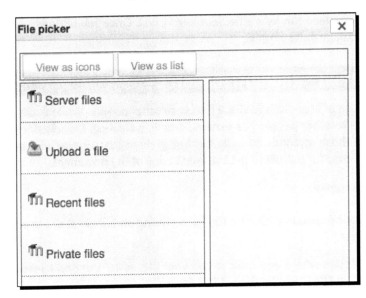

6. To add a new file, select **Upload a file** from the menu on the left. Browse for the file you want to add. You can also edit the Author input box and choose a license for distribution. Most of the time, you will want to leave the license on All rights reserved.

 Moodle 2.0 enables you to select a copyright license for the material you are uploading. By default, any content in Moodle is yours and you keep all rights to the content. The open source license does not extend to your content, just the Moodle code. The other licensing options allow users of your course some rights. Public Domain allows the users to do whatever they want with the content. The Creative Commons licenses allow the users to do more with the content, but reserve some rights to the authors. You can get more information about the Creative Commons licenses at http://www.creativecommons.org.

7. You can then select a display option for your file. The options are:

   - **Automatic**: Moodle will select the display option automatically.
   - **Embed**: Your file is displayed within the page, using a plugin if necessary. Moodle wraps the file with its own navigation.
   - **Force download**: The user must always download the file to their personal computer.

□ **Open**: The file is displayed in the window, with no Moodle navigation around it.

□ **In pop-up**: The file is displayed in a new browser window with Moodle underneath.

8. The display resource name option allows Moodle to display the original file name (along with the name of the resource you just set).

9. The other settings determine who can see the file. We will cover these in a later chapter. For now, click on **Save and display** to see your file in Moodle.

10. The example below shows an image file with the embedded option and display description turned on.

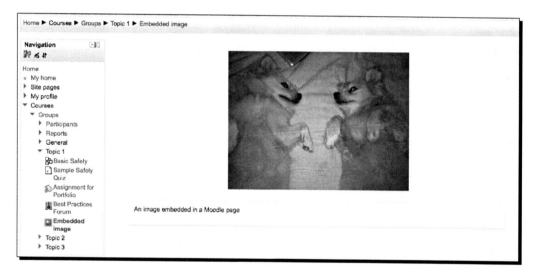

What just happened?

We just uploaded a single file to Moodle that can be viewed by anyone with access to the course. The link to the file appears in the section where we added the resource.

Have a go hero – organizing resources

Now that you have uploaded a single resource, you can begin to experiment with the file system in Moodle. Your challenge is to add three different resource types, and select the appropriate display option. Word Docs, PowerPoint files, and PDF files are common file types, but experiment with media files such as MP3s as well.

Creating a forum

Forums are the basic collaboration and communication tool in a Moodle course. Many people are familiar with web forums; most popular news sites have comment sections with reply capabilities attached to their news stories. Moodle's forums are threaded discussions, which is a fancy way of saying you can keep them organized by discussion topics.

You may have noticed there is already a forum in the course you just created. Moodle creates a special News Forum by default. This forum only allows teachers to create posts, and is meant as a place to post course announcements.

Beyond simply distributing course news, forums can be used for discussing learning activities, be the learning activity, or for general collaboration within a community of practice.

Time for action – creating your first forum

Let's start by creating a simple forum for our learners to discuss a case study in a course. We'll want everyone to post to the forum and have an open discussion.

1. In the section where you would like to add a forum, select the **Add an activity** drop down and then select **Forum**:

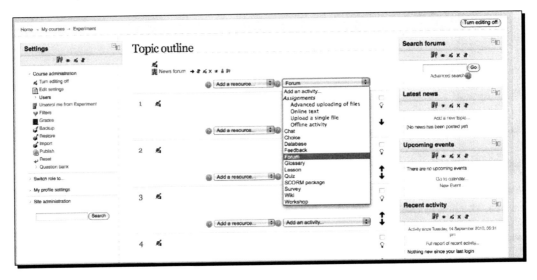

2. You will then be taken to the **Adding a new Forum** screen. Enter a name for your forum. Like the resource link above, the name of the forum will become the text of the link to access the forum.

3. Select the **Forum type**; these are your choices:

- ❑ **Standard forum for general use**: This is a standard threaded discussion board where anyone can start a new discussion topic.

- ❑ **A simple single discussion**: A forum with only one discussion topic.

- ❑ **Each person posts one discussion**: A forum where each person in the class can post a single discussion topic.

- ❑ **Q and A forum**: A question and answer forum where the participants must first post a question before they can see other user's questions.

- ❑ **Standard forum displayed in blog-like format**: A standard forum where anyone can post a discussion topic, but the topics are displayed in a blog-like format.

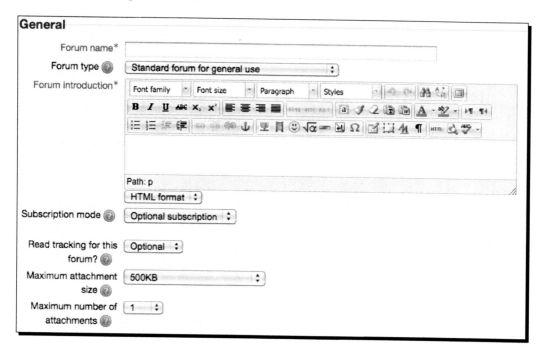

4. Enter a **Forum introduction**. Remember, the introduction is displayed at the top of the forum when participants first enter. Explain the purpose of the forum and any particular requirements for posting or participating.

5. Choose a **Subscription mode**, either optional or forced subscriptions. Forum subscriptions are one of the great features of Moodle. When users subscribe to a forum, they will receive a copy of each message in their e-mail. It's a great tool for staying involved in the conversations.

6. Choose whether **Read tracking** is optional, on, or off for this forum. Read tracking tracks read and unread messages for participants. I find this a useful tool and generally recommend it turned on.

7. Set the **Maximum attachment size** for the forum. Participants can attach files to their forum posts (we use it to share screenshots of bugs and problems). This setting keeps them from attaching truly massive files (or sharing audio and video where it really isn't appropriate). If you want your users to attach word processing documents, set this to under 50 MB. However, if they are supposed to attach slide decks or video, set it to the maximum setting.

8. The **Maximum number of attachments** determines how many attachments a user can add to a forum post. If this is set to 0, they can't add any attachments at all. In our example, we might want the participants to attach their analysis of the case, so we'll set this to one.

9. The next three settings cover blocking thresholds for people who are abusing the system with too many posts (it also prevents runaway forum spam should someone get on a public forum for those purposes). The time period is the time over which the number of posts is counted for the Post threshold for warning and the Post threshold for blocking. If a user exceeds the warning threshold within the blocking time, they get a warning on the screen. If they exceed the blocking threshold, they are prohibited from posting for the blocking period.

10. The **Grade category** determines where in the gradebook any scores for the forum are recorded. Forum posts are not graded by default. In our example, we don't want to give a grade on an open discussion of a case study.

11. If you did want to use ratings, you would set how the grade is set in the next section. The score for a forum is determined by the aggregation type for the ratings. The options are:

    ❑ **No ratings**: There are no ratings in the forum.

    ❑ **Average of ratings**: The average of all the scores for all of the participant's forum posts.

    ❑ **Count of ratings**: The number of posts with ratings.

    ❑ **Maximum ratings**: The post with the highest rating determines the score.

    ❑ **Minimum ratings**: The post with the lowest rating determines the score.

    ❑ **Sum of ratings**: All of the ratings for the participant are added together to determine the score for the forum.

12. You can then restrict the ratings to within a range of dates.

13. Again, we will cover groups and access permissions in a later chapter. For now, click **Save and display** to see your new forum.

What just happened?

We have now created a forum for our users to communicate with each other in a Moodle course.

Reflection

Forums in Moodle can be rated by either a facilitator or by participants in the class. In an educational setting, this can be used to give a participation grade or determine the students' score on an assignment. In a corporate setting, forced participation in a discussion can be de-motivating. How could you use the forum rating system to encourage participation in your online discussions? What other settings could be used to tune the discussion to meet a specific need?

Have a go hero – doing more with forums

Create a forum of a type other than the standard forum for general use. How is it different from a user's perspective? How could you use it in your organization?

An eLearning framework for implementing Moodle

Implementing Moodle on a technical level can be relatively easy. The difficult part is using Moodle to impact organizational performance. There are many more factors beyond software to consider when planning to roll out a learning system. While we have discussed the advantages of Moodle relative to other LMS systems, the organizational challenges are the same as rolling out any other piece of enterprise software.

There are many factors to consider when considering enterprise software decisions: the business strategy or goals the software is meant to help enable, development of a solution, solution implementation, training, measurement, and finally circling around back to the goals to ensure an appropriate ROI.

To help structure the task of implementing business solutions in Moodle, we have developed a simple framework for analyzing your proposed application and measuring the results. The framework is designed to help you think through what you want to achieve with your Moodle solution, how you will implement it, and how you will measure whether you have been successful.

Our implementation framework has five main steps: Align, Develop, Implement, Measure, and Evaluate (ADIME). The framework is designed as an iterative process. The analysis in the Align phase determines what will be measured in the Evaluate phase. The data from the Evaluate phase is used to improve the alignment analysis as part of a continuous process.

Align

The purpose of the Align phase is to explore the potential organizational impacts of your Moodle initiative. Your initiative needs to be aligned with larger business strategy and organizational procedure to ensure a positive impact. During this phase, you will also determine the success criteria for the project. These criteria will form the basis of the Evaluation phase after you have rolled-out the first version of the project.

- What business problem are you solving with Moodle?
- How is your Moodle initiative aligned with your larger organizational strategy?
- How can you support your organization's practices, policies, and procedures with the use of Moodle?
- How can we enable the organization to meet its goals faster / cheaper / better using Moodle as a learning and communication platform?
- Is this initiative an opportunity to improve rather than simply translating existing practices?
- Who in the organization needs to be involved? Who will be impacted by your initiative?
- What is the budget for the project?
- What are the anticipated savings / additional revenue from the project?

Develop

During the Develop phase, you will develop the solution to meet the objectives outlined in the Align phase. The Develop phase creates the Moodle course or collaborative area for other people to use.

Before beginning development there are some basic questions you need to answer to ensure you are developing a useful solution:

- Where will people access your solution (office, home, road, client premises)?
- How will people access your solutions (Desktop, laptop, mobile, in class)?
- What Moodle tools will meet your audience's needs and deliver the expected business results?

- What content do you need to develop? Who are the experts you need to work with to get the information you need?

- How will you prompt or support any needed collaborative work?

- How will you assess learning or change?

- Does your solution require the participants to create something? How will they share or submit their creation?

- Do you need to support reflection on the part of the learner?

- How will you support transfer of the online experience to the job (assuming the online experience is not the job itself)?

Implement

In the Implementation phase, you will roll out your solution to your intended audience. Implementing your solution will probably be at least as difficult as developing it, but this is where we start to see the real-world impact of your solution on the business.

- How will you give the right people access at the right time?

- Are there special roles or permissions you need to define for various groups of users?

- Do you need to set things to happen at certain dates or times?

- How will you market your solution within your organization? How will you get the word out?

- Does your solution solve a "job to be done" for your target audience?

- Who will provide technical support for participants?

- Have you tested your solution with a sample of your target audience?

Measure

Once people start to use your solution, you need to measure how they are doing within the context of the solution itself. You are not measuring the business impact yet, as we need to first determine if the solution is valid. In the Measurement phase, we look to see if participants are using the solution as it was intended. In the Evaluate phase, we will look to see if what they have learned impacts the organization:

- How will you measure if participants are successful within your solution?

- Will you measure assessment results, usage statistics, and time on task?

- What are the benchmarks for successful participation?

- How will you remediate if your participants are not successful?

- How will you ensure continued engagement with your solution?

Evaluate

In the Evaluate phase, we begin to measure the impact of your solution on the organization and the goals you set out in the Align phase.

- How will you measure the impact of your solution on the organization?
- How will you measure change in performance by participants and compare it to prior performance or a control group?
- How will you measure the financial impact of your solution?
- How will you measure the schedule / time impact of your solution?
- How will you measure the impact your solution has on quality?
- How will you measure the impact your solution has on customer satisfaction?
- How will you use the data you gather to decide how and when to improve your solution?

Obviously there are many possible answers to these questions, most of which will lead to even more questions to answer. The trick is to do enough analysis so you know what you want to achieve while avoiding "paralysis from analysis". Moodle makes it easy to try things, figure out what works, change what doesn't, and move on. So use the framework to sketch your solution, then go ahead and implement a pilot. Learn quickly, improve what you can, and roll out to achieve business success.

Case Study—OpenText

OpenText Corporation is an enterprise software company and leader in enterprise content management. It helps organizations manage their business content. OpenText began as a spin-off company from the University of Waterloo and over the following 20 years became the market leader in providing Enterprise Content Management solutions that bring together people, processes, and information.

What was the business problem(s) for which Moodle was chosen as the solution?

OpenText has over 140 different product variations within its product portfolio. It was becoming too difficult to manage the product knowledge training through face-to-face instructor-led training, so management wanted to test online training to deliver a more paperless training. They also recognized the need to help the 800 strong sales force to understand and keep up-to-date with the product set through more accessible training.

What was the solution and how did they arrive at the solution?

Initially OpenText looked at the target audience and focused on a small subset to begin with: the 800 strong sales team which was spread across the globe. They proceeded to evaluate over 30 different corporate LMS in the marketplace and finally settled on one. This was used for six months to roll out an online college for the sales team, with assignments, Scorm objects and chat, but the project didn't go as well as expected.

However, they found challenges with administration, user navigation and collaboration tools which sent them looking again. This time Moodle was identified internally as a viable option which delivered on all the core features required.

Why did they choose Moodle?

One of the reasons, although not the primary reason was budget. The cost of rolling out Moodle was within the budget levels that had been assigned for the first project. However, the things that stood out for OpenText were the collaboration tools such as the forum and chat were impressive. The assignment types and interactive correction tools were comparable to a top corporate LMS. The intuitive user navigation interface and administration underlined the difference in platforms. Crucially the system was also a stable platform, and any time that any issues did arise, the Moodle Partner Remote-Learner were able to solve them quickly.

Was the project a success?

Rahmat explains that the move to Moodle was a huge success for OpenText. They moved from just sales "field enablement" to a corporate-wide delivery of training. Then OpenText included external sales partner companies and built a partner portal within Moodle for knowledge sharing.

They built a professional development series of 120 different courses which were developed in-house, all working in Moodle. This was in addition to the deployment of over 2,500 off-the-shelf Scorm and AICC courses, including a range from Skillsoft which enabled easy delivery and consistent reporting.

What were the benefits gained?

The flexibility and ease of customization of the system was one of the biggest benefits as Rahmat explained, "you can bend Moodle to work the way that you want to, rather than having to bend to work the way it wants you to".

The ROI was significant with corporate wide adoption of e-learning, saving time and money. "Moodle is a cost effective choice for delivering learning across the company and partners", concluded Rahmat.

What lessons were learned?

Through experience Rahmat felt that whether it is open source or proprietary systems you are evaluating, you need to focus on the feature set in your LMS analysis and on the level of support that's available both commercially and within the community.

"You don't need an in-house programmer to roll out Moodle", Rahmat explained, "as much of the changes you need to do just don't need it, but when its something major you can get a specialist Moodle Partner in."

Do you have any advice for future businesses who plan to implement Moodle?

Rahmat had a few bits of advice for potential Moodlers:

- As with any project that involves people's data, it is important to involve the IT and security departments as early as possible to ensure that critical data is managed correctly
- Before you start deploying users into the system, take the time to analyze your ERP system to see what user fields you want to be using in Moodle, so you customize them before you have a lot of user accounts already created

Any other thoughts or comments?

The help you can get in the Moodle community is invaluable. Don't be afraid to get involved.

Summary

We learned a lot in this chapter about open source software, the advantages of Moodle, and how to install and begin to use it.

Specifically, we covered:

- Moodle, as open source software, is free to download, install on any machine, and use with as many people as you want.
- Moodle Partners provide professional support for Moodle, so if you want someone to train you, provide Moodle hosting, or customize it to meet your needs, there are a number of companies out there to help.
- It is easy to set up a course and add static resources to Moodle to share with others.
- Adding basic activities in a course, like Forums, is easy to do with a simple web interface. There is also a lot of hidden power to customize the application to meet your needs.

We also discussed a framework for planning your Moodle solution. The ADIME framework provides a simple heuristic for thinking about how to implement a Moodle solution in your organization.

Now that we've learned about the basics of Moodle, we're ready to begin using Moodle to support one of the most important business functions, hiring the right people—which is the topic of the next chapter.

2
Moodle in Hiring and Interviewing

In the previous chapter we introduced a framework for thinking about how to implement Moodle in your organization. We also created a Moodle site, a course, and a forum in Moodle. In this chapter, we will build on these skills and teach you some new ones, while investigating ways to use Moodle to support the hiring process.

One of the key strategies necessary for a successful business is recruiting and retaining good employees. Moodle can be used as an effective tool in implementing these processes. This chapter will teach you how to use Moodle to facilitate the hiring processes. We will look at how to receive resumes and applications from candidates and evaluate them. We will also learn how to administer competency tests, schedule interviews, and collect reactions from multiple interviewers during the selection process.

In this chapter we shall:

- ◆ Learn how to set up a Moodle site to facilitate the hiring and interviewing process
- ◆ Learn how to create a Moodle assignment where candidates can upload their resumes or job applications
- ◆ Learn how to enable applicants to create new accounts
- ◆ Learn how to rate candidate's applications by using the grade assignments as an initial screening process
- ◆ Learn how to create and administer competency tests using the Moodle quiz module

◆ Learn how to coordinate an interview schedule using the choice module.

◆ Learn how to create interviewer resources and forums to assist interviewers and decision makers

So let's get started...

 Recruiting and retaining good employees is critical to the success of a business. This chapter will focus on managing the recruiting process using tools in Moodle.

Creating an assignment for submitting resumes/CVs

Before we get into specifics it is necessary to agree on a framework for how we will set up our Moodle site for recruiting new employees. For simplicity, we recommend setting up separate Moodle sites for internal and external processes. There are ways to enable both on the same site, but it adds a level of complexity. Additionally, there are some add-ons for Moodle to help you manage multiple sites. We will explain these in *Chapter 8, Integrating Moodle with Other Systems*. For the purposes of this chapter, we will assume that we are using a Moodle site just for the hiring process.

In the previous chapter, you learned how to create a course. On our Moodle site, there will be a course for each position available. Creating a course for each position will simplify the course creation process and make the interface simpler for the applicant.

Time for action – creating the assignment

Collecting resumes or CVs is the first step in recruiting new employees. Moodle can be used to collect resumes from potential new candidates for an open position. In this example, we will use the **Upload a single file** Assignment type in our Moodle Course to enable users to submit applications.

1. Log into Moodle as the Moodle admin and create a course on your test Moodle site by following the course creation instructions in *Chapter 1, Getting Started with Moodle*. For our example, I've entitled the course, **Available Position**. When you create the course, select the **Topics** format from the course settings.

2. Go into the course created for the new position and turn editing on.

3. We'll start by creating a label for section 1, so the user knows what they are supposed to do in each area of the course. Click the edit button at the top of the section.

4. Uncheck the **Use default section name** checkbox at the top of the **Summary of Topic 1** screen.

5. Type the name of the section in the **Section Name** field. For this example, we'll call this section **Resume Submittal**. The section name will appear in bold at the top of the section.

6. The **Section Description** field enables you to add text under the section label to provide more context. We will leave this blank for the purpose of this example.

7. We will create the Assignment under the first Topic section so it appears at the top of the page. To do this, at the bottom of section 1, click the **Add an activity...** menu, and then select **Upload a single file**.

8. The next screen, entitled **Adding a new Assignment to Topic 1**, shown in the following image, will then open. In this screen, under the **General** section, enter the name of the Assignment, for example, "Please submit your resume for the available position here".

9. Then in the **Description** box enter instructions for the applicant explaining how to upload their resume and any due dates applicants should know.

10. After the **Description** box, you will see the **Available from** and **Due date**. Here you can enter the time period you will be accepting applications for the open position.

11. At the bottom of the **General** section, you will see **Prevent late submissions**. Select **Yes** here so applicants will not be able to submit resumes after the due date.

12. In the same screen, the **Grade** section follows the **General** section. We will be using 'grades' to evaluate the applications. The scores will also enable us to create conditions for the next activities in this course. Here you can enter what scale you want to use for grading. The default is 100 and is what we will use for the example in this chapter.

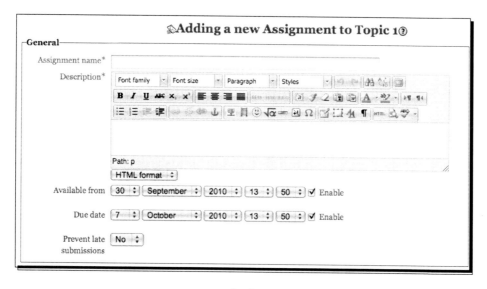

13. After the Grade section, in the **Upload a single file** section, you can decide if you will allow resubmitting. For this example, we will not allow resubmitting. This means that once the resumes have been reviewed and scored to determine if they will move on to the next stage in the hiring process, they will not be able to resubmit a different resume.

14. Under **Email alerts to teachers**, select **Yes** so when a new resume/CV is submitted you will receive an e-mail.

15. Once you have entered all the settings for the assignment, scroll down to the bottom of the screen and select **Save and display**.

16. When a new applicant selects the assignment they will see the following screen:

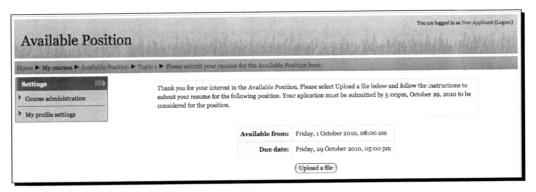

What just happened?

You have just created an activity where applicants can now upload their resume/CV for consideration for the open position. Once a new applicant has logged on and submitted their resume/CV, you will receive an e-mail notification and can begin your initial screening process.

Have a go hero – adding an application form to the assignment module

How could we use the Assignment module to allow an applicant to upload an application form created by your company instead of their own resume?

This is an easy addition. You can still use the Upload a file Assignment module, however you will need to create a link to the Application Form. To do this you could create a link to download the application form in the **Description** box. It is easy to create a link using the tool available in the **Description** box, as shown in the following screenshot:

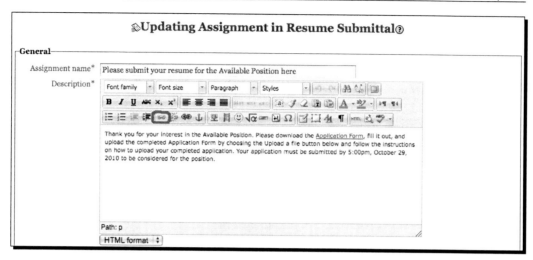

1. Highlight the text you want linked to the downloadable form and then select the **Insert/edit link** icon from the tool bar. In the previous screenshot, it is the icon that looks like a chain link.

2. The **Insert/edit link** window will then open. Select the browse icon to the right of the first empty field, Link URL, then browse and select the application form file that the applicants will need to download. Once you have selected the file, click the **Insert** button found at the bottom of the window.

3. You will then be back in the **Updating the Assignment file** window. Select **Save and Display** at the bottom of the window. You should then see the assignment you created and test the link to the application form.

Many companies find it is good practice to require applicants to submit both a resume and an application form to make sure they receive all the information they feel is necessary to make a good hiring decision. Is there a way to create an assignment where the applicant can upload two files? Yes, there is. Moodle also provides an assignment type that allows the uploading of multiple files. To create an assignment to allow multiple file uploads, follow these steps:

1. When you create the activity, under the **Add an activity...** drop-down menu, simply select **Advanced uploading of files** rather than **Upload a single file**.

2. Then it is very similar to the Upload a single file setup, except this assignment type allows you to select the maximum number of files to be uploaded by the applicant. In this case it would be two their completed application form and their resume/CV.

3. Don't forget if you get stuck you can always get help by clicking on the yellow question mark icons next to each setting. If you need more information try clicking on the yellow information icon at the bottom of the page, which will take you directly to the Moodle documentation for this activity.

Enabling user account creation

Future applicants will need a way to log on to our system, so before we can test the application process, we need to make sure we have enabled user self email-based registration on our Moodle site.

Time for action – how to enable self registration

Follow the steps below to enable self registration:

1. Log in to your Moodle site as the admin.

2. On your home page, go to the **Site administration** menu under the **Settings** block, and select **Plugins**, as shown in the next screenshot:

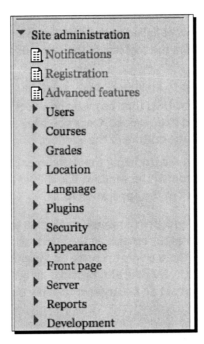

3. Then select **Authentication** and then **Manage authentication**. You will then be at the screen shown below:

Manage authentication

Available authentication plugins

Name	Enable	Up/Down	Settings
Manual accounts			Settings
No login			Settings
Email-based self-registration	👁	↓	Settings
LDAP server	👁	↑	Settings
CAS server (SSO)	◡		Settings
External database	◡		Settings
FirstClass server	◡		Settings
IMAP server	◡		Settings
Moodle Network authentication	◡		Settings
NNTP server	◡		Settings
No authentication	◡		Settings

4. In the **Manage authentication** screen, first make sure that the **Email-based self-registration** is enabled. You will know if something is enabled if the eye next to it is open.

5. Click the **Settings** link to the right of the **Email-based self-registration** setting. This will take you to the settings page for the plugin.

6. On the plugins setting screen, set the **Enable reCAPTCHA element** to **Yes**. ReCAPTCHA is a system for preventing spammers from using programs to create accounts on your system. It generates a random string of numbers and letters that are difficult to process with code.

7. Next, on the same screen, scroll down to the **Common Settings** and set the **Self registration** option to **Email-based self-registration**.

8. At the bottom of the form are two fields **ReCAPTCHA public key** and **ReCAPTCHA private key**. You will need to register your site on the ReCAPTCHA site to get these keys. Go to `http://www.recaptcha.com` and fill in the registration form. You will then be given the two keys. Copy and paste them into these fields.

9. Then scroll down further on the same screen to the **Instructions** field. The instructions that you type here will appear on the log in screen. You will want to remind users to follow the instructions to create a new account or to log in if they have already created an account. Once you have written your instructions, select the **Save Changes** button at the bottom of the screen.

Avoiding spam filters

When your site goes into production, you will need to make sure your Moodle e-mail configuration is properly set up. In the Site Administration menu, under the Server heading you will find the Email settings form. Talk to your IT department to make sure you have the proper settings here to make sure Moodle is using the right e-mail server. If this isn't set up, Moodle will use its internal e-mail method which is much more likely to be caught by a spam filter.

Now let's set the site up so that once the applicants have created an account and logged on to the site, they will see the list of courses/open positions:

1. Under the **Site administration** menu, from step 2 above, select **Front page**, and then select **Front page settings**.

2. You will then be on the **Front Page Settings** screen. Scroll down to **Front page items** when logged in and select **List of courses** from one of the menus.

3. Remember to scroll down to the bottom of the page and click **Save changes**.

Before we can test this we need to make sure that the course is set up for self-enrolment.

1. Go to the course and under the settings block find the **Course administration** menu. Select **Users**, and then **Enrolment methods**.

2. You will then be at the **Enrolment methods** screen. Make sure that **Self enrolment (Student)** has been enabled. The eye should be open if it is enabled as shown in the next screenshot:

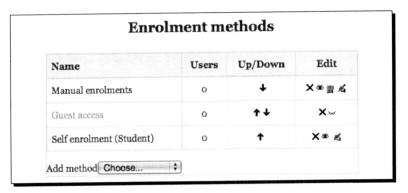

3. Let's see if it worked. Log out of the admin account and then select the Login link at the top right-hand corner of your screen where it says, **You are not logged in. (Login)**. You should now be at the login page. Following is an example of what it should look like:

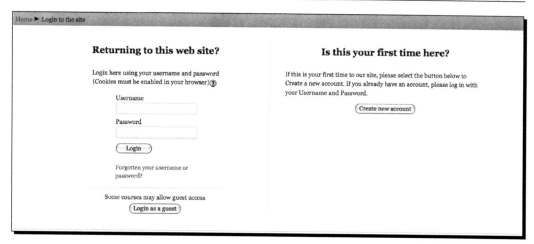

Home ► Login to the site

Returning to this web site?

Login here using your username and password
(Cookies must be enabled in your browser)

Username

Password

(Login)

Forgotten your username or
password?

Some courses may allow guest access
(Login as a guest)

Is this your first time here?

If this is your first time to our site, please select the button below to
Create a new account. If you already have an account, please log in with
your Username and Password.

(Create new account)

> When we were writing the book, we frequently had two different browsers
> open (Firefox and IE on Windows, Firefox and Safari on Mac). If you login as
> a student user in one browser, you can log in to Moodle as the admin in the
> other browser, so it's easy to switch back and forth between users. You need to
> use two separate browsers, and not the windows or tabs of the same browser.

What just happened?

You just set up your Moodle site so users can self enroll. When a potential applicant goes
to your site now they will be able to create an account and enroll in any of the available
position courses you created.

Standard Moodle is focused on education and the standard labels reflect this. When using
Moodle for business purposes, you may want to change these labels to something more
applicable to the context. For example, in this chapter we are creating a course for each
open position and when you choose to show the available courses on the home page the
heading is "Available Courses", but for this case a heading such as "Available Positions"
would be more appropriate. It is possible to change these language strings and we cover
how to do this when we discuss creating custom themes in *Chapter 9, Integrating Moodle
into Enterprise*.

Assessing submitted resumes/CVs

Once a new applicant has created a user account, enrolled in a course, and submitted their resume/CV through the Assignment module created at the beginning of the chapter, the HR manager or hiring manager, will then receive an e-mail notifying them that a new application has been received. The first step in the hiring process is to screen the applications. Typically the HR manager will go through all the resumes, see if they meet the requirements for the position, and submit a score for each one. A perfect score would mean that the resume meets all the requirements for the job. The lower the score assigned, the poorer the match. For this first screening process, a company may decide that only the applications that have a score/match of greater than 85% will move on to the next stage in the hiring process. In this section you will learn how to assess and grade an assignment.

Be sure your HR or hiring manager is registered as a teacher in the course. Only teachers get notified when an assignment is submitted.

Time for action – screening the resumes/CVs

Imagine you are the HR manager for a company. You have advertised the job opening, set up your Moodle course for the open position, and created an Assignment where applicants can submit their resume/CV. Today you just received an e-mail notifying you that someone has submitted his or her resume by uploading it to the assignment you created previously. Now you need to conduct the initial screening to see how good a match the candidate is for the open position.

1. Go to the course created for the position and select the assignment you created for applicants to submit their resumes. You will be brought to the assignment page. In the top right-hand corner you will see a link, **View # submitted assignments**. Select the link. You will then be brought to the window shown in the following screenshot:

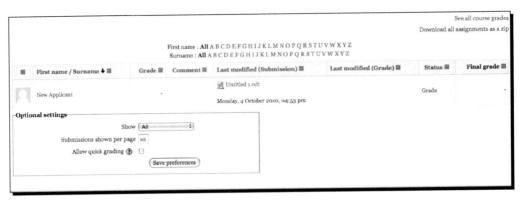

2. You will then see a table of the applicants who have submitted a resume/CV or application form. You can review their submission by selecting the **Grade** link. Read the applicant's submission and rate their resume. Click **Save** when you have given them their score.

3. You will then be brought to the **Feedback** page which will be titled **Feedback: Name of Applicant**. This page will show the name of the applicant, the date they submitted their resume, and the first section will contain their submitted file.

4. The next section on the page is entitled **Grades**. In the **Grades** section, select the score for the resume. The last section is the **Feedback** section. Here you will be able to give feedback to the applicant. For our example, if an applicant receives a grade of greater than 85/100 you may want to give them instructions on how to proceed to the next step whether it is an aptitude test, cognitive ability test, personality test, or scheduling an interview.

5. Once you have entered a grade and any feedback don't forget to select **Save changes** at the bottom of the screen. An e-mail will then be sent out to the applicant with a link back to the course so that they can get their grade and feedback.

6. You will then be brought back to the table shown in the previous screenshot. More of the table is now completed with the grade you assigned the applicant shown and the feedback you gave the applicant displayed in the second and third columns labeled **Grade** and **Comments** respectively. Notice that in the **Status** column there is no longer the highlighted Grade, but it has now changed to **Update** in case you later want to make changes to the grade or feedback provided to the applicant.

What just happened?

You now know how to score an assignment activity and use that score to conduct the initial screening process. Applicants who receive a score of greater than 85% will now move on to the next stage in the hiring process.

Have a go hero – evaluating cover letters

Create an Advanced Uploading of Files assignment and allow the applicants to upload multiple files. Log in as your test user and upload both a cover letter and a resume. Evaluate both as the HR manager and give the applicant a score.

Time for reflection

Reflect on the hiring process at your company. What modifications would you make to what has been discussed in this chapter so far to suit your company's hiring process?

Creating competency tests with the Moodle quiz module

Many companies do not like to just rely on resumes and the interviewing process. With increasing frequency companies are requiring applicants to also take competency tests. These could include aptitude tests, cognitive ability tests, personality tests, and so on. The main requirement is the test should prove to be a good indicator of success in the position for hire. Moodle's quiz module can be used to administer a wide variety of tests.

Using Moodle to create competency tests

You have gone through all the resumes submitted by applicants and have scored them based on how well they meet the job requirements. You want the top scorers to move through to the next stage of your hiring process, which is the competency test. Moodle 2.0 allows conditional access to activities based on achieving a minimum score in a previous activity. In our example, access to the competency test will depend on the grade the hiring manager gave the applicant's resume in the previous example.

Time for action – enabling conditional activities

Before we begin to create the quiz, we need to enable conditional activities at the site level. Conditional activities are a new feature in Moodle 2.0 and not everyone will want to use them right away. So the developers created a switch to allow Moodle admins to turn the feature on when their users were ready.

1. Login to Moodle as a Moodle administrator.

2. In the **Site administration** menu, select **Advanced features**.

3. Toward the bottom of the **Advanced features** settings page, check the box for **Enable conditional access**.

4. Click on **Save changes** at the bottom of the page.

What just happened?

We have just enabled conditional activities which will enable course developers to restrict access and visibility based on participant scores, dates, or other parameters.

Time for action – creating a quiz

Your first step in creating the competency test using the Moodle quiz module is to create a quiz and set up the conditional availability to the competency test. We will set it up so that only applicants with a score greater than 85% will be allowed to move on to the next step and take the competency test.

1. Create a label for Section 2 using the process you used for Section 1. Call Section 2 **Competency Test**.

2. Under the **Add an activity...** menu in Section 2, select **Quiz**.

3. You will then be brought to the **Adding a new Quiz** page. On this page you will enter the title of the quiz in the **Name** field. For our example, we will keep it simple and call it **Competency Test**.

4. In the **Introduction** field, enter the instructions for the quiz. These usually cover any instructions or tips you would like to give the user. For our example, we've listed the number of questions and the time they have to take the exam. Refer to the next screenshot.

5. The next two fields are **Open the quiz** and **Close the quiz**. These allow you to enter the dates from which the quiz will be available to applicants. To set the open and close dates for the quiz you must first select the **Enable** checkbox, and then enter the dates. For the purposes of this example, we will choose the date all resumes had to be submitted by as the start date and close the quiz a week later.

6. Next is the **Time limit** field. Here you can enter the amount of time that the applicants will be given to complete the exam. If you want to set a time limit, click the **Enable** checkbox and then enter the amount of time allotted for the exam. If you enable the **Time limit** feature, then during the exam the applicant will see a timer window with the countdown. After time is up, the quiz will be submitted automatically. For our example, we will give them 60 minutes to complete the competency test.

7. The **Attempts allowed** field allows you to enter the number of times an applicant is allowed to retake the test. If no retakes are allowed, then enter 1.

8. If you have entered more than 1 in the **Attempts allowed** field, then you will need to select the **Grading method** in the drop-down menu found at the end of the **General** section. There are four different grading methods:
   - Highest grade: The final grade given will be the highest grade of all attempts.
   - Average grade: The final grade given will be an average of all attempts.

❑ First attempt: The final grade given will be the grade received in the first attempt.

❑ Last attempt: The final grade given will be the grade received in the last attempt.

9. In our example, we are only going to allow one attempt, therefore we will not need to enter anything for the **Grading method**. The next screenshot shows the General section completed with our example:

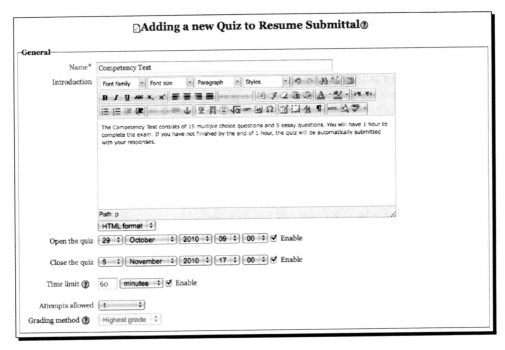

10. The **Layout** section comes after the **General** section. **Question order** allows you to select if the questions will be displayed randomly or in the order in which you enter them into the quiz. We will select **As shown on the edit screen** from the drop-down menu because you will probably want to have control over the order of the questions.

11. The **New page** field under the **Layout** section allows you to select the number of questions displayed per page. We will leave it at **Every question** so that there is one question per page.

12. In the **Question behavior** section, you can select whether you want possible answers to be shuffled for the questions. If you have a test with a lot of multiple choice questions, with responses that don't need to be in a particular order, then it is good practice to select **Yes** for this and shuffle the question answers.

Beware of "All/None of the above" responses.

We once had a client for whom we were converting quizzes from print to Moodle quizzes and the client wanted the answers to shuffle with every attempt. There were several questions that had "All/None of the above" responses. This is fine in print or if you are not going to shuffle the answers. However, when the answers are shuffled and "All/None of the above" ends up somewhere other than the last option, it can be confusing.

Unfortunately, we did not catch this until many of the quizzes were already done. We then had to go back over several questions and change all these responses to "All/None of these are correct". It is a silly mistake, but it can be very time consuming to correct.

13. The **Adaptive Mode** setting is applicable if you are allowing multiple attempts, which for a competency test is unlikely, so we will set this to **No**.

14. Under the **Review options** section, you can select what type of feedback/results you want the applicants to have and when you want them to receive their feedback/results. This can be an effective tool in a learning process; however in a competency test this is not as important. We will select to let the applicants view their score on the test immediately after their attempt and later, while the quiz is still open. To set this up you simply select the checkboxes next to the review options you want applied. See the following screenshot for this example:

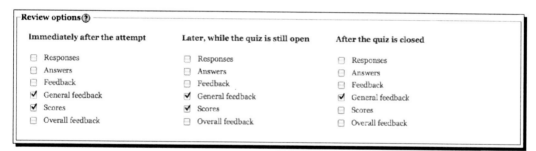

15. Below the **Review options** section is the **Display** section. The first field, **Show the user's picture**, can be very useful in a proctored exam because while the user is taking an exam their picture will show up on the screen making it easy to confirm their identity.

16. The other two fields in the **Display** section relate to the number of digits displayed after the decimal point when showing grades. The grades stored in the database are calculated to full accuracy; these settings just refer to the display of the grade. There are two fields: **Decimal places in grades** (which refers to the display of overall grades) and **Decimal places in question grades** (which refers to the display of your grade on a question). For our example, we will leave the default, which is 2 for both overall and question grades.

17. **Extra restrictions on attempts** is the next section. For our example we don't need any extra restrictions so we will skip this section.

18. In the **Overall feedback** section, you can provide feedback based on the score achieved on the quiz. It is likely that you will require a minimum score on the Competency Test before the applicant can move on to the next stage in the hiring process. The Overall feedback section is a good place to let the applicant know if they have passed the requirement and will move on to the next stage. Let's say the passing grade for the Competency Test is greater than 70%. You will set up an additional grade boundary to the first 100%. For the second **Grade boundary** enter 70%. In the first Feedback box, enter the feedback the applicant will receive if they obtain a grade between 70% and 100%. In the second Feedback field, enter the feedback the applicant will receive if they score below 70%. The following screenshot shows these fields completed for our example:

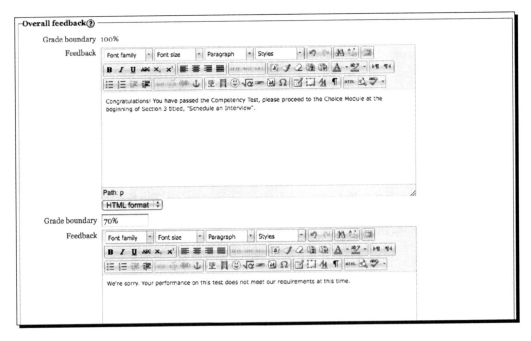

19. Finally in the last section, **Restrict access**, we will set up the condition for being allowed access to the Competency Test. Under the **Grade condition** field, select the activity from which a minimum grade is required. In this example it will be the activity created to submit their resume/CV, entitled, **Please submit your resume for the Available Position here**. Then enter the minimum grade requirement, which is 85% for our example.

20. In the **Before activity can be accessed** field, select whether you would like the activity to be grayed-out with the restricted information listed or whether you want it to be invisible before the activity is available to applicants. We will let it be grayed-out for this example.

21. Click on **Save and display** at the bottom of the page. You will then see a screen as shown in the following screenshot. You have now created a quiz and set up the conditions, but now we need to add questions!

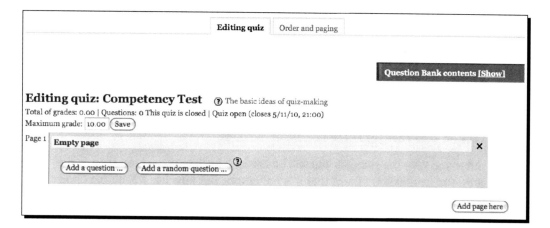

Time for action – adding questions to the quiz

We've set up the shell for our Competency Test and applied the conditional access. Now let's create the questions that will be covered in the exam. Moodle 2.0 has 11 different question types. For now we will focus on the two question types you are most likely to use to set up a Competency Test: Multiple Choice and Essay.

1. From the page you ended at in the previous screenshot, select **Add a question…**. The **Choose a question type to add** window will then pop up. Choose **Multiple choice** from the menu of question types and select **Next**.

2. Accept the default setting for **Category**. Later in the next section you will learn how to create a new category.

3. Enter the title of the question in the **Question name** field. We will call this Question No. 1 in our example.

4. Enter the question in the **Question text** field.

5. In the **Default question grade** field enter the score for each question. We will leave it as the default and the question will be worth one point.

6. The next field is **Penalty factor**. We are not using adaptive mode or penalty factors in this section; therefore just leave that value alone.

7. In the **One or multiple answers?** field towards the bottom of the **General** section, you can set the question type to be a **One answer only** multiple choice question or to a **Multiple answers allowed** multiple choice question.

8. The last step is to enter the choices for the multiple choice question next to the **Answer** field for each Choice. For the correct answer, under the **Grade** drop-down menu, select 100%. If you have a multiple answers question, then you would select a grade depending on the number of correct answers. For example, if the test taker was suppose to select two correct answers, then you would place a 50% in the grade for those choices.

9. Click on **Save changes** at the bottom of the page.

10. After you save the changes you will be brought back to the screen seen in the previous screenshot, except that it is not empty, but now has a Multiple Choice question in the quiz. See the following screenshot:

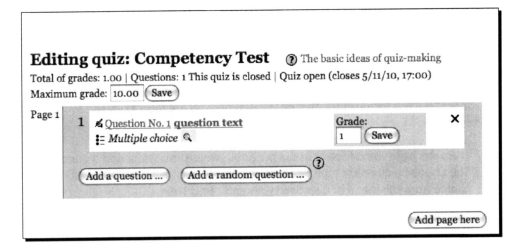

11. Now let's add an Essay question to our quiz. Essay questions can be handy for learning more about an applicant; however they do need to be manually graded after the user takes the exam. Again select **Add a question....** This time from the pop-up window, select **Essay** and then click **Next** at the bottom of the window.

12. You should now be at the **Adding an Essay question** window. Similar to creating a multiple choice question, under the **General** section, select the **Category** you wish to store the question in, enter the **Question name**, **Question text**, and **Default question grade**. Then scroll down to the bottom of the page and select **Save changes**. As mentioned previously, essay questions will need to be manually graded so there is no section to enter the correct answers.

13. After you save the changes you will see a screen, similar to the next screenshot, with two questions created in your quiz:

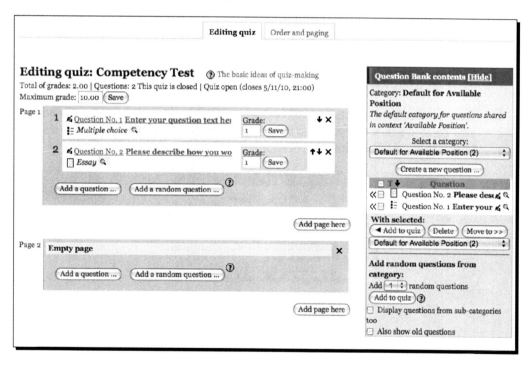

What just happened?

We just created a new question and added it to our competency test. We could create all of the questions for the quiz this way. But it would be difficult to keep everything organized. In the next section, we'll explore how to create question categories.

Time for action – creating a Question Bank

Many times we will want multiple competency exams, to reuse questions in multiple exams, or we may need to create different question banks for each competency test. The best way to do this is to create a category for each question bank and add your questions to the corresponding question bank.

1. From the course home page, with editing turned on, go to the **Course administration** menu and select **Question bank**.

2. From the drop-down menu select **Categories** from the Question Bank drop-down menu. You will be brought to the **Edit categories** page. Here you can edit existing categories or add new categories.

3. To add a new category, go to the **Add category** section towards the bottom of the page.

4. In the **Parent category**, select the parent category for the category you are creating. For this example we will select **Top** beneath the course we are working in. Then enter the name of the category and any category information.

5. Once you are finished, click on **Add category** at the bottom of the page. You have now created a new category and will see it on the **Edit categories** page. See the following screenshot. The Competency Test is the category we created.

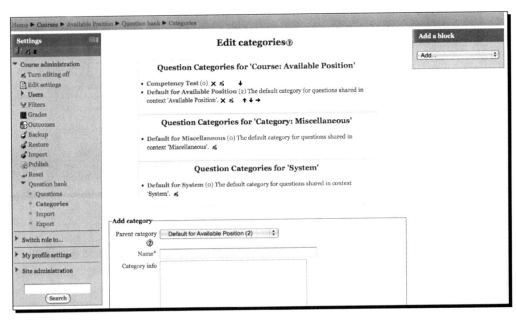

6. Now let's add questions to the category we created. From the **Course administration** menu, select **Questions** from the **Question bank** drop-down menu. You will now be on the **Question bank** page. At the top of the page, select the category you would like to add questions to from the drop-down menu.

7. Click **Create a new question....**You will then be brought to the **Choose a question type to add** window and will follow the steps in the previous section to add questions to your question bank. Refer to the next screenshot for the **Question bank** page:

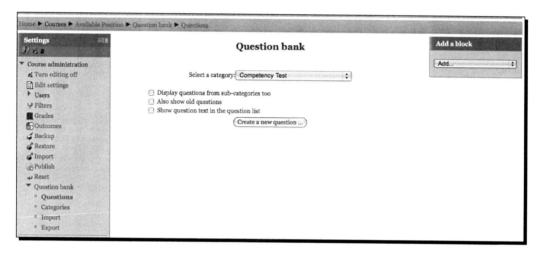

8. Now we need to add our questions from the question bank we just created to our quiz. From the course home page, select the quiz you want to add the questions to. You will now see the **Quiz administration** menu in the **Settings** block. From the **Quiz administration** menu, select **Edit Quiz**.

9. You should now be at the **Editing quiz page** as shown in the next screenshot. This is a very handy page. On the left, notice the Quiz administration menu. In the center you will see the questions already in your quiz and can rearrange or delete the questions as necessary. In the right column you will see the Question Bank contents block. This is where we will select the questions we want to add to the quiz. From the **Select a category:** drop-down menu, select the category you just created.

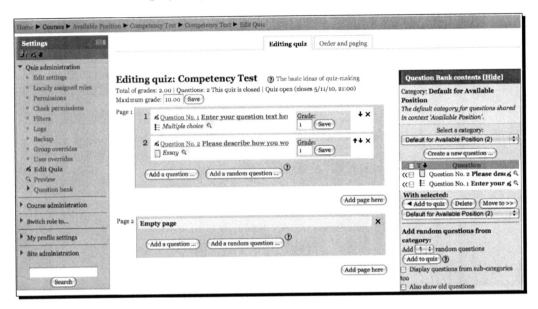

10. Then in the **Question** section you will see all the questions in your category. To the left of the questions are checkboxes. Simply check the box next to the questions you wish to add to the quiz. Then from the **With selected:** menu at the bottom of the question list click **Add to quiz**.

What just happened?

We have now created a simple question bank and added the questions to a quiz. You can use question banks to create large pools of questions organized by topic or skill.

Have a go hero – creating other question types

Go back to your question bank and add a question of a type other than essay or multiple choice. How could you use another question type to evaluate an applicant's abilities?

Time for action – grading competency test responses

If you have used Essay questions in your competency test, you will need to evaluate the applicants' responses and give them a score on each essay question. Unfortunately, artificial intelligence hasn't reached the point of automatically evaluating open response questions, so we still need to do it ourselves.

Once applicants have begun to take the assessment, you begin to evaluate their responses. To grade an essay question:

1. From within the course, select the **Competency Test** link. When you select the quiz as the admin role, you will be taken to the quiz administration page.

2. In the **Settings** menu, select **Results** for the quiz.

3. The next screen will display the quiz results report. See the next screenshot. At the top of the page there are options to filter the display. Make sure **Marks for each question** is set to **Yes**. This will make it easier to see which questions need grading.

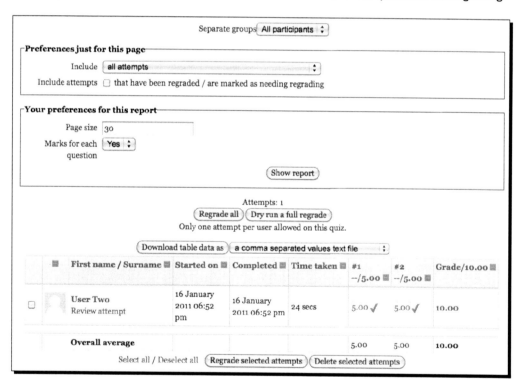

4. Below the Options, each quiz attempt appears after users have made attempts. With the Marks for each question option selected, you will see a column for each question. The ungraded essay questions will have "Requires grading" in the cell for that question. Click the **Requires grading** link.

5. Moodle will then display the question and the applicant's response in a pop-up window. Below their response you will see a link labeled **Make comment or override grade**. Select this link to enter the applicant's score on this question.

6. A new pop-up window will then open with a text box for your comments and an entry field for the score. Make any comments you wish to make on their response and enter your score. When you select the **Save** button, the window should close.

7. Close the window with the user's response and go back to the window with the quiz results report. When you reload the screen, the score you just entered will appear. Repeat steps 4-7 for each question you need to evaluate for the applicants.

What just happened?

You now have a shell for your competency test and know how to create multiple choice and essay quiz questions, categories, and question banks. You also know how to evaluate the essay questions. These are the basic tools you will need to create competency tests.

While Moodle can evaluate multiple choice questions, providing an applicant with just multiple choice questions can constrain the depth of the competency evaluation. Using essay questions requires you to evaluate the applicant's response, but gives the applicant an opportunity to provide a more nuanced response.

Time for reflection

Pull out the map of your hiring process you created earlier. What modifications would you make to what has been discussed in this chapter so far to suit your company's hiring process?

Have a go hero – adding randomized questions to a quiz

You now know how to create quizzes, categories, and question banks. In the last section we discussed how to add questions from a question bank to a quiz. What if you have a very large question bank and you only want to randomly add twenty questions from the question bank to your quiz? Well give it a go! Here is a hint...you will find the last screenshot in the *Creating a Question Bank* section very useful.

Creating a choice module to schedule interviews

You have gone through the resumes and chosen the ones who best meet the job requirements. Those applicants have taken the competency test and now you want to schedule interviews with all the applicants who have received a score greater than 70% on the competency test. There are several ways you could facilitate this process in Moodle, but we're going to do it by creating a choice module!

Time for action – creating a choice module

All the top applicants have passed the competency test by the quiz close date. You now want to schedule interviews with these applicants during the following week. To facilitate this, you need to know when applicants are available for interviews. We'll create a choice module in Moodle where we let applicants select the best times available for them:

1. From the course home page, with editing turned on, go to the section you would like to add the choice module to and from the **Add an activity...** drop-down menu select **Choice**. For this example, we are going to create this module in Section 3, for the third stage in the hiring process, which I have entitled **Interviews**.

2. You are now on the **Adding a new Choice** page. See the next screenshot. In the **General** section, enter the **Choice name** and **Introduction text**:

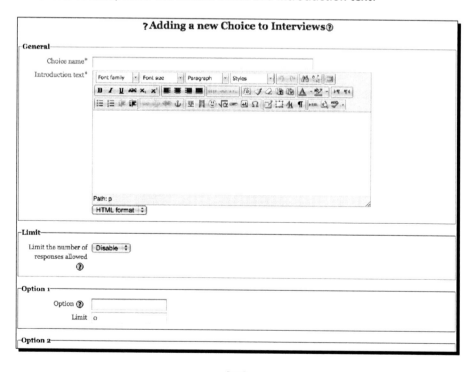

3. The **Limit** section is the next section on the page. Here you can limit the number of applicants that can select each choice. If you want to enable this option, then choose **Enable** from the drop-down menu. This option is extremely helpful in scheduling interviews because we only want one applicant per time slot, so we will enable this option in our example.

4. The next step is to enter our time slots for the interviews. For this example, imagine we want to interview eight people. Therefore, we will want to fill in eight **Options**, which can be found below the **Limit** section. In each **Option** section, we will enter a four hour time window and a **Limit value** of 1. There are only five option sections available as a default. To add more click **Add 3 fields to form**, which is found below the options.

5. The next section is **Restrict answering to this time period**. If you want to restrict the module to a certain time period, select the checkbox and enter the dates.

6. The next section is for **Miscellaneous settings**. The first field is **Display mode**. Here you can select whether you want to display the choices horizontally or vertically. For our example, it will look better to be displayed horizontally. Select **Display horizontally** from the drop-down menu.

7. The next field is **Publish results**. You have four options from the drop-down menu:

   ❏ Do not publish results to students

   ❏ Show results to students after they answer

   ❏ Show results to students only after the choice is closed

   ❏ Always show results to students

8. We are going to select **Do not publish results to students** because we don't want applicants to see responses from other applicants. Only the teacher/HR manager needs to know the schedule and then send e-mails confirming the interview times to the applicants.

9. Under **Allow choice to be updated**, select **Yes**. We want applicants to be able to change the best time for them if necessary.

10. Finally we will go to the **Restrict availability** section, where we can restrict the availability of the choice module only to applicants who have achieved a grade greater than 70% on the competency test. This is similar to what you did when you restricted access to the competency test. Under **Grade Condition**, select the **Competency Test**, and enter the grade requirements.

11. Click on **Save and display** at the bottom of the page and you're finished! The next screenshot shows the Choice module we just created. Remember to test your choice by logging in as a student user:

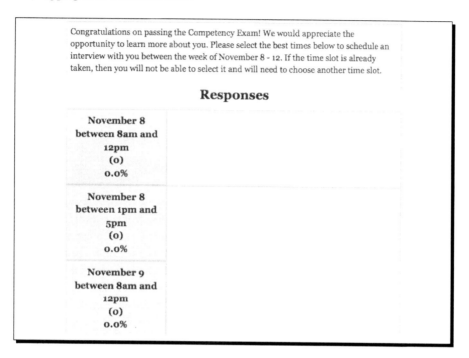

Congratulations on passing the Competency Exam! We would appreciate the opportunity to learn more about you. Please select the best times below to schedule an interview with you between the week of November 8 - 12. If the time slot is already taken, then you will not be able to select it and will need to choose another time slot.

Responses

November 8 between 8am and 12pm (0) 0.0%	
November 8 between 1pm and 5pm (0) 0.0%	
November 9 between 8am and 12pm (0) 0.0%	

What just happened?

You have just created an automated way to schedule interviews. So far, in the first two screenings there has been no direct contact with the applicants. After the choice module where applicants have selected the time they would prefer for the interview, direct contact will begin. Note that you have been able to cut down on a lot of time by automating the first two screenings. You could automate the process even more by only having a multiple choice competency exam so no manual grading will be required.

Time for reflection

At the beginning of this section we mentioned you could coordinate the interview process using several different activities in Moodle. What is another way you could coordinate your interview process?

Creating resources and forums for the decision makers

The interview process and interview style can vary greatly from company to company. Some companies will interview the applicant with several different people individually, some conduct panel interviews, and some may just have one individual conduct the interview and make the hiring decision. Additionally there are several different interview styles: behavioral, structured, directive, non-directive, patterned, and stress. No matter how your company formats its interview process, documents for the interviews need to be available for the interviewers. In order to facilitate this process, we will discuss how to add resources and forums to your course.

Time for action – creating resources and forums for the decision makers

You now have eight interviews with potential new hires scheduled for the available position. As the HR manager, you will need to make sure you have provided the interviewers with the materials they need. Depending on the interview style this may entail a list of topics to be covered during the interview. If it's a structured interview it will include a predetermined set of questions to be asked of all applicants. If it's a non-directive interview, then it will contain a set of less structured, broad questions. You get the idea. There may also be other resources such as the organization's mission statement, information regarding the culture of the company, and information regarding the position for hire. These are all easy to make available in your course using the **Add a resource...** feature. In the first chapter you already learned how to create a file resource so you know how easy that is. This time we are going to put all of our documentation for the interviewer in a folder and upload a folder resource to the new section we created entitled "Resources for the Interview".

1. From the course home page, select **Folder** from the **Add a resource...** drop-down menu in Section 4.

2. You will now be on the **Adding a new Folder** page. In the **General** section, enter the name of the folder and a description. For this example, we will name the folder **Interview Resources** and in the description list some simple instructions for the interviewer.

3. Next is the **Content** section. Click the **Create folder** button. A pop-up window will open asking you to **Please enter folder name**. I am going to use the same name I used in the **General** section in step 2.

4. Once you have created your folder, make sure it is selected so that the Path shows **Files | Folder Name**; then in the same **Content** section click the **Add** button. A **File picker** window will pop up and from here you will follow the instructions to add your files. My files are on my computer so I will click on **Upload a file** button, then

browse to locate the file I want to add. Once selected, click the **Upload this file...** button. You have now added one file to your folder and you will now see it listed in the **Content** section. Repeat this step until you have uploaded all the files you wish to upload to your Moodle course. The next screenshot shows you what the **Adding a new Folder** page should look like once you have filled in the first two sections:

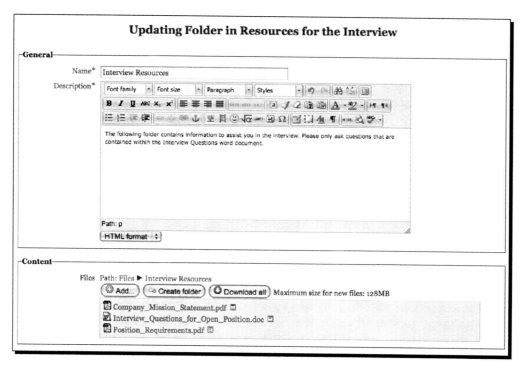

5. Don't worry if you have added the file, but forgot to add it to the folder. Or if you added the wrong file. All you need to do is select the file showing in the content section, and then a menu will pop up with four options: **Download, Rename...**, **Move...**, and **Delete...**, and you will be able to make any necessary changes.

6. There is a **Restrict access** section in the **Adding a new Folder** page, but since this documentation is only being made available to the interviewers who would have more of a teacher/non-editing teacher role, then we are not going to restrict availability based on date or grade. We will leave this section blank.

7. The last step is to click **Save and display**. Your resource will look like the window shown in the following screenshot:

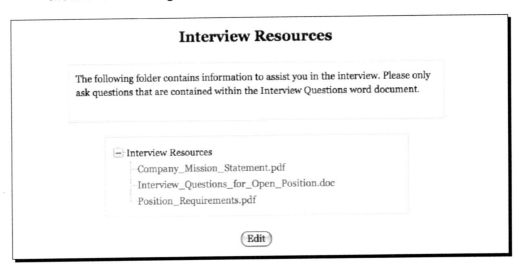

So far, in this chapter we have added four sections to our course, Available Position. The first three sections, Resume Submittal, Competency Test, and Interviews, contain activities in which we want the applicant to participate. The fourth section, Resources for the Interview, is a section we do not want visible to the applicant. We only want the interviewers/teachers to see this last section. How do you make a section visible to interviewers/teachers and not to applicants/students? It's easy. First, turn on Editing. On the course home page, scroll down to the section you want to be only visible to teachers. Then on the right-hand side of the section you will see an eye icon. Select the eye. When the eye is shut, the section is only visible to teachers. When the eye is open, the section is visible to teachers and students. Note that every activity also has an eye icon next to it in case you want to hide just a particular resource, not an entire section.

What just happened?

We added an area to our course for interviewers to store and share resources for the interview process.

Time for action – creating question and answer forums

You learned how to create a general forum in *Chapter 1, Getting Started with Moodle* and you could certainly apply that here for simplicity purposes. For this application let's look at another type of forum Moodle offers—the Question and Answer Forum. Let's go back to our example. You are in a company that has several people interview the applicants. After the interviews, all these people need to come to an agreement on whom to hire. You want everyone's unbiased opinion on the applicant. The Question and Answer Forum is a good tool to use for this. This type of forum requires people to respond to the questions in the forum before they are allowed to view other people's responses. So each interviewer can give their opinion without being influenced by others.

1. From the main course page, in the same section we entitled, "Resources for the Interview", from the **Add an activity...** drop-down menu select **Forum**.

2. You are now on the **Adding a new Forum** page. In the first section, **General**, enter your **Forum name**. Next, from the **Forum type** drop-down menu select **Q and A forum**. At **Forum introduction**, enter the introduction for your forum as in the image. Now there are a couple of ways we could set up this forum for our example. We could create one forum per applicant, with each topic being a question we want the interviewers to answer regarding the applicant they interviewed. Or, we could create one forum, with one topic per applicant. Then within the text of the topic, list all the questions we want the interviewers to answer. For our example, we have chosen to set up one forum per applicant, but keep in mind you could set it up differently if you prefer.

3. The remaining items in the **General** section to be filled out are **Subscription mode**, **Read tracking for this forum?**, **Maximum attachment size**, and **Maximum number of attachments**. Subscription mode allows you to have optional, forced, auto, or disabled subscription. Read tracking refers to whether participants are able to track read and unread messages. Optional allows the participants to decide. This is the option we are going to select for our example. We are looking for interviewers' opinions in this forum so we are not going to allow attachments. The screenshot shows the **General** section filled out for this example:

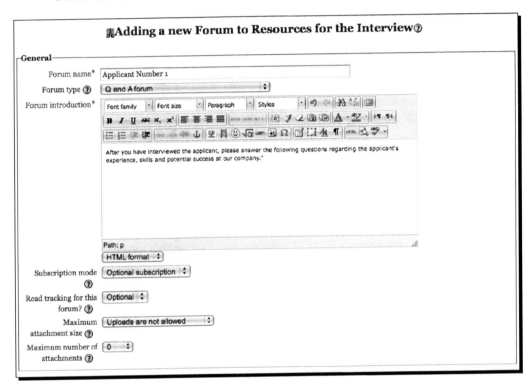

4. For this example, we will leave the rest of the settings as their defaults and click on **Save and display** at the bottom of the page. If you would like more detail regarding these settings please refer to *Chapter 1, Getting Started with Moodle*.

5. You are now on the forum page you just created. At the top of the page you will see your introduction text. Now it's time to add our questions to the forum. Click on the **Add a new question** button located below the introduction text.

6. The **Your new question** page will open and here you will create your question. Enter the **Subject** and in the **Message** field the question you want interviewers to answer regarding the applicant.

7. Under the **Subscription** drop-down menu select if you want to be e-mailed copies of forum posts or not. Then select **Post to forum** at the bottom of the page. The following screenshot shows the **Your new question** page:

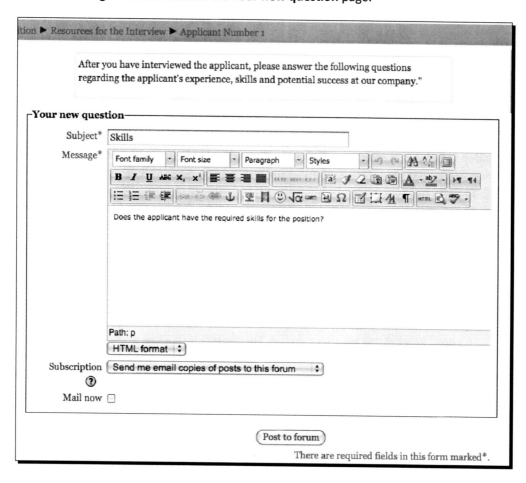

We've created the forum, but we're not done. This format is targeting the interviewers and we don't want applicants to have access to the forum. Let's talk about roles. We set it up earlier in the chapter so that when applicants enroll in the course, they will be enrolled as students. What roles should the interviewers and human resources manager have? Should they be different? Let's talk specifically about the student and teacher roles. A student is a participant in a course; they do not have any editing privileges and can only view what the course creator has allowed. The default teacher role has complete control and editing privileges in a course.

How does this apply to our example? We have applicants, who are students in the course. We have a human resources manager, which has the teacher or admin role, who is responsible for creating the course and grading competency tests. What about the interviewers? Where do they fit in? The human resources manager wants to get unbiased opinions regarding the applicants from the interviewers. If the interviewers are given the teacher role, then they will be able to see and edit everything in the course and therefore the purpose of the Question and Answer Forum will be lost. We need to assign the interviewers a separate role. Roles can be customized to suit a wide variety of needs. We review the basics of role customization in *Chapter 6, Communities of Practice in Moodle*. The non-editing teacher role is perfect for this example.

The non-editing teacher is not allowed to edit anything in the course, but they are able to see hidden sections and activities. Therefore, they will be able to see the Resources for the Interview Section we hide from students. However, we can now set it up so that only non-editing teachers will have access to the question and answer forums that the HR manager is creating to collect the opinions of the interviewers on each applicant. To set up the Q & A forums so that only non-editing teachers will be participants, follow these steps:

1. Select the Q & A forum you created from the main home page. Then in the Settings block you will see the **Forum administration** menu. Select **Permissions**.

2. To prevent the interviewers/non-editing teachers from being able to see other interviewer's responses before they post their own, scroll down to the **Activity forum** section, and towards the bottom of the section you will see **Always see Q and A posts**. Refer to the next screenshot. The default is to allow non-editing teacher, teacher, and manager roles to be able to see the posts. We need to remove the non-editing teacher from this permission. To do this, select the **X** to the right of the **Non-editing teacher**. Now non-editing teachers won't be able to see other posts until they have posted a response.

Always see Q and A posts mod/forum:viewqandawithoutposting	Non-editing teacher✗, Teacher✗, Manager✗ ✚	✚

3. Since we have hidden the section, we know that students will not be allowed access to the forum.

What just happened?

In this section you learned how to set up a section directly targeted at your interviewers. You added any resources they would need to conduct the interview and created a Q & A forum allowing you to collect the opinions of all the interviewers on each applicant. You could use a variety of tools to achieve this, including the quiz module, or forums. You also learned how to use roles to restrict access. You now have all the basic tools you need to facilitate the hiring process.

Time for reflection

Reflect on the hiring process at your company. Take a moment and sketch out the process. Who is involved in making the hiring decision? How do they collaborate to make decisions? Could you make this process better, faster, cheaper with an on-line tool?

How could you support your hiring process with the Moodle skills you have learned so far? What other activities could you use to support your organization's hiring process?

Case Study—A&L Goodbody

A&L Goodbody is Ireland's premier law firm, having recently been named 'Law Firm of The Year' for the fifth consecutive year at the Who's Who Legal Awards. They have over 350 staff and total headcount of 525. Although their primary office is in Dublin, they are an all-island law firm with offices in Dublin and Belfast, and international offices in London and the USA.

Such accolades make the Firm a popular choice for law students seeking traineeships, a prerequisite in Ireland for those who want to become solicitors.

What was the business problem(s) for which Moodle was chosen as the solution?

The solicitor application and assessment process is detailed and involves a number of key stakeholders in the Firm. Previously, each applicant applied by submitting a handwritten Application Form downloaded in PDF format from the Firm's website. The information was then collated manually by an administration team and distributed to the stakeholders for review and interview selection. This process became increasingly cumbersome and time consuming as the number of applicants increased. A more efficient process was required.

What was the solution and how did they arrive at the solution?

A&L Goodbody investigated an online solution in 2007 in order to streamline the recruitment process and cut down on administrative work. Hazel Mullan, Assistant Director of Training and the e-learning project manager at the Firm, had previous experience with Moodle while studying for her Masters in Training & Education Management in Dublin City University and working as a lecturer. Hazel had already successfully piloted Moodle as a Learning Management System within the Firm and thought it might be a good option for the recruitment process, given its extensive functionality.

"We looked at a number of off-the-shelf commercial packages", commented Hazel Mullan, "However we were attracted to Moodle as we could heavily customize it to suit our specific requirements. The fact that we could maintain control of the software and manage the site ourselves proved very attractive".

The solution was a customized version of existing activities within Moodle, namely the questionnaire, quiz, and reporting modules. A&L wanted potential trainees to initially fill out personal details in the questionnaire module. From there they would be directed to a Moodle quiz to test key competencies via an online assessment and then back to the questionnaire to complete and submit the form. The administration team had specific reporting requirements for selection and assessment purposes.

"We were able to extrapolate information from Moodle via an excel spreadsheet which significantly simplified the backend processing work. A printed or e-mailed version of each Application Form could be passed around for review—a significant improvement on its handwritten predecessor!" commented Mullan.

A&L Goodbody was one of the first law firms in Ireland to have their online Application Form up and running in 2008.

Key development work included removing all the navigation options from the site. This locked down the site and steered applicants, 'with a heavy hand' through the application process to completion while removing any possibility of browsing within the site. The main objective was to make the completion of the Application Form a seamless process between the Moodle activities and the user login profile. The site was also branded using the Firm's logo. Enovation worked with A&L to achieve this.

The uniqueness, and in some ways, complexity of the project meant that A&L were keen to engage with a service partner that had extensive knowledge of Moodle to enable them to bring the project to a successful completion. Enovation not only had the Moodle knowledge and experience that A&L were looking for, but also a proven reputation in the legal sector with their long term customer, The Law Society of Ireland.

Why did they choose Moodle?

Selection of a suitable solution should be based on defined needs; both immediate and long term. The Firm chose Moodle for a number of reasons:

- The previous success of Moodle as a learning management system within the Firm.

- It was easy to customize. It could accommodate the Firm's specific requirements: commercial off-the-shelf solutions allowed much less flexibility and control.

- It is easy to use. Through her knowledge of Moodle, Hazel was confident that applicants and those processing the Application Forms would find it easy to use and navigate.

- From a cost benefit point of view it was the best option for the Firm.

- Applicants had more control of the process. They could log in and out, completing their Application Form in different sections until they were happy to submit it.

- It enabled the integration of an online assessment as part of the Application process.

- It provides excellent backend processing facilities and reporting features.

- Law students are already familiar with the software as it was used in universities in Ireland and the Law Society of Ireland.

Was the project a success?

A&L Goodbody successfully piloted the application process with a number of existing trainees in early 2008 and, based on positive feedback, officially launched the system in September 2008.

Hazel continued: "Moodle has proved to be a very effective solution for a very important process. Applying for a traineeship is a daunting and intense process for applicants and we wanted to provide them with a user-friendly online experience which not only improved the process, but gave applicants more control over the process. Using Moodle involved some degree of risk as it hadn't been used for this purpose before but it worked and it has been a resounding success."

The value of e-learning, including A&L Goodbody's use of Moodle, has been recognized with the following nominations and awards:

- A&L were nominated for the 'Best Commercial Initiative Under 1000 Employees' in the 2009 UK Training Journal Awards for ALG e-learning

- A&L Learning & Development won an 'outstanding achievement' award at the IITD National Training Awards for the second year in a row 2008 and 2009

- A&L e-learning receives 'highly recommended' commendation for the IITD Pearse Walsh Award 2009

- A&L e-learning won second place in the Managing Partner Forum Awards: 'Best use of Technology' 2008

What were the benefits gained?

A&L Goodbody's online Application Form site hosts several different types of Application Forms seamlessly and the application process is completely automated and streamlined:

- The administration time associated with the recruitment process has been greatly reduced.

- Applicants now experience a much more user-friendly and cutting edge application process.

- The reporting features, such as those on the Moodle quiz, give key stakeholders a breadth of information which benefits the selection process and was previously unavailable.

- Applicants can print submitted Application Forms from their own computers for their records. An HTML editing box allows applicants to edit their applications (for example, Spell check) before submitting them.

- Completed applications can be e-mailed between stakeholders.

- The administration team can produce crucial reports from every data field in the system for the purposes of mail merges and trainee application follow ups.

What lessons were learned?

Hazel Mullan: "We used Moodle in a way that it had never been used before. We came at Moodle from a different angle and harnessed its unique functionality to meet our requirements. Release the potential; throw away the box!"

Summary

We learned a lot in this chapter about setting up a Moodle course to implement the process of hiring for a new position.

Specifically, we covered:

- We learned how to create an assignment to allow users to submit a document.

- We created a basic competency test with multiple choice and essay questions.

- We looked at how to use the choice module to schedule interviews and support the interview process with a Q and A forum.

- We also learned how to manage the application process by linking activities together with conditional access. Only applicants who are qualified are allowed to pass on to the next activity.

- We also took a look at overriding permissions to enable you to customize the behavior of the modules.

Now that we've learned about using Moodle to support hiring great people, we're ready to begin training them—which is the topic of the next chapter.

3
Rollout Products and Services with Moodle

Across an organization, there is a continual need for providing product knowledge internally and externally. Many layers of staff need to know the business products from various perspectives. In addition to the internal audiences, an organization's clients and product end users need to understand more about the product to use it effectively.

Moodle can be a key component in meeting the challenge of providing efficient and cost effective knowledge training to this diverse set of constituents. This chapter covers some of the techniques that you can employ to meet this business goal.

In this chapter, the reader shall:

- ◆ Understand how to set up a Moodle course to cater for the wide range of roles which need product knowledge
- ◆ Learn how to create terminology glossaries to help accustom the participants to the new key phrases
- ◆ See how to organize a real-time role-playing chat between participants
- ◆ Learn how to create a Product Knowledge Sheet database using Moodle and how to use this in the knowledge program
- ◆ Use the Random Glossary Block to provide extra context to your course content

So let's get on with the show.

Using Moodle to support rolling out products and services

Developing and maintaining product knowledge is core to the success of a business in many departments but especially in sales and support. This chapter will focus on some techniques of using Moodle to help deliver product knowledge training and development of a product knowledge community.

Some points to keep in mind

As already discussed, there are a wide range of roles in an organization which require adequate product knowledge to be effective in supporting the rollout of a product.

The sales force needs access to up-to-date product knowledge, descriptions, and benefits, so they can be effective in providing solutions to existing and new customers.

The support staff needs access to not only product knowledge used in sales, but also a deeper knowledge in other areas so that they can respond effectively to internal and external queries.

The finance department needs access to the underlying principles of the product, the costs of creation, delivery, and support, so they can manage and understand the impact to the bottom line.

The marketing staff needs access to the whole range of product knowledge to deliver supporting advertising and promotion.

The end users need product training on how to use the product effectively.

While going through each of the sections, keep in mind all of these different target audiences and how this could work for them as well.

To cater for this diverse set of constituents, you have two options:

- ◆ Create a different Moodle course for each target audience
- ◆ Use the Moodle topic structure to allow each role to focus just on their needs

In this section we will implement the second option, creating a course which takes advantage of the new navigation options in Moodle 2.0 by focusing on just one topic at a time.

In previous chapters we have touched on adding in resources and uploading content files to the course. So we won't be covering this during the rest of this chapter. We will focus on laying out the course in a structured manner, and on implementing three activities which help support product knowledge learning.

The sample course outline will be available throughout 2011 for all purchasers of the book on http://www.moodleforbusiness.com/.

Setting up a course for a new product

For the purpose of an example product for this chapter, I have selected the open source ePortfolio product Mahara from http://www.mahara.org.

Before you set up a course it is important to know what the goals of the training are; that is, what are the learning objectives for each part of the course. Traditionally this has been done for face to face with a curriculum structure of a Scheme of Work. This becomes the map which you configure your online course with.

Below we will go through a sample extract from a Scheme of Work for an introduction course on a product called Mahara. This is an online product used for e-Portfolios, but this approach can work for all product types.

There are many layouts used for creating a Scheme of Work for a class, but they all generally cover the structure and the content of a course.

There are two key aspects of the Scheme of Work structure.

Firstly, there is an overall summary section; this abstracts all the objectives and reasons for the course. Some of the data it usually includes is:

- **Module Name**
- **Module Level** (This can be a standard set of definitions or a custom scale such as basic, intermediate, and advanced)
- **Requirements and Assumptions**
- **Technical Requirements** (The requirements for a course online are often different to those offline. Are you using technologies which they will need such as Flash? Will they need MS Office or PowerPoint? Will they need a microphone or speakers?)
- **Required Outcomes**

There can be a lot more options here and you may have an organizational standard already as to what information is recorded. Below is an example of the Scheme of Work's first page:

Scheme of Work Overview	
Module Name	Introduction to Mahara
Level	This is a basis introduction to the product and is aimed at sales and internal support staff.
Requirements and assumptions	• Everyone will have a computer with internet access for accessing the training online. • Everyone will have knowledge of the learning/training& Development sector.
Technical requirements	• A computer with soundcard with headphones/speakers • Internet access • Modern Web Browser with standard plugins including flash, adobe acrobat reader.
Required Outcomes	1. Understand what an ePortfolio is 2. Understand the key components of Mahara 3. Understand the terminology of Mahara 4. Understand some of the use cases of Mahara 5. Be able to create a simple profile 6. Be able to create a simple view

Secondly, there is the summary detail of each distinct lesson. This summary is usually enhanced greatly for the full lesson plan. This is often a table with a number of columns:

- Lesson Number
- Lesson Name
- Lesson Objectives
- Lesson Resources
- Lesson Activities
- Trainer/Facilitator Guidelines

Having this basic information is really helpful as it can be used as the map for the online course. Following is a brief sample of content for the second page of the Scheme of Work as outlined above.

#	Topic	Outcomes	Resources	Assessment
	Topic Name	Understand Y Able to do X	Presentation on aaaa Case study on bbbb Worksheet on cccc Video on dddd	Discussion on topic at end OR MCQ Quiz on topic OR Create something OR ...
1	ePortfolios	Understand what an ePortfolio is	Presentation on ePortfolios	Discussion about concept of eportfolios.
2	Background of Mahara	Understand the background to Mahara Understand the terminology of Mahara	Overview on Mahara Glossary of Terminology	Quiz testing terminology and understanding of the product.
3	Using Mahara	Understand the key components of Mahara	...	...

Time for action – creating a Scheme of Work

Identify a product or service that you want to improve the training for within your organization. You are tasked with creating the training for this product. So let us begin. For simplicity, take an existing product or service that you know well and go through the following steps. For this exercise, choose one or two audiences that you will focus on, to keep the objectives short and concise:

1. Using MS Word, OpenOffice, or even on paper lets create the summary page as described above.

2. Once this is done, on a second page, create a list of lessons that you want to deliver.

3. For each lesson create a table as in the example above with the lesson name, learning objectives, resources, and activities.

4. Review your work to ensure you are happy that the lesson summaries tackle your overall objectives and none were left out.

What just happened?

With the Scheme of Work created, you now have an outline for your course which you want to implement.

Now we can go on to take the Scheme of Work document and turn it into a Moodle course structure.

Creating the course

Looking at the Scheme of Work document we can now look at each of the distinct lessons and make them into a topic within your Moodle course.

Time for action – creating the course

There are a number of built-in formats in Moodle which help you lay out your course. The most commonly used include:

1. **Weekly format**: This course is organized week-by-week starting with the date that you enter in the course settings.

2. **Topics format**: This course is broken up into topic sections where you put a set of resources and activities.

3. **Social format**: This course type is designed around the use of one main forum and arguably isn't even a course, just a social discussion area.

4. **Scorm format**: This is a pre-packaged course format usually used when you have a large bundled course bought off the shelf from a supplier like Skillsoft (for example).

From my experience, the most used course format is the **Topic format** and that is what we are going to use for this example. Now we will go through the basic settings that you would want to use in creating the course itself.

In *Chapter 1, Getting Started with Moodle,* we went through the process of creating a course, so here we will focus on the key fields that you will want to use, and skip the rest.

1. From within **Course categories**, click on **Add a new course** which brings you to the **Edit course settings** page.

2. For **Course full name** enter in the name of your training course.

3. The **Course short name** is a shortened course name that is used in the navigation which should be short and snappy, but meaningful. Feel free to use X123 or similar if that is meaningful to your organization.

4. You can ignore the **Course ID number** and now fill in the **Course summary**. This can fit many purposes, but most often is the advertising or marketing "pitch" of what the course covers, its objectives, and requirements. So your summary sheet from the Scheme of Work is a good starting point for text.

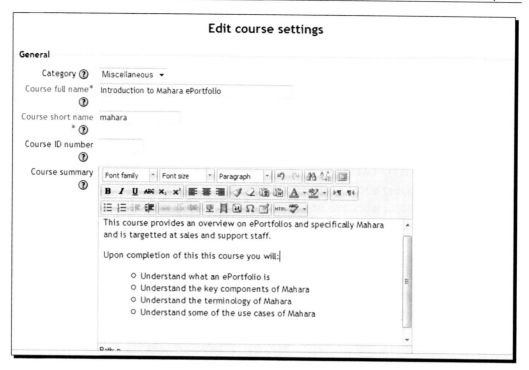

5. When you scroll down, make sure that the **Format** is **Topics format**.

6. You can set the **Number of weeks/topics** to whatever you want, but as a general rule, if you have three lessons, add two extra topics, so this would need five: One topic for introduction, one topic per lesson, and one for wrap up. You can ignore most of the other settings for now. However, the last section on **Role renaming** can be edited at this point to whatever language you use with your organization. Here I have changed the role names from **Manager** to **Supervisor**, from **Teacher** to **Trainer** and from **Student** to **Participant**. This is the text that appears in places during the course, so having familiar wording is important.

7. Click on **Save changes.**

8. When you get prompted to **Enroll users** on the **Enrolled users** page, you can simply skip this by clicking on the **Course short name** in the **Navigation** block. You can come back and enroll participants at a later stage when the course is ready.

What just happened?

We have set up the course the way we need it. The course name is meaningful and the description outlines what the course is about. The course has enough topics for the course purpose, but nothing extra. The wordings of the roles have been changed to reflect the organization.

Now we can continue to create the overall structure.

Creating the structure

When a course is created it is very empty. You have just walked into the digital equivalent of an empty room with four walls and no furniture, desks, chairs, carpet, windows, flipchart, projector, whiteboard, and so on. Now we need to add the structures to the course.

Time for action – editing topic summaries

The Topics Format as you can see is just a list of numbered topics with no context. This allows you to decide how to structure and order the content. First, let us put some structure to this empty course by adding the titles to each topic.

From my sample lesson plan I have my three lesson titles, so I will use these to name my topics as follows:

1. In Topic 1 (with the number one beside it) click on the **Edit icon**.

2. Un-tick **Use default section name**. This allows you to customize the topic title for navigation.

3. Type the lesson name into the **Section name** field. I always use topic1 as the introduction to a course rather than topic0, so let's put **Introduction** here. However, why I recommend this needs explanation.

    When you use the facility to focus on one topic at a time in a Moodle course, it shows topic0 and the topic you are focusing on. So if you put much more than the course name, and perhaps the intro forum in topic0, it pushes the topic you are looking at further down the screen.

4. Ignore the **Summary** field. I recommend using a Label to hold this type of information. When the content is in a label, it is identified within the course structure as a resource, which can help if you need to move the information around within the course or set up conditional visibility.

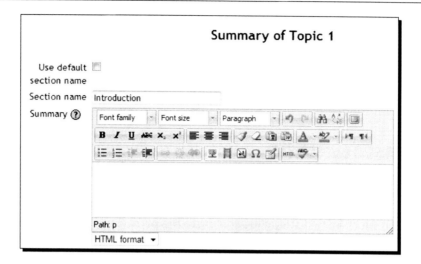

5. Click on **Save changes** and repeat steps 1 through 5 for the other topics.

6. You will have noticed that the area above topic1 (known as Topic0) hasn't been edited and has a news forum in it. Using the same approach, edit this section and just give it a name, the same as the course name.

7. Then using the **move icon** on the News forum, move it into topic1.

8. Rename the **News forum** to **Course announcements** as this is the primary usage of the forum. This helps avoid confusion for learners.

9. Now **Turn editing off**, and you can see the course layout as follows:

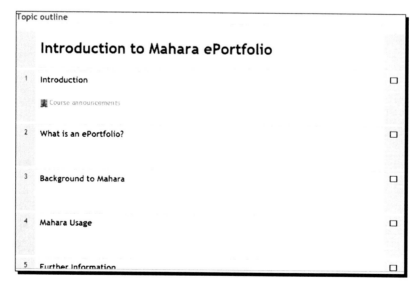

What just happened?

Now when you look at the course page you can see the overall structure starting to appear through the section titles. These titles also will help the navigation but this is just the first step, so let's keep moving.

The next step is to add some context to those titles.

Adding lesson objectives

Topic titles alone give just an indication of what the topic contains. To avoid that "am I in the right place?" question from participants, this is where a general description of the topic lesson comes in. The lesson objectives from the Scheme of Work can help form the basis for this description which immediately gives context to the participant. However, there are many other uses for this first label including inspirational quotes related to the material. There are a few ways of structuring the description and objectives; this is just one way.

Time for action – adding labels to each topic

Let's start with the first topic.

1. Make sure editing is on. If not, click on **Turn editing on**.

2. As in *Chapter 1, Getting Started with Moodle*, to add a resource label, click on the **Add a resource** drop down and select **Label**.

3. In the introduction text include the lesson objectives for the lesson when it's a lesson topic. These objectives would be the same as the ones you wrote in the Scheme of Work.

4. When you are finished, click on **Save and return to course**.

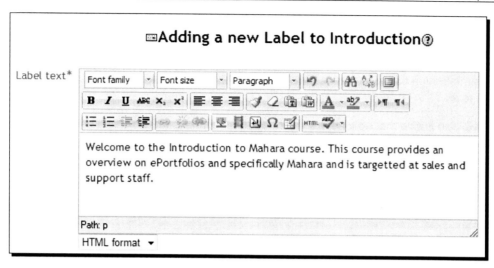

5. Now repeat steps 2 through 4 for each topic.

6. In topic 1 you will want to move the forum below the label. Do this using the move resource icon as before.

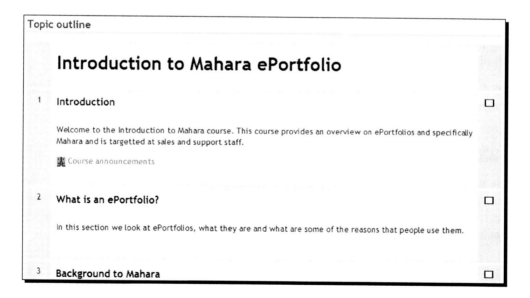

What just happened?

Now look at the course. It is starting to take shape. Anyone looking at this page will know the purpose of the course, the goals, and see how it is broken down. Clarity in layout and contextualization can help reduce the stress of the participant and provide direction on what to do.

You will also notice that now once a topic has some content, the summary name which we added forms the navigation tree in the navigation block. This is a really powerful aspect of Moodle 2.0; with just one click a participant can focus in on the topic they want, and also swap to other topics quite easily.

Reflection

Think about the existing product development and implementation at your organization. After completing this section, what changes to the process would you recommend? What additions do you think would help maximize the success of a product rollout?

Have a go hero – adding more topics

Once you have the course created, you suddenly realize that you need to add another lesson for another target audience or constituent. So we need to add in another topic.

Doing this is very straightforward, and just requires us changing the existing course settings and editing in a summary name, and a descriptive label.

Don't forget that you will need to move that topic above the last one using the move icon on the right side of the topic.

Creating a glossary of terminology

Often in business there is product-related terminology and abbreviations which need to be known to understand the product. It is essential to add in a glossary of these terms to enable users to look up complicated or unknown wordings for clarification. This is achieved with the Moodle activity type "Glossary".

Time for action – creating a glossary

Now that you know that you need a glossary, the steps for creating a glossary for your course terminology is straightforward.

1. Ensure that editing is turned on (click **Turn Editing On**).

2. In Topic 1 (**Introduction**) click on the **Add an activity** drop down, and select **Glossary** from the options.

 Although there are a lot of options, to create a simple glossary we just need to focus on a few of the fields.

3. This glossary will be for **Product Terminology**, so fill this in as the **Name** of the glossary.

4. Description is very important in most activities, and the glossary is no different. This provides the context around the content which appears in the glossary. So fill in some text explaining why the glossary is here and for what purpose it is added.

5. Leave the default **Entries shown per page**, as ten is a good amount. However, you may want to change this to more or less depending on the size of each entry to avoid too much scrolling.

6. As this glossary is related to the Mahara course, leave the **Is this glossary global** un-ticked. With a Global glossary you can have the terminology auto-linked from throughout Moodle and not just this one course. However, as that can lead to confusion if lots of courses have global glossaries, let's keep it local.

   Auto-linking is a powerful feature of Moodle. When this is enabled, any time the wording appears in the Moodle course content, it will automatically become a link to the entry in the glossary. This helps users get immediate access to words they don't understand.

7. You can leave all of the other settings as they are, except for **Approved by default** which you will want to set to **No** before the course is live. This is just in case you encourage participants to add in entries that you have to approve before they are seen by others.

8. Click on **Save and display** to create the empty glossary:

The terminology around ePortfolios and Mahara can sometimes be quite unusual and will be new to those not familiar with the area. This glossary contains all of the key phrases related to the product.

Search ☐ ☑ Search full text

Add a new entry

Browse by alphabet Browse by category Browse by date Browse by Author

Browse the glossary using this index

Special | A | B | C | D | E | F | G | H | I | J | K | L | M | N | O | P | Q | R | S | T | U | V | W | X | Y | Z | **ALL**

No entries found in this section

What just happened?

Now you have added in a glossary to your course. It has no entries yet, but it provides the framework for you to add entries in and should you want to, you can allow participants to add entries in as well.

You will see in the image before that it is possible to browse by alphabet, category, date, and author. This helps users get access to the information that they want in a direct manner.

Adding terms to the glossary

Now the glossary is set up, but it is empty. It is time to add some of the terms or acronyms to the glossary.

Time for action – adding entries to the glossary

To start adding items into the glossary please ensure that you are in the glossary and not in the course page.

1. Click on the button **Add a new entry**. This brings up the form which we need to fill out.

2. The two required fields here are **Concept** and **Definition**, so select one of the terms related to the product and enter it in here.

3. If the definition can apply to a number of words that are used as an alias for the **Concept**, you can add those extra aliases in the **Keyword(s)** section; otherwise leave this empty.

4. If the definition benefits from a file attachment, such as an image, video, or even a document, you can attach it here under **Attachment**. However, for this example we will leave it empty.

5. One of the very powerful aspects of using the glossary is where it can **auto-link** the phrase to the definition wherever it appears in the course content. However, for now leave that un-ticked. The other two options relate to the logic of how it is auto-linked.

6. Click on **Save changes**.

7. Repeat steps 1 through 7 to add some more definitions if you wish.

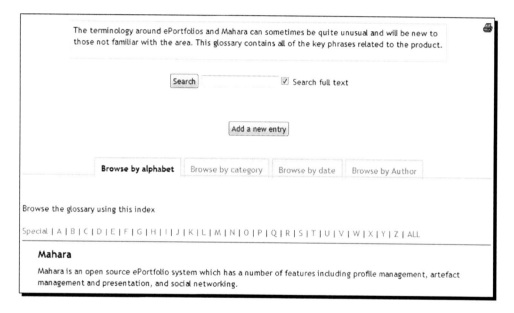

What just happened?

We just went through the process of adding in one entry to the glossary. As you can see it is quite quick as long as you have your concepts and definitions to hand.

While having a simple glossary of terminology helps provide some important content and context to the resources in the course, you can use the glossary to test the participant's understanding of the material by asking them to take two terms and create their own definitions.

Creating flashcards

Once you have some content in the glossary you can have one of the entries display randomly as part of the course page using one of the standard blocks.

Time for action – adding the random glossary entry block

Make sure you have returned to your course page by clicking on the short name in the navigation block. When creating a course I usually remove all of the blocks except for the **Navigation** and **Settings** blocks. This forces you to justify to yourself on which blocks to add from a teaching/learning point of view.

1. To add this new block we need to scroll down so we can see the **Add a block** option:

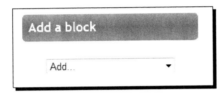

2. Click on the drop down and select the **Random glossary entry** from the list (it is near the bottom of the list).

3. Once it is added you will need to configure it using the edit icon, so click on the **edit** icon in the new block immediately above the **Add a block** menu box.

4. Some of the settings are already filled in, and in fact you don't need to change many settings. However, to start, change the **Title** to **Important terms**. This is the name that the block has in the course view page. Often people choose to have no block name, but this may not work with your theme.

5. The second field **Take entries from this glossary** allows you to select which glossary to use as the source of content for this block. This is great when you have more than one glossary available.

6. If the course is running over a lengthy period, and you want to have the same content item appear in the block for a few days, put that number of days in the **Days before a new entry is chosen** field. I seldom do this as I like the dynamic daily changes.

7. **How a new entry is chosen** is a very powerful option. If you have a set of ordered content (such as daily steps to achieve a task), then selecting **Next Entry** from the drop down is the best choice. If you are having students create entries, then using the **last modified entry** option from the drop down is the most appropriate to use.

8. If the entry is a definition, then you should leave **Show concept (heading) for each entry** set to **Yes**. However, if it is a quote, image, or different context, you may wish to set this to **No**.

9. The three text options **When users can add entries...**, **When users can view the glossary...**, and **When users cannot edit...** can be removed, so the links to add quotes or browse quotes don't show. This is what I have done below. However, if you want to prompt users to submit entries, or browse around the content from the block, leave the text in, although you will probably want to edit it.

Configuring a Important Terms block

┌Block settings─

Title	Important Terms
Take entries from this glossary	Glossary of Product Terminology ▾
Days before a new entry is chosen	0
How a new entry is chosen	Random entry ▾
Show concept (heading) for each entry	Yes ▾

You can display links to actions of the glossary this block is associated with. The block will only display links to actions which are enabled for that glossary.

When users can add entries to the glossary, show a link with this text	
When users can view the glossary but not add entries, show a link with this text	
When users cannot edit or	

---

10. Click on **Save changes** and you return to the course.

What just happened?

Now when you look at the course page, you can see a glossary entry appearing on the bottom-right, below the other active blocks. This randomly-changing content block not only provides extra content on the page, but also helps to keep the page fresh and new.

Breaking up a glossary into categories

We have talked about different types of entries that you may have in your glossary. However, even just with terminology, you may want to enable the participants to separate the different terms and browse them by category. By default there are no categories, so you will need to decide what categories you want and then create them.

Time for action – adding a category

Categories are managed within the glossary activity itself. So if you are on the course page, click into the glossary so you can see the browse by options.

1. Click on **Browse by category**. This will show the category list.

2. Click on the button **Edit categories**. This brings up the **Category manager** page.

3. Initially there are no categories here, so to create one click on **Add category**.

4. You will be prompted to enter a category **Name** and decide if you want this auto-linked. So type in the category **Name** and leave the **Link** option at **No** for now.

5. Click **Save changes** to return to the **Category manager** page.

6. Repeat steps 3 through 5 to add some more categories as required.

7. Click on **Back** to return to the glossary category view.

8. Although we have added categories, none show on this **Browse by category** view. The entries have not been tagged with a category as the category needs to be added when the entry is created, or by editing an existing glossary entry. So let's add a new entry by clicking on the **Add a new entry** button.

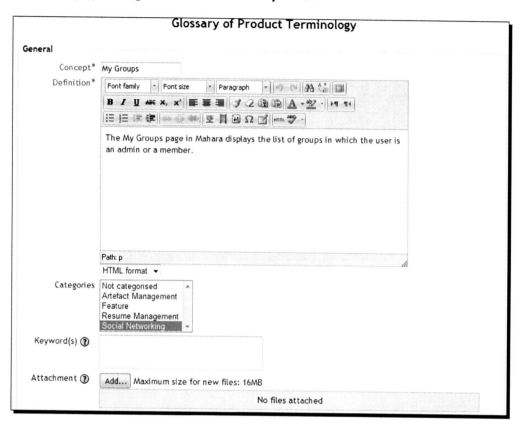

9. Now you can see the list of categories from which you can select none, one, or many to tag the **Concept**. Create a new entry by adding the **Concept**, **Definition**, and selecting one or more **Categories**, and then click on **Save changes**.

What just happened?

Now that we have added some categories, and added in a new entry with a category selected, we can look at the glossary **Browse by category** page. As you can see there is now the **Social Networking** category and the **My Groups** entry, as shown in the following screenshot:

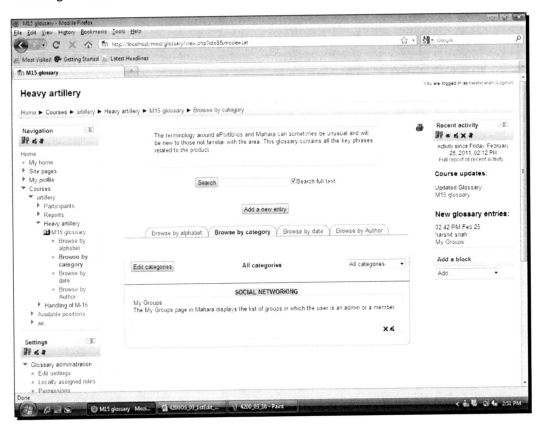

Have a go hero – adding different glossaries

A **glossary** and the **random glossary entry** block can be used to present other types of content on the page and not just terminology.

Suppose you wanted to add a selection of product images into the course which would change each time the page loaded. How would you go about configuring the glossary and its entries for this use case?

Maybe your sales team could benefit from having the key unique selling points of the product appearing like a "quote of the day" on the page; how would you go about doing this?

What other use case for the glossary can you think of that would help support the product knowledge acquisition process?

Complex terminology seems to be everywhere now. How is complex terminology currently handled in your organization? Think about the products in your organization. Which would benefit from having a distinct glossary of terms to help reduce misunderstandings? Which already have printed glossaries but could use improvement?

Implementing role-playing

One way to assess someone's grasp of the product is to conduct a role-play where one participant tries to sell the product to another. As a sales training role-play, it can be useful to run a few different role-plays where the potential buyer knows more or less about the product to see how the discussions progress.

Once you have the role play scenario thought out, the next step is to choose which of the activities available online are suitable for the delivery.

There are multiple ways to run such role-playing online:

- You can use a real-time audio tool, where people speak but have no visual cues
- You can use full video conferencing, where the visual aspect always comes into play
- And you can use a text chat where there is only what is written, and no audio or visual cues

Moodle integrates with a wide range of third-party conferencing software which can cater for the first two scenarios, but it has a very strong real-time chat activity which is suitable for tackling the third method. This is what we will focus on here.

Time for action – creating a chat

Using a Moodle chat for a sales role play scenario has a few strong benefits. The first is that before people send the message to the chat, they are able to edit it and so can be happy with what they are saying. It's a bit less immediate however, when just learning a product. This can help support that learning process. Secondly the chat sessions can be logged and kept for a long period of time, either just for the trainers' access or for the participants too. This provides people with options to go back through the role-play and analyze what was said and reflect on them after the fact.

1. We are going to create a chat session in Topic 4. So before we begin, go to the course view page and make sure that editing is turned on.

2. Scroll down to **Topic 4** and click on the **Add an activity**.

3. Select **Chat** from the drop-down menu.

4. As with all **activities** and **resources**, the name field is very important. This is the text that appears on the course view. Type **Role-Play: Want to buy a Mahara**? into the field **Name of this chat room**.

5. The **Introduction text** is very important for the chat session. This sets the scene of the chat, so be sure to enter text which explains the scenario that will be role-played and any guidelines that you want participants to follow.

6. The **Next chat time** is a great way to schedule the chat. The chat gets put into the course calendar. Set a time within the next day.

7. **Repeat sessions** allow for holding a chat daily, weekly, or just once. For this chat, choose the second option in the drop down: **No repeats – publish the specified time only**.

8. Click on **Save and return to course**.

9. You will now see the chat entry **Role-Play** has appeared in **Topic 4** with a chat icon beside it.

What just happened?

We have now just scheduled a role-play scenario using the Moodle chat session. This appears both on the course view page as demonstrated and on the calendar with the date that we have chosen. The calendar is available as a block that can be added to the course using the same steps as adding the random glossary entry.

However, what if someone misses the chat session? What if someone wants to go back and read the session from before and reflect upon what went well and what could be improved upon?

Recording the role-play

By default, chat sessions are saved forever, although only the trainer has access to the session. While this is useful from the trainers' point of view, participants often want to replay what happened and see what can be improved.

Time for action – a look at chat logging

To enable the participants to view the old sessions we must edit the chat settings:

1. Click on the **edit icon** for the existing chat session in Topic 4.

2. Change the **Everyone can view past sessions** set to **Yes**.

3. Click on **Save and display**.

Role-Play: Want to buy a Mahara?

In this chat session two people will conduct a role play exercise.

One of the people will be playing the part of a sales person trying to sell Mahara as an ePortfolio solution.

Their counterpart will be playing the part of a lecturer in a college who is looking for a solution for students showcasing their project work.

The role play will last up to 10 minutes with everyone contributing to a discussion afterwards.

Click here to enter the chat now

Use more accessible interface

---

4. This is what the user will see when they click on the chat from the course view. We need to enter the chat and type some lines.

5. Click on the **Click here to enter the chat now** link.

6. This will pop up a chat window. As you can see in the following screenshot, the area on the left is where the text from the discussion appears, and on the right is the list of attendees. You use the box at the bottom to type in your text.

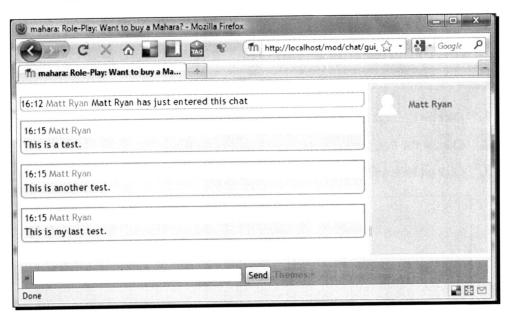

7. Each of the text messages are stamped with the time and name of the participant who contributed. Type a message into the text box and click **Send**.

8. Type two more messages into the textbox, clicking **Send** after each one.

9. Close the pop-up chat window.

10. Reload the chat activity page. You will see that a new option has appeared: **View past chat sessions**. Click on this link.

11. Since we did not have a full session, it will state that it found no complete chat sessions. Click on the link **List all sessions** to access a list of every session, whether complete or not.

12. The page will display all sessions, and in each session box it will list the participants and the number of messages they contributed in brackets after their name. For example **Matt Ryan (3)** in the following example.

13. Click on the link for **See this session**. You now get a list of all the messages sent during the sessions, with the name and timestamp for each message.

Role-Play: Want to buy a Mahara?: Chat sessions

Listing all sessions. List just complete sessions.

Saturday, 30 October 2010, 04:15 PM --> Saturday, 30 October 2010, 04:19 PM

Matt Ryan (3)

See this session
Delete this session

What just happened?

By creating a chat session in Moodle we have enabled participants to role-play a sales scenario and hold a discussion afterwards about the role-play.

By providing access to past sessions to all participants, even those who were unable to attend are able to benefit from the role-play and the subsequent discussion.

Have a go hero – different chat options

In a fast changing business marketplace, it may be useful to only keep logs for a shorter period of time. How would you go about doing this?

In one of the chat discussions something confidential was mentioned, but the chat is keeping logs forever. What would you do to remove the chat history?

A product manager wants to make himself available for regular weekly-chat sessions to answer any queries on the product that people may have. How would you go about setting this up?

Reflection

Do you currently use role-plays in face-to-face training? If you do use them, how do people react to role-playing? Reflect on the difference between face-to-face and online role-playing. What are the benefits of one over the other, and when is it best to use face-to-face, or best to use online?

Creating and assessing product knowledge sheets

Different staff within organizations use product information (or product knowledge) sheets in different ways. The sales team use product knowledge sheets to help provide the key information to a potential lead while support staff use knowledge sheets to help tackle and understand the challenges a user may have.

Once participants have gone through the various information brochures, product manager and subject matter expert's presentations, listened to the podcasts, and perhaps even used the product, asking them to create a product knowledge sheet and thus distilling the information that they have acquired is often a good test of their knowledge understanding and acquisition.

There are many ways that this could be done in Moodle, but in this example we will use the **Database activity** which allows you to create customized forms into which participants fill in information.

Once an entry has been reviewed by the trainer, the submissions can then be opened up to other users for peer review through comments.

This dual approach of both creation and assessing other's product sheets should give the participants a better rounded understanding of the purpose of the sheet and the information they hold.

Time for action – creating the outline of the product knowledge sheet

Before we start configuring a database we need to know what we are doing with it, what the plan is. A product knowledge sheet can have quite a lot of different types of information depending on the product and the target audience of the sheet.

Some of the possible information that you could find include Description, Product properties and features, Product capabilities, Product applications, Product advantages, Typical users, Opening questions, Closing statements, and Competition products.

So before we build this form for participants we need to decide which fields we want them to be filling in. For the purpose of this example, we will just use four fields:

1. Choose what product information fields that you will want to test the participants on (we will use description, capabilities, applications, and advantages).

2. Decide what order you want them in, and what level of detail you expect the participants to provide.

What just happened?

As with all of the more complicated activities in Moodle, preparation is paramount to not lose yourself in settings and options, and end up having to start from scratch.

Having prepared manually what you are going to apply to the database, now you are ready to move forward.

Building a structure

The database activity is one which has so many use cases that it sometimes can be overwhelming to start off using it. However, as we have a very clear purpose in what we want to achieve don't be put off by the number of options and just stay focused on what we need to achieve.

The process of creating a database is as follows:

1. Create the structure with the settings.
2. Add fields to the database.
3. You may at this point edit the templates from the default ones but this is totally optional. You will probably come back later and edit them to add in context.
4. Add in sample entries.

So let's get on with the first step, creating and configuring the database activity itself.

Time for action – creating the database

Before we start, return to the course view page and make sure editing is turned on. It is a good habit to turn editing off whenever you are not editing the course as this can help reduce mishaps of deletions, or moving items around.

1. We want to create a product knowledge test form in Topic 4. Scroll down to Topic 4.
2. Click on **Add an activity** and select **Database** from the drop down.
3. Enter **Product Knowledge Assessment** into the **Name** field.

4. As with other assignments it is important to use the **Introduction** field to explain the purpose of the activity and to clarify what exactly is required from the participants. Please fill out the **Introduction** along those lines:

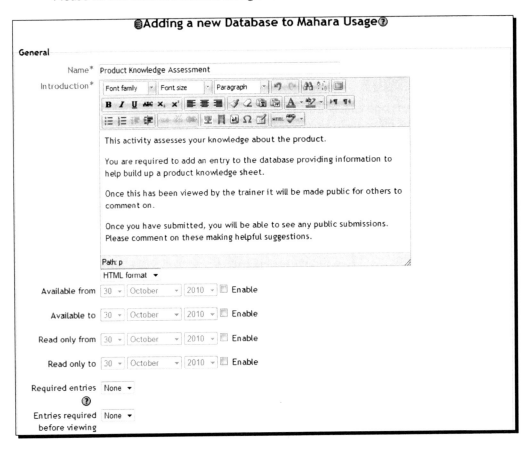

5. The four date options can be ignored for now. They are required in different use cases.

6. The **Required entries** should only be enabled if you are using course tracking for completion. If not, like now, just leave it at **None**.

7. Set the **Entries required before viewing** to **1**. This requires the participant to submit one entry before he can view the submission of anyone else.

8. For this activity, ignore the **Maximum entries** setting.

9. Set the **Comments** option to **Yes**, as this will allow students to comment on each other's submissions once they are approved.

10. Likewise, set **Require approval** to **Yes** so that the trainer has to approve entries before they are open to comments.

11. The rest of the settings can be ignored too for this set up.

12. Click **Save and display** to enter the database configuration page.

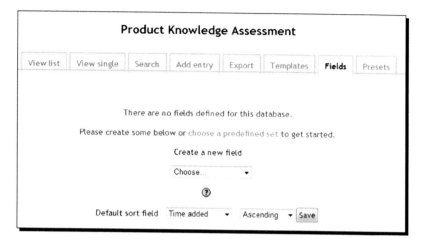

What just happened?

The database by itself is not usable yet, but it has been configured to the point that we can now start adding fields. It is very important that you go from the settings page and then directly into creating fields, or you may end up lost.

Adding fields

There are a number of different field types available to you, to add to the, as of yet, empty database structure. The options are:

- Checkbox
- Date
- File
- Latitude/longitude
- Menu
- Menu (multi-select)
- Number
- Picture
- Radio buttons

- Text
- Textarea
- URL

We will not be using most of these now, but later when you are feeling brave you can play around and see how they are used, or check out the Moodle Docs explanations on `http://docs.moodle.org/en/mod/data/field/`.

Time for action – adding a field to the database

We have already selected the four fields that we are going to ask the participants to complete, so now we need to decide what format they will be; for the four fields chosen they will all be text areas. The four fields we will use are going to add Product Description, Product Capabilities, Product Applications, and Product Advantages. However, as it is clear this relates to the product, we drop the word Product from the field names.

It is very important to know the order you want them created in, or it will require some complicated HTML and template editing later to alter the presentation of the information.

1. From the **Fields** tab, click on the **Choose** drop down and select **Textarea**.

2. Put the first field name (**Description**) into the **Field name** field.

3. Put the same information into the **Field description** field. Although with complicated names these two fields can be different, I like to keep them the same to remove confusion later on when editing.

4. Leave the default **Width** at 60 columns.

5. Change the **Height** to 10 rows as the default 35 is quite a lot.

6. Click on **Add**.

7. Repeat steps 1 through 6 for each of the fields you want to add (use a different type if you want to).

8. Once you have added all your fields, you are now ready to proceed.

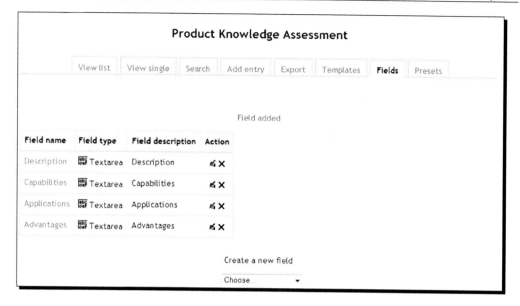

9. Click on **Templates** and have a look at the different layouts, especially the List template and the Single template. You will probably want to alter these later.

What just happened?

By adding in some fields into the database we have now prepared the activity for participants to start submitting their abstracted product knowledge.

Adding entries

It is always good to add a few entries to check that it is working the way that you intend before you release it to participants.

Time for action – adding an entry to the database

1. Click on the **Add entry** tab.

2. You will now see the form for adding in the database entry. Each of the Textarea fields has a WYSIWYG HTML editor to aid layout of the text. You may want to add an image in here as blocks of text can be boring to look at.

3. Fill some text into each block to check if the space given is enough.

4. Review your work and then click on **Save and view** when you are finished.

If you have not looked at the **Single template** (under **Templates tab**), it will not have been initiated, so quickly do that now and you can then view the list of entries or the single entry options.

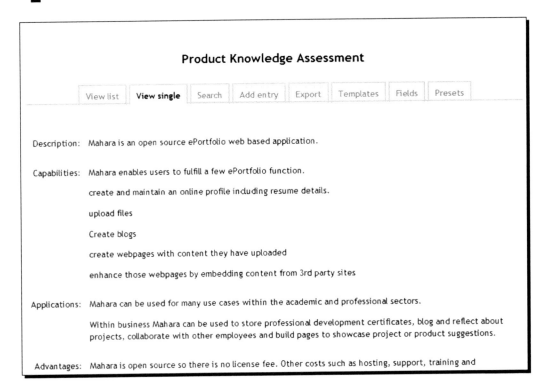

Product Knowledge Assessment

| View list | **View single** | Search | Add entry | Export | Templates | Fields | Presets |

Description: Mahara is an open source ePortfolio web based application.

Capabilities: Mahara enables users to fulfill a few ePortfolio function.

create and maintain an online profile including resume details.

upload files

Create blogs

create webpages with content they have uploaded

enhance those webpages by embedding content from 3rd party sites

Applications: Mahara can be used for many use cases within the academic and professional sectors.

Within business Mahara can be used to store professional development certificates, blog and reflect about projects, collaborate with other employees and build pages to showcase project or product suggestions.

Advantages: Mahara is open source so there is no license fee. Other costs such as hosting, support, training and

What just happened?

You have now completed the creation of the database activity. You went through the configuration, added fields, checked the templates, and created a test entry.

Before releasing to students you will want to remove the test entry, and perhaps alter the templates so that the **view list** and **view single** pages look more to your taste.

If you want to do a bit more reading on the database templates, Moodle Docs is where to look: `http://docs.moodle.org/en/mod/data/templates`.

The Moodle community also share quite a few different database formats which can be seen in the Exchange Samples Moodle course on the demo site `http://demo.moodle.net/course/view.php?id=604`, and also available for download in the Database for Databases on moodle.org site itself: `http://moodle.org/mod/data/view.php?id=7303`.

Reflection

Think about how product knowledge sheets are currently created within your organization. Who creates them? How are they distributed? Are they used and are they effective?

Reflect upon how you could improve and increase their use to support product rollout. Think about how you would go about measuring and evaluating their success rate.

Have a go hero – different database options

The database is a very powerful feature within Moodle and can be used for many different applications.

How would you go about configuring and setting up a database for people to submit their profile for an icebreaker? What data fields would you use? What field types would you choose for that data?

Think about a use case which would use the **Latitude/longitude** field type. When would this type of data be useful?

Although we haven't touched on it, when people have built a database for a specific use case they often share it with others in the community. These can be found in the Database for Databases section of moodle.org: `http://moodle.org/mod/data/view.php?id=7303`.

Case Study—AA Ireland

As mentioned at the start of the chapter, it is often a good idea to use Moodle for initial and on-going provision of product knowledge training. One such organization which does this is AA Ireland.

AA Ireland has been the 'Champion of the Motorist' since 1910 with over 550,000 customer relationships and employing over 480 employees. AA Rescue is Ireland's premier roadside assistance product and uniquely in Ireland, over 80 % of breakdowns are handled by their patrols.

AA Roadwatch is Ireland's premier traffic and travel information service, where updates can be heard across Ireland's national and local radio network and accessed on their travel and traffic portal, `http://www.aaroadwatch.ie`.

AA Ireland worked with the Irish Moodle partner Enovation Solutions to implement Moodle in their organization. Now that they have been using Moodle for a number of years, Mary Dempsey, the training manager with AA Ireland says, "Moodle has become a critical tool for AA Ireland."

What was the business problem(s) for which Moodle was chosen as the solution?

The training department at AA Ireland administer new customer service agent training, as well as keeping existing agents up-to-date with information about rate changes, and product and procedure changes. The main problem for AA Ireland was the amount of paperwork that was associated with the processes, particularly around the training assessment process.

What was the solution and how did they arrive at the solution?

The idea of a learning management system was introduced to help the training team reduce the paperwork and make as much material as possible available on-line in an easy-to-access environment for agents on their desktops.

Why did they choose Moodle?

Selection of a suitable solution should be based on defined needs; both immediate and long term needs should be taken into account. "We considered a number of options", said Mary Dempsey, training manager with AA Ireland. "However, what attracted us to Moodle was the fact that it suited our department's needs with its wider uses as an HR intranet and general information repository."

Was the project a success?

Often the success of a project can be measured by whether the solution which has been implemented has actually been adopted fully, and is being used for the purposes defined. For AA Ireland, Mary explained, "Moodle has become an invaluable tool for the training team, and the wider organization."

What were the benefits gained?

Mary explains that AA Ireland administers the majority of the courses through the online environment, including attendance and assessments. "We are at the stage where our agents are accessing it regularly for product updates. We are utilizing databases for data collection and collation which was previously a paper-based task. The AA Roadwatch team is even using the Moodle forum option for internal traffic updates, which is great."

What lessons were learned?

AA Ireland, like many organizations, feels that it is not just about putting paper-based work online. Two lessons which they draw from the project are:

- Design and presentation require consideration if replacing paper-based solutions with system-based solutions
- Training of key administrators and ensuring content is kept up-to-date is vital

What advice does AA Ireland have for businesses that plan to implement Moodle?

AA Ireland have one key bit of advice for those who are considering implementing Moodle and that is to plan ahead and to try and put a structure in place pre-launch, particularly if there are a number of departments involved.

Reflection

Implementing a product strategy is not a one-off task. Each of the different activities and resources that can be implemented to provide initial training also need to be assessed for on-going product knowledge maintenance.

Even with supporting product knowledge development, it is important that all aspects of the training aim to tackle defined problems. Having recognized goals can foster cross-organizational support for the effort, and help ensure successful rollout.

As touched on earlier, development of the resources and activities need to take into account all dependencies including the target audience and how they will use the site, both for creation and assessment.

Having strong support throughout the organization can aid implementation, but having good relevant content, activities, and resources can bolster re-use. As the AA Ireland case study demonstrates, the benefit of having an up-to-date product knowledge system centrally available can lead to where it becomes a mission critical system where people depend on it and even expand its usage beyond original terms.

With product knowledge training, measurement of the training can be tackled in many ways; for example, how many completed the training? It is also important to measure immediately with the trainees to identify ways to support on-going training and provide corrections and improvements to the course at every stage. Products evolve and change and so should the training for the products that change and evolve.

Ultimately, impact on the business is where training is evaluated. How many extra sales were generated from the training? How many satisfied customer support queries? Are support calls getting resolved in a shorter time? Did things improve immediately and tail off indicating the need for more on-going training? You need to have set realistic goals, measureable goals, and preferably short-term goals so you can evaluate early and often.

Summary

Throughout this chapter we learnt techniques about implementing product knowledge training. We looked at a case study from AA Ireland and their successful implementation of Moodle as a product knowledge intranet and training centre. We saw how their product knowledge system became a mission critical tool in keeping staff up-to-date with product change.

Specifically, we covered:

- ◆ When creating a course, the structure and layout is important to aid understanding and provide context to the learning resources and activities. A good curriculum structure or course scheme of work can aid in this endeavor.

- ◆ You can reduce the complexity of the course by providing a glossary of terminology and including the random glossary block as a flash card learning tool.

- ◆ Role-playing can help create understanding of the different types of product knowledge and how it is applied by different departments. This can be facilitated and logged by using the Chat module.

- ◆ Presenting the facts and figures relating to a product needs to be done in a way that aids retention. Applying tests for comprehension and memory soon after using the lesson can aid the learning process.

It is important to clearly identify the business need for each area of the organization regarding product knowledge to understand what the goals are.

We also discussed that when building a course for a range of constituents we must focus on delivering on the specific objectives to the set target audiences.

Now that we've learned about applying Moodle to help facilitate Product Knowledge Management, we're ready to move on to the next chapter which covers managing compliance training.

4

Moodle for Managing Compliance Training

Companies must find a way to successfully manage many kinds of risks including legal compliance, health and safety, security risks, and privacy risks. Training can be an important part of a risk management program or process. Depending on the industry there could be several external regulations as well as internal company mandates. Human resource managers must develop programs to ensure legal compliance and the mitigation of risk. In this chapter we will build on what you have already learned and introduce you to several more Moodle tools that can be used for risk management and compliance training.

Throughout this chapter think about how Moodle can help manage risks and ensure regulatory compliance through training.

In this chapter we shall:

- ◆ Learn how to use the Moodle lesson module to deliver compliance training
- ◆ Learn how to create hide and show activities based on group membership in Moodle
- ◆ Learn how to track student completion in your Moodle course
- ◆ Learn how course completion reports can be used to facilitate compliance training

So let's get started...

> **Using Moodle to manage compliance training**
>
> Compliance training is a very important part of an organization's risk management strategy. Moodle has a number of tools that you can use to deliver and manage required training for your employees. In this chapter we will explore the lesson module as well as some useful user management tools to ensure your employees receive the training they need.

Using the lesson module as a training tool

Every human resources manager must understand and comply with a multitude of regulations and establish policies and procedures to ensure their company is in compliance. Additionally, there are several internal risks to consider including work-life discrimination, protection of confidential information, workplace privacy risks, and so on. Many companies develop training programs as a way to mitigate and avoid certain risks by making employees aware of the company policies and procedures. Moodle's lesson module is a useful tool for this type of training. Using Moodle's inbuilt lesson module is also a time and cost-effective alternative to relying on third-party authoring tools that publish Scorm.

The lesson module uses two different page types, which can be implemented in several different ways to create an interactive learning experience for the user. First, the question page asks the user a question and then provides the user with feedback based on their response. The question pages are graded and contribute to a user's grade. The second page type, the content page, presents content and navigation options without grading the user's response.

Creating a lesson module

Let's take a business case study example. You are developing a lesson module on basic office safety. To train employees on basic fire safety, you decide to use a common active training method—the case study. Before we dive into the lesson module, let's take a moment to decide how we're going to implement this. First, we are going to use a content page to present a realistic building fire scenario and have the learner choose their first action. Second, we will create a question page to present the learner with a scored choice regarding fire safety. Third, we need to then come up with feedback based on their responses.

In reality, the fire safety plan would probably be part of a larger emergency action plan. However, for the purposes of this chapter we are going to keep things simple and address a scenario that may be used when training employees on fire safety.

Lesson modules can get quite complicated if you let them, depending on how many choices the reader has for a given scenario and how long the chain of reasoning is. Many experts suggest developing a flowchart to plan out your lesson module before creating it in Moodle. For our purposes, we will just take it through the first choice to show you how to use the content page and then a question page. Once you have that down, it will be easy to keep repeating the process to make your lesson module as simple or complicated as you'd like.

Time for action – creating a lesson module

1. Log in to your Moodle site as an administrator. Create a course for your compliance training by following the instructions in *Chapter 1, Getting Started with Moodle*.

2. Click the **Turn editing on** button in the top-right corner.

3. Go to the section you want to add the lesson to and from the **Add an activity...** drop-down menu, select **Lesson**. You should now be on the **Adding a new Lesson** page.

4. The first section of the page is the **General** section.

   - In the **Name** field, enter the title of your lesson, for example "Fire Safety".

   - If you want to enter a time limit for the lesson, click the checkbox to the left of **Enable** at the **Time limit (minutes)** field and enter the time limit you want implemented, in minutes, for the lesson. For the purposes of this example, assume that if I do not give you a specific value to enter for a field, leave it set at the default.

   - If you want to restrict the availability of the lesson to certain dates, then click the checkboxes next to **Enable** and enter the **Available from** date and **Deadline** date.

   - Under **Maximum number of answers**, select the maximum number of answers that may be used in the lesson. For example, if it only consists of True/False questions, this would be 2.

There are a lot of settings in the lesson module. You are not expected to remember them all. I don't! Next to most of the settings is a ? icon. Select this icon for a description of the setting anytime you can't remember what its purpose is.

5. **Grade** is the next section on the **Adding a new Lesson** page.

   ❑ For **Grade**, select the maximum score that can be given for the lesson from the drop-down menu. If there is no grade, then select **no grade** from the drop-down menu. We are not going to use question pages for our case study example, so for here select no grade.

   ❑ The **Grade category** refers to the category in the grade book. We have not set the grade book up yet, so leave this as the default **Uncategorised**. There will be nothing else available yet in this drop-down menu if you have not set up categories in the grade book.

6. Next go to the **Grade options** section and select your settings.

   ❑ In the **Practice lesson** setting, select **No** from the drop-down menu if you want the grades for this lesson to be recorded.

   ❑ The **Custom scoring** setting allows you to give a score (positive or negative) for each answer. For our example, select **No**. This could be a useful tool if there are different levels of right and wrong answers and you wish to capture this in the grade book.

   ❑ If you want to allow re-takes, select **Yes** from the drop-down menu at the **Re-takes allowed** setting.

   ❑ If you selected **Yes** in the previous setting and are allowing re-takes, then you need to select the method for grading in the next setting—**Handing of re-takes**. Your two choices from the drop-down menu are **Use mean** or **Use maximum**.

   ❑ The **Display ongoing score** setting, if **Yes** is selected from the drop-down menu, will allow the user to see their current score out of total possible thus far in the lesson. The following screenshot shows the **General**, **Grade**, and **Grade options** sections of the **Create a lesson** page.

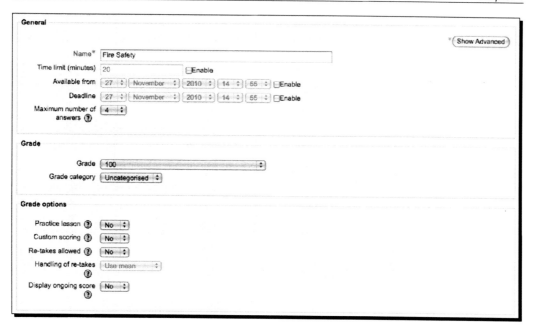

7. Now go to the **Flow control** section and select your settings.

   □ **Allow student review**, if **Yes** is selected, gives the user the option of going through the lesson again from the start after they have completed the lesson.

   □ **Provide option to try a question again**, select **Yes** from the drop-down menu to give the user the option to take the question again for no credit or continue with the lesson if they answer a question incorrectly.

   □ If you selected **Yes** for the previous setting, then in the next setting, **Maximum number of attempts**, you must select the number of attempts allowed from the drop-down menu. If the user answers the question incorrectly repeatedly, once the maximum number of attempts is reached the user will proceed to the next page in the lesson.

   □ If you want the default feedback for correct and incorrect answers to be shown when no feedback has been specified for the question, then at the **Display default feedback** section, select **Yes** from the drop-down menu. Default feedback for a correct answer is "That's the correct answer" and for an incorrect answer is "That's the wrong answer".

   □ If **Yes** is selected for the **Progress bar** setting, then a progress bar is displayed at the bottom of each page.

❑ When set to **Yes** the Display left menu setting provides a list of all the pages in the lesson on the left side of each lesson page.

8. The **Pop-up to file or web page** section allows you to choose a file to display in a pop-up window at the beginning of a lesson. It also displays a link to reopen the pop-up window in every subsequent page in the lesson.

9. The **Dependent on** section allows you to restrict access to the lesson based on performance in another lesson in the same course. Restrictions can be based on any combination of completion, time spent, or minimum grade required.

❑ Under **Dependent on**, select the lesson required before access to this lesson from the drop-down menu.

❑ **Time spent (minutes)**: If time spent is one of the requirements, then enter the minimum number of minutes required.

❑ **Completed**, if completion is a requirement, then check the box.

❑ If a minimum grade is required, then for the **Grade better than (%)** setting, enter the minimum grade required. The following screenshot shows the **Flow control, Pop-up to file or web page**, and **Dependent on** sections of the create a lesson page.

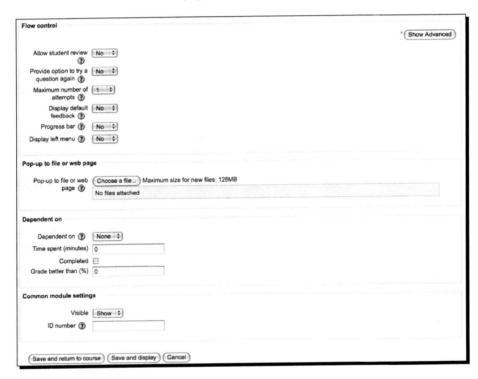

10. Once you have entered all your settings on the lesson page, click on the **Save and display** button at the bottom of the page. You are now on the editing page for the lesson you just created. See the following example:

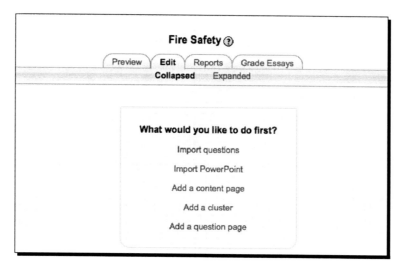

What just happened?

We have just created the shell of a lesson activity for our learners. In the next steps we will add content to the lesson and learn how to ask the learner questions.

Time for action – creating a content page

Now that we have the shell of the lesson, we can begin to add content. We'll start with adding a simple content page.

1. From the editing page for the lesson you just created, select **Add a content page**.

2. Enter a descriptive title in the box next to **Page title**. For our example, we will enter **Building is on fire**.

3. Enter the content for this page in the **Page contents** text area.

4. If you want the user's choices for the lesson page to be displayed horizontally, then check the box to the left of **Arrange content buttons horizontally**? You have now filled in the **Add a content page** section; see the following screenshot for our example:

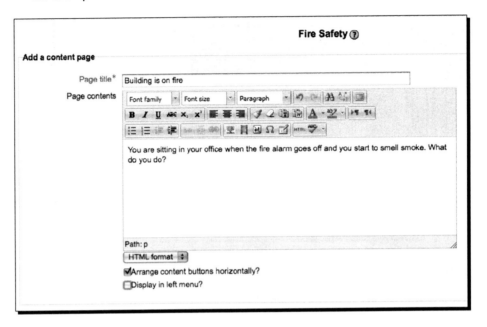

5. In the **Add a content page** section you will find sections for **Content 1**, **Content 2**, and so on. This is where we will create the choices for the user. For our example, we will enter "Grab the fire extinguisher and look for smoke" in the **Description** text area for **Content 1**. Leave the drop-down menu below the text area on the default **Moodle auto-format**. For now leave the Jump drop-down menu as is; we will come back to this later.

6. In the **Content 2** section, enter your second choice in the **Description** text area. For our example, we will enter "Walk calmly to the exit and exit the building."

7. Now scroll down to the bottom of the page and select **Add a question page**. This will save the content page you just created. You will now be on the editing page for the lesson you are creating and you should be able to see the content you just added. See the following screenshot for our example:

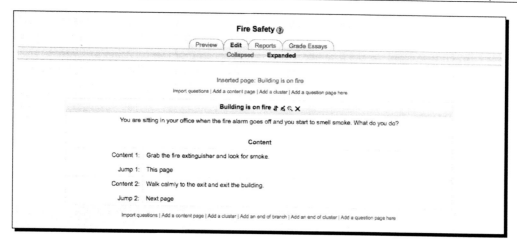

What just happened?

We have now added a content page to our lesson. Content pages can include a wide variety of media, including text, audio, video, and Flash. Next we will look at how to add a scored Question page to test the learner's understanding.

Time for action – creating a question page

Now we are going to create a question page in our lesson. Question pages are scored and provide the user with feedback on their choices.

1. From the edit page, click the **Expanded View** option at the top of the page. Then select the **Add a question page here** link below the content page you just created.

2. From the **Select a question type** drop-down menu select the question type you want to use. For our example, we are going to select **Multichoice**.

3. Next click on the **Add a question page** button.

4. For **Page title**, enter a title for your question page. For our example, we will enter "Why is this a bad idea?".

5. In the **Page contents** text area, enter the question you want to ask the learner. For our example, we will enter "Why is grabbing the fire extinguisher and heading for smoke a bad idea?".

6. Below the **Page contents** text area you will see an **Options** field; check the box next to **Multiple-answer** if you are creating a question with more than one correct answer. Our example is going to be single response; therefore we will not select this box.

7. Below the **Add a question page** section, you will see the **Answer 1**, **Answer 2**, and so on, sections where you will enter the possible list of answers the learner will have to choose from. In the **Answer 1** section, enter one of the possible answers to the question in the **Answer** text area. For our example, we will enter "It's dangerous. You should leave it to the professionals".

8. Next in the **Response** text area, enter the response you want the learner to receive if they select this choice. For our example, we will enter "Firefighters are trained to put out the fire and have the necessary protective gear".

9. Then move to the **Answer 2** section and put your second choice and response. For this example, we will have "You can't put out an office fire with a fire extinguisher" for the **Answer** and "You might be able to put out the fire, but without a respirator you might be overcome by smoke" for the **Response**.

10. For the correct answer, enter a "1" in the **Score** field located at the bottom of the corresponding **Answer** section.

11. Once you have entered all your answers, scroll down to the bottom of the page and select **Add a question page** to save. Now you are back on the Lesson edit screen and will see the Content page and the Question page you just created. See the following screenshot.

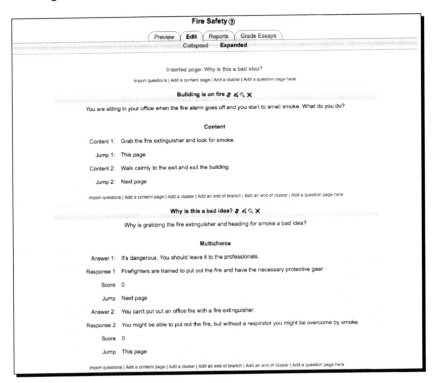

What just happened?

We have now created a question page to test the learner's understanding of the lesson material. We now need to go back and begin to link our pages together with page jumps.

Time for action – creating page jumps

You have now added a content page and a question page, but you're not done yet. Now we need to link the question page to the content page using a page jump. The page jump is simply the link between pages. We need to go back to the Jump field we skipped previously:

1. Go back to the content page you created by selecting the edit icon to the right of the **Building is on fire** page. The edit icon looks like a hand holding a pencil.

2. Scroll down to **Content 1** and from the **Jump** drop-down menu, select the question page you created. For our example, it was **Why is this a bad idea?**.

3. Set the jump for **Content 2** to the **End of the Lesson**. If the user selects this option, they will end the lesson.

4. Scroll down to the bottom of the page and click on the **Save page** button. You will now be back at the edit lesson page and the **Jump 1:** field will now read **Why is this a bad idea?**.

What just happened?

We have now linked our pages together using page jumps. In a lesson module, page jumps are used for both navigation and to provide feedback pages for questions. Now we need to go through and test our lesson to make sure everything works.

Time for action – testing your lesson

We have now gone over all the fundamentals you need to create a lesson. Before we move on, we should test what we have created to make sure it is working properly.

1. Currently you should be on the **Edit** tab for the lesson you created. To the left of the **Edit** tab is the **Preview** tab. These are located at the top of the page. Click on the **Preview** tab.

2. You will now be on the 1st page of the lesson, which was the content page we created. You will see the two choices displayed horizontally below the content as we specified earlier. See the following screenshot:

Fire Safety ⑦

Preview | Edit | Reports | Grade Essays

Building is on fire

You are sitting in your office when the fire alarm goes off and you start to smell smoke. What do you do?

(Grab the fire extinguisher and look for smoke.) (Walk calmly to the exit and exit the building.)

3. Select the first choice, **Grab the fire extinguisher and look for smoke**.

4. Now you will be on the question page. This is correct. We created this jump in the previous section. Select an answer and see if you get the response we created earlier in the question page.

What just happened?

You just set up a scenario based lesson on fire safety. In the process, you learned the basic tools needed to create a lesson: how to create a content page, how to create a question page, and how to create lesson jumps. You can now use these tools to develop any lesson you would like. Maybe start by taking the example lesson we just created and fill in all the content and questions needed to train employees on your company's Emergency Action Plan or Fire Prevention Plan.

Have a go hero – creating flash cards

In the Moodle lesson module, you have the option of adding a cluster. A cluster is a group of question pages from which a random question page can be selected. The default is an unseen question within a cluster jump. We did not go into this with our example, but it could be a useful tool for creating flash cards. Flash cards would be a useful study tool for employees preparing for a compliance exam.

The unseen question within a cluster jump would keep randomly selecting a question that has not yet been seen by the user until it has gone through all the questions.

Take a moment and think of a useful purpose for flash cards at your company and create a flash card lesson module. Go on have a go!

Reflection

Reflect on the internal mandates and external regulations your company needs to address. What is your organizational strategy for compliance? How could you use Moodle to support your organization's compliance policies and practices?

Creating groups and groupings to manage employees going through training

Many companies have different levels of training for different job classifications. For example, in a construction company everyone in the company needs basic safety training. Employees in the field will need more advanced safety training for working around heavy equipment. Finally, a few employees who handle hazardous materials will need very specific, advanced safety training on the handling of hazardous materials. In this section, we will explore how to use groups and groupings to filter the resources and activities in a course so that only the employees who need certain training will receive it.

In Moodle, a group is a group of users who can work together on an activity while remaining separate from other groups. For example, if a forum is set up for groups, members of the group will only be able to reply to forum postings from members of their own group. If you choose this option, you can even prevent them from seeing any posts from members of other groups.

Groupings are used to restrict access to activities based on group membership. A grouping is composed of one or more groups. Once you have created a grouping, you can limit access to an activity to members of one or more groupings. In our example in this section, we will restrict access to advanced training to only those users who need it based on their group membership.

Creating groups

The first step is to create the different groups in your course. For our example, we have three different groups of employees who require different levels of safety training. Therefore, we will create three groups: Safety Level 1, Safety Level 2, and Safety Level 3.

Time for action – creating groups in your course

To create a group in your course follow these steps:

1. Make sure you are logged into your course as an administrator or teacher and editing is turned on.

2. From the **Course administration** menu under the **Settings** block, select **Users**, and then select **Groups**.

3. Click on the **Create group** button located at the bottom left of the screen.

4. Enter the group name in the **Group name** field. For our example, enter "Safety L1".

5. Enter a group description in the **Group description** text area if needed.

6. Leave the **Enrolment key** blank for this example. In the future, if you add an enrolment key to your group and a user enrols in a course with that key, they will be automatically added to that group. This could be helpful once you have your course set up and want to automate enrolment in a track.

7. If you want, you can assign a picture to a group. This is what the last two settings are about. If **No** is selected for the **Hide picture** setting, then if there is a picture associated with the group it will be displayed. The last setting, **New picture**, is where you can upload the picture you want associated with the group. The following screenshot shows the Create group page for our example:

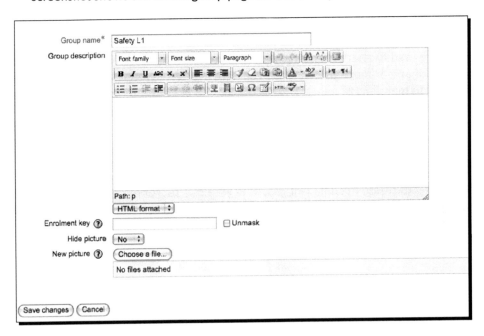

8. Scroll to the bottom of the page and click the **Save changes** button.

9. For our example, go through steps 1 to 8 two more times to create the following groups: Safety L2 and Safety L3. Once you have created three groups, you should see them listed on the **Groups** page as shown in the following screenshot:

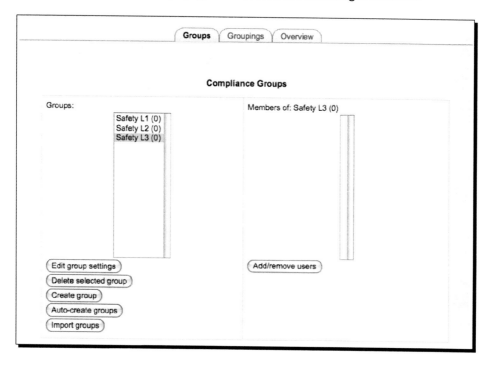

What just happened?

We have now created groups of users in our course. Using groups allows Moodle course creators to use the same activities for multiple user populations.

Time for action – enabling groupings in your course

Before we get into creating groupings, which are groups of groups, we will need to make sure we have enabled groups and groupings in the course. Follow the steps below to enable groupings.

1. Under the **Settings** block, select **Site Administration**, select **Development**, select **Experimental**, and then select **Experimental settings**.

2. On the **Experimental settings** page, select the checkbox next to **Enable group members only**. This enables activities to be restricted to only members of a certain group. See the following screenshot:

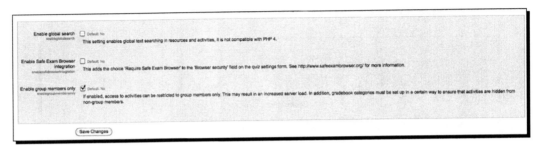

3. Don't forget to click on the **Save Changes** button at the bottom of the screen.

What just happened?

We have now enabled groupings. Groupings allow us to filter activities based on the user's membership in a group. It is a useful method for using the same course for multiple user populations when you only need a few activities to vary by group.

Time for action – enabling group mode

Now go back to the course and set group mode in the course.

1. From the course home page, go to the **Course administration** menu and select **Edit settings**. You will now be on the **Edit course settings** page.

2. Scroll down to the **Groups** section and set the **Group mode** to **Separate groups**.

3. Scroll down to the bottom of the page and click the **Save changes** button.

What just happened?

We have now enabled group mode in the course. This is a necessary step to fully enabling groupings.

Time for action – creating groupings

Now we are ready to create groupings in our course. To create a grouping, follow these steps.

1. From the **Course administration** menu select **Users** and then select **Groups**.

2. At the top of the new screen, select the **Groupings** tab.

3. Click on the **Create grouping** button.

4. Enter a grouping name of Basic Safety in the **Grouping name** field.

5. If desired, enter a description in the **Grouping description** text area.

6. Click on the **Save changes** button.

7. Then follow steps 1 to 5 again and create two more groupings for our example. Name the groupings: Intermediate Safety and Advanced Safety.

8. Now we need to add the groups to the groupings. From the **Groupings** page, under the **Edit** column, select the **show groups in grouping** icon. It is the icon that looks like a group of people. Since the **Advanced Safety** grouping is first, we will add the groups to this grouping first.

9. Once you select the show groups in grouping icon, you will be on the **Add/remove groups: Advanced Safety** page. In the list of **Potential members**, you will see the list of safety groups you created earlier. Safety L3 is the only group that should be a member of Advanced safety. Select **Safety L3** from the **Potential members** list, and then click on the **Add** button. You should now see **Safety L3** in the **Existing members** list and no longer see it in the **Potential members list**. See the following image:

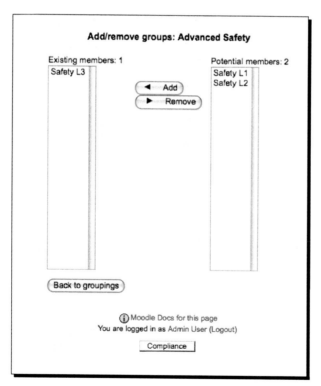

10. Click on the **Back to groupings** button, and then repeat the steps to add **Safety L1**, **Safety L2**, **Safety L3** to the **Basic Safety** grouping and **Safety L2** and **Safety L3** to the **Intermediate Safety** grouping.

What just happened?

We have now created the groupings necessary for our course. The final step in the groupings configuration is to filter activities based on the user's group membership.

Time for action – filtering activity access via groupings

So now you have created groupings in your course. Next we will learn how to filter access to an activity via grouping. For the purposes of this example, imagine we have created three lessons in our course entitled Basic Safety, Intermediate Safety, and Advanced Safety.

1. From the course home page, with editing turned on, go to the **Basic Safety** lesson and select the **update** icon, the hand holding the pencil, next to the lesson.

2. Scroll down to the **Common module settings** and click on the **Show Advanced** button located on the right.

3. Select the checkbox next to **Available for group members only**.

4. From the **Grouping** drop-down menu, select **Basic Safety**. See the following screenshot:

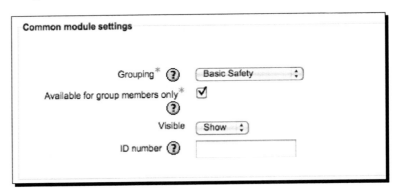

5. Click the **Save and return to course** button.

6. If the Intermediate Safety and Advanced Safety lessons existed, the next step would be to assign the Intermediate Safety grouping to the Intermediate Safety lesson and then assign the Advanced Safety grouping to the Advanced Safety lesson.

What just happened?

You have now filtered activities by group membership. Now, only members of the intermediate and advanced safety groups will see those lessons.

Time for action – adding users to groups

In previous chapters you learned how to create users; now let's cover how you add users to groups.

1. Log in to your course as a teacher or administrator.

2. From the **Settings** block, select **Course administration**, select **Users**, and then select **Groups**.

3. From the Groups page, select the group you want to add users to. For this example, let's select the **Safety L1** group we created previously.

4. Next click on the **Add/remove users** button located on the bottom right. You will now be on the **Add/remove users: Safety L1** page. See the following screenshot:

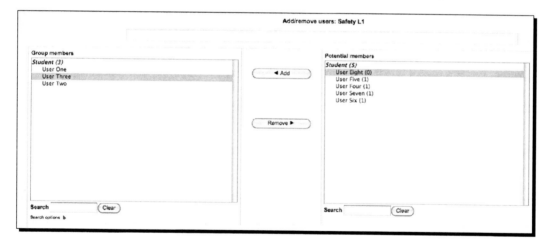

5. On the right side of the page you will see a list of **Potential users** you can add to the group. This lists participants in the course who are not already assigned to the group.

6. To add a user, select the user you want to add from the list of **Potential members** and click the **Add** button. The user you just added should now appear in the left **Group members** column.

7. You can search for users in either column from the **Search** box below each respective column. This comes in handy when you have a large number of users.

 In the **Potential members** column, you will see a number in parentheses next to the username. This is the number of groups the user is already a member of in the course. If you click on a user who is already a member of a group, the groups that they belong to will appear on the far right under **Selected user's membership**.

What just happened?

You have just restricted access to training activities based on the level of training a user needs. When an employee, who only needs basic safety training, logs into your course, they will only see the basic safety training lesson. Likewise, when an employee who needs all three levels of training logs into the course, they will see all three safety training lessons. With groups and groupings you have filtered access to course activities or resources based on the needs of the employee, and with the addition of an enrolment key you could also automate enrolment into groups.

Have a go hero – adding an enrolment key

In the beginning of this section, we briefly mentioned the enrolment key when creating groups. This is a useful tool if you want users to self enrol in a course. You create a group enrolment key and when it is time for the user to take the required training, give them the enrolment key and then they can self enrol in the course. It saves you from having to do it for them!

Try adding an enrolment key to one of the groups you created in the beginning of this section.

Reflection

Reflect on the implementation of training at your company. What groups and groupings would help you best facilitate compliance training at your organization?

Using completion tracking

Completion tracking is a way for users to track their progress through a course. In our safety course, someone who needs to take all three safety lessons would need to know they have finished Lesson 1 before they can move on to Lesson 2. With completion tracking, once an individual has completed part of the training, a check mark will appear next to that activity.

Time for action – enabling completion tracking

The first step is to enable completion tracking on your site.

1. Log in to your Moodle site as the admin.

2. Go to the **Site Administration** menu located in the **Settings** block.

3. You will see a search box at the bottom of the **Site Administration** menu. Type "completion" and click on the **Search** button. The following screenshot shows the first three search results that will be displayed, which are the three we need to configure:

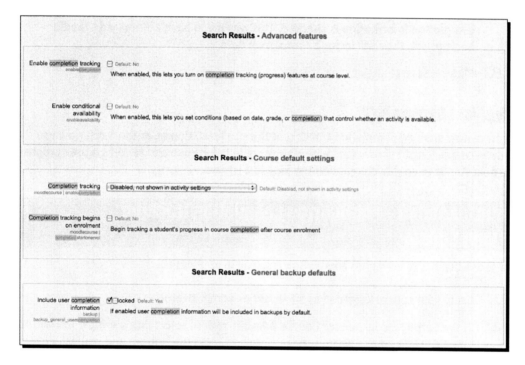

4. Under **Advanced features**, select the checkbox next to **Enable completion tracking**.

5. Under the **Course default settings**, for the **Completion tracking** setting select **Enabled, control via completion and activity settings** from the drop-down menu.

6. The next setting, **Completion tracking begins on enrolment**, allows you to start completion tracking when the user is first enrolled in the course. If you leave this disabled, completion tracking will start when a user enters an activity for the first time. This is important because some completion tracking options are time based and Moodle needs to know when to start tracking time. For our example, we will leave this unchecked.

7. Under **General backup defaults**, make sure both checkboxes are selected next to **Include user completion information**. The first checkbox is to include user completion information in course backups and the second checkbox is to lock this feature so teachers cannot choose to not include completion data.

8. Under **Automated backup setup**, make sure the checkbox next to **Include user completion information** is checked. This way if you have automated Moodle backups set, they will include completion data.

9. Click on **Save changes**.

What just happened?

We have now enabled completion tracking at the site level. Course authors can now use completion tracking to show users where they are in the course and report on user progress. The next step is to enable completion tracking in a course.

Time for action – configuring completion tracking in your course

The second step is to configure completion tracking in your course.

1. Go to your course logged in as a teacher or administrator.

2. In the **Settings** block, under **Course Administration**, select **Edit settings**. You will now be on the **Edit course settings** page. Scroll down to the bottom and you will now see a new section called **Student progress**.

3. For the **Completion tracking** setting, select **Enabled, control via completion and activity settings** from the drop-down menu.

4. The next setting is **Completion tracking begins on enrolment**. If you enabled this at the site level, then it should already be selected here. If you uncheck it, you can override the site default and not have it enabled for this course.

5. Select the **Save** button at the bottom of the page.

6. Now if you go back to the course home page, under **Course administration**, you will have a new option called **Completion tracking**. Select **Completion tracking**. You will now be on the **Edit Course Completion Settings** page.

7. The first section is **Overall criteria type aggregation**. This sets up how the completion for the course is calculated. There are two options: **All** or **Any**. If you set it to **All**, then all of the completion settings you set on this page must be completed before the course is complete. If you set it to **Any**, then the course is complete if any of the criteria for the completion settings are met.

8. The next section is **Course prerequisites**. If you have other courses with completion criteria set, then you can set them as prerequisites for this course. For example, if we set up our previous safety training example into three separate courses: Basic Safety, Intermediate Safety, and Advanced Safety, then we could make Basic Safety a prerequisite for Intermediate Safety and so on.

9. **Manual self completion** is the next setting. If this is **Enabled**, then students can mark the course as complete on their own. This is the equivalent of an employee checking a form that says, "I have read this". An example where you may want to use this feature is if you have a course for your Employee Handbook. Once an employee has read the handbook, they can then mark the course complete to indicate that they have read it.

10. The **Manual completion by** section allows you to set the roles that can manually mark the course as complete. The **Aggregation method** setting allows you to set whether **All** the roles selected have to mark it complete or if **Any** one of the roles can mark it complete. Imagine a course being taught by multiple teachers, for example a training course taught by multiple departments. If you select All here and check the box next to the Teacher role, then every teacher from every department would need to mark the course complete for every participant.

11. The **Activities completed** setting is where you can mark which activities need to be completed before a course can be completed. This section will only display activities that have activity completion set. We will cover this in the next section.

12. The **Date** setting, if **Enable** is checked, means the course is marked complete after the date specified.

13. The **Duration after enrolment** setting, if **Enable** is checked, means the course is marked complete after being enrolled in the course for the specified number of days.

14. The Grade setting, if Enable is checked, allows you to set a minimum passing grade for the course to be complete.

15. The **Unenrolment** setting, if checked, says the course is marked complete when a user is unenrolled. The following screenshot shows the Edit Course Completion Settings page that was discussed in steps 6 through 14.

Edit Course Completion Settings

Overall criteria type aggregation

Aggregation method [All ⬍]

Course prerequisites

Course completion is not enabled for any other courses, so none can be displayed. You can enable course completion in the course settings.

Manual self completion

Enable ☐

Manual completion by

Aggregation method [All ⬍]
Manager ☐
Course creator ☐
Teacher ☐
Non-editing teacher ☐

If you enable **Manual self completion** in the course, you will need to make sure you add the **Self Completion** block to the course. To do this go to the block in the right column titled **Add a block** and select **Self Completion** from the **Add...** drop-down menu. When the students log on, they will see the **Self Completion** block in the right column and will have a link that says **Complete Course...** When they click on this link they will receive a confirmation page that reads **Confirm self completion**. To confirm, they will click on the **Yes** button.

What just happened?

We have enabled completion tracking at the course level. Users can now see whether they have completed a course or not.

Time for action – configuring completion tracking at the activity level

After you have enabled completion tracking at the site level, and configured it at the course level, the next step is to configure it at the activity level.

1. Go to the course home page and turn editing on.

2. Select the edit/update icon next to the lesson or other activity you want to configure for completion tracking.

3. Scroll down to the bottom of the settings page for your activity to the **Activity completion section**.

4. From the **Completion tracking** drop-down menu, there are three options available:

   □ **Do not indicate activity completion**: Obviously this is what you would select if you do not want to enable completion tracking for this activity.

   □ **Students can manually mark the activity as completed**: We discussed this in the Employee Handbook example.

   □ **Show activity as complete when conditions are met**: Use this when you want to control the conditions of completion.

5. The next two settings, **Require view** and **Require grade**, are the possible conditions that can be set if you have selected **Show activity as complete when conditions are met**.

6. The **Require view** setting, if the box is checked, means that the activity will be complete as soon as the student views the activity.

7. The **Require grade** setting, if the box is checked, means the student must receive a grade in the activity before it will be complete.

8. The **Expect completed on** setting, when enabled, only appears in the activity completion report. It is not viewable by students in the course.

What just happened?

We have just enabled completion tracking at the site, course, and activity level. We have also set up course completion criteria in our course so that both employees and managers can measure progress.

Have a go hero – blank questions

Sometimes a score on a quiz isn't enough to complete a course. There are times when an expert in the field is required to judge whether a student has successfully met the requirements. Or we may want to mix both face-to-face and online training. For example, a Sexual Harassment course may have both an online reading and quiz component and a face-to-face role-play offline assignment. The moderator for the face-to-face portion of the training would need to judge whether the employee successfully applied what they have learned.

For this *Have a go hero*, create a course that requires both a score on a quiz and moderator approval to pass.

Reflection

You now have a few more tools in your Moodle toolbox, but don't forget that the modules you learned in previous chapters can also be very useful when delivering compliance training. Take a moment and reflect on what you learned previously and how forums, databases, quizzes, and glossaries could also be useful in compliance training at your organization.

Course completion reports

In the previous section we went over how to set up completion tracking. This is a very useful feature in Moodle that can be used to keep track of what training an employee has completed and what training they still need to complete. Once you have set up completion tracking, as the administrator or teacher of the course, you will be able to view the course completion reports for each employee. In this section, you will learn how to enable course completion reports and understand what information they provide.

Time for action – adding the completion status block to your course

Before you can have access to the completion reports, you need to add the Course completion status block to your course.

1. Go to the course homepage logged in as a teacher or administrator and turn editing on.

2. In the right column you will see a block titled **Add a block**. From the **Add...** drop-down menu, select **Course completion status**.

3. You will now see a new block in the right column entitled **Course completion status**. When logged in as the administrator or a teacher, the block will contain a link to **View course report**, as shown in the following screenshot:

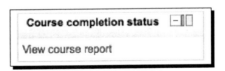

4. Select the **View course report** link.

5. On the **Course completion report** page, you will see a table that lists all the course completion requirements across the top and all the users down the left column. If a user has met a completion requirement, you will see a check mark in the table cell. In the following example, you will see there are eight users enrolled in the course and four completion elements. **User Five** has completed the **Basic Safety** lesson and so far has a passing grade of 80% or higher. They still have to complete the Safety Quiz and the Intermediate Safety Lesson.

All participants: 8

First name: **All** A B C D E F G H I J K L M N O P Q R S T U V W X Y Z
Surname: **All** A B C D E F G H I J K L M N O P Q R S T U V W X Y Z

Criteria group	Activities			Grade	Course
Aggregation method	All			-	All
Criteria	sic Safety	ple Safety Quiz	rmediate Safety	% required	rse complete
First name / Surname					
User Eight					
User Five	✓			✓	
User Four					
User One					
User Seven					
User Six					
User Three					
User Two					

First name: **All** A B C D E F G H I J K L M N O P Q R S T U V W X Y Z
Surname: **All** A B C D E F G H I J K L M N O P Q R S T U V W X Y Z

6. At the bottom of the **Course completion report** page you will find two options to download the report into a spreadsheet. The first option, **Download in spreadsheet format (UTF-8.csv)**, allows you to download a csv file for non-Excel spreadsheets. The second option, **Download in Excel-compatible format (.csv)**, allows you to download in an Excel format.

7. If you are logged in as a student, you will see your course completion status in the **Course completion status** block. Refer to the following screenshot for an example:

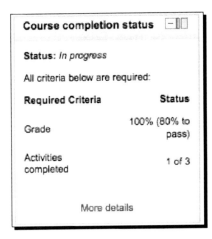

8. If you select **More details** at the bottom of the block, you will be brought to the **Completion progress details** page. You will see all the course completion requirements set in the course completion settings. In the following example, you can see that the learner is required to complete the **Basic Safety** lesson, the **Sample Safety Quiz**, and the **Intermediate Safety** lesson. Additionally, they are required to get a passing grade of **80%** or higher.

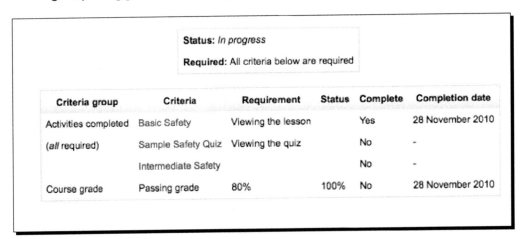

Status: *In progress*

Required: All criteria below are required

Criteria group	Criteria	Requirement	Status	Complete	Completion date
Activities completed	Basic Safety	Viewing the lesson		Yes	28 November 2010
(*all* required)	Sample Safety Quiz	Viewing the quiz		No	-
	Intermediate Safety			No	-
Course grade	Passing grade	80%	100%	No	28 November 2010

What just happened?

We set up the course completion status block to access course completion reports and looked at how the completion data is displayed for both the student and course instructor.

Reflection

How will you measure the impact of your training on your company's compliance and other risks? Can you develop measures to correlate training with reduced accidents or lowered risks of fines?

Case Study – Aer Lingus

Aer Lingus was founded by the Irish Government in April 1936 to provide air services to and from Ireland. Aer Lingus' low-cost, low fares model is centred on maintaining low unit cost, offering one way fares, maintaining effective fleet utilisation, and developing the Aer Lingus brand.

Aer Lingus operates operates over 80 routes to and from the United Kingdom and Continental Europe, and a long haul network to six destinations in the United States.

What was the business problem(s) for which Moodle was chosen as the solution?

The business challenge was the logistics and costs associated with the annual refresher training for 500 pilots. Called "Ground School", the training programme incorporates simulator training with procedural and aircraft operation training. All 500 pilots must complete the course each year in order to maintain their flying status in accordance to EU regulations.

What was the solution and how did they arrive at the solution?

The solution was to move the ground school element of the programme into an online environment to allow pilots who spend a lot of time travelling to access the training material from anywhere in the world that their works finds them. Online training offers much more flexibility than classroom training and is becoming more prevalent in the airline industry as a result.

Why did they choose Moodle?

Aer Lingus researched a number of learning management systems from other providers but found that proprietary offerings varied in what they could do and were not as flexible as open source solutions. Moodle satisfied requirements in terms of features and functionality, but also had the open source flexibility which allowed Aer Lingus to customise it to suit their own needs. The reporting aspect of Moodle also meant that Aer Lingus could meet one of their key requirements—the ability to report on user activity to demonstrate regulatory compliance to the relevant authorities. Other requirements included security and the ability to deliver third-party content.

Was the project a success?

In October 2008, the project was successfully piloted to a group of instructors in a classroom environment. Aer Lingus then went on the launch the live site in January 2009 for the first round of 2009 training schedule. The pilots had three months to complete the course with the end of March being the cut-off date.

Feedback from Conor Rock, Training Captain at Aer Lingus, is a positive validation of Enovations work on the project: "Enovation delivered on all of our requirements. Moodle has been universally well received by the pilots and we have reduced our training costs, and from what can I say—the project has been a huge success."

What were the benefits gained?

There were a number of benefits gained:

- Logistics: The pilots can now access the training content from anywhere in the world, reducing the need to coordinate attendance at training headquarters in Dublin.
- Cost reduction: Online courses reduce the need for trainers and other related costs.
- Reporting in accordance with EU regulations: The Aer Lingus training department can produce reports to show that users view and complete all tasks within Moodle by a specific date.

Summary

We have covered one of the most powerful Moodle modules and implemented several Moodle features that will help facilitate compliance training. Take a moment to review these one more time before moving on to the next chapter.

Specifically, in this chapter, we have covered:

- How the Moodle lesson module works and how it might be used to deliver compliance training
- How to create groups and groupings in Moodle to manage all the different levels of training required
- How to set up completion tracking and completion status reports to let employees and human resource managers know where individuals stand in their training

As you know, training is not just important for compliance and risk management; it is also just as important in continuing professional development. Keep in mind what you have learned in this chapter as you move on to the next chapter regarding continual professional development and competency tracking.

5

CPD and Competency Tracking with Moodle

In Chapter 3, Rollout Products and Services with Moodle, we looked at using Moodle to help build product knowledge among staff. Outcomes can be used to help map the product knowledge of your staff as it is acquired. To do this, you will need to think about what Outcomes you are looking to map in each learning area. Some professions have gone through extensive processes and research to help define a set of competencies which can be applied to their industry.

However, when it comes to products rather than skills you do need to think about the definition and come up with a set of **Outcomes** *that you want people to be able to do after the training. These may be different for each profession and role, and often can go down to great detail. However, you do need to consider what level of detail is practical for training and assessment.*

After product training, you may want someone to be able to:

- ◆ Describe the product
- ◆ Explain what the product can be used for
- ◆ Explain what are the benefits of the product
- ◆ Understand what are the Unique Selling Points of the product
- ◆ Explain the sales process for the product
- ◆ Explain the support options available
- ◆ Explain the pricing structure and payment terms

These can be viewed as **Outcomes** for pretty much any product, so to have **Outcomes** related to a product, it must be specific. So, using the product example from *Chapter 3, Rollout Products and Services with Moodle*, let's redo these options making them specific:

- Describe Mahara
- Explain what Mahara can be used for
- Explain what are the benefits of Mahara
- Understand what are the Unique Selling Points of Mahara
- Explain the sales process for Mahara
- Explain the support options available for Mahara
- Explain the pricing structure and payment terms for Mahara

Now that these are clear, you can think about how you would assess these **Outcomes**.

However, if you were to search through Moodle, you would not find competencies. The feature is there but it is called **Outcomes**, which is synonymous with competencies and goals. This is an advanced feature which needs to be enabled by administrators. Moodle defines **Outcomes** as:

"**Outcomes** are specific descriptions of what a student is expected to be able to do or understand at the completion of an activity or course."

This definition is certainly close enough to the usual competency understanding, so it can be used in a similar way.

Once the `Outcomes` function is enabled in Moodle, you are then able to grade activities using one or more scales that are linked to the **Outcomes**.

In this chapter, we shall:

- Learn how to enable **Outcomes** for use in competency tracking throughout the Moodle site
- Learn how to create site-wide competencies/**Outcomes**
- Learn how to import/export competencies/**Outcomes**
- Learn how to select competencies for a specific course
- Learn how to add extra competencies at a course/module level
- Learn how to use competencies in assessments
- Learn how to view competencies in the gradebook

So let's get on with the show.

Some points to keep in mind

As already discussed, Moodle calls competencies by a different name—**Outcomes**. So from here onwards, we will stick to the Moodle terminology in this chapter. However, do remember they are equivalent.

It is important to note that there is no hierarchy to the **Outcomes** within Moodle. It's a flat list. Other systems like ELIS from Remote-Learner provide tree options. However, without that, you need to be careful how you name your **Outcomes**.

To help you navigate a long list, I recommend inverting the preceding examples. So instead of Describe Mahara, use Mahara Description so that all the Mahara **Outcomes** come at M in the list, rather than spread out at each point like at D for description and so on.

- Describe Mahara
- Describe Moodle
- Explain benefits Mahara
- Explain benefits Moodle
- Explain Mahara Use
- Explain Moodle Use

If you order it, as suggested, reversing with product first you get:

- Mahara Benefits
- Mahara Description
- Mahara Uses
- Moodle Benefits
- Moodle Description
- Moodle Uses

As you can see, you can easily find the correct **Outcomes** now. This can be annoying at first, but you will soon become familiar with it.

In previous chapters, we have touched on setting up a quiz and other activities, so we won't be covering this during the rest of this chapter. We will focus on applying the settings related to **Outcomes** and how they impact setup.

The sample course outline will be available throughout 2011 for all purchasers of the book on http://www.moodleforbusiness.com/

> **Using Moodle for continual professional development**
>
> Helping staff to maintain, improve, and widen their skills and their knowledge, more often than not, falls into the lap of the employer. The capability to demonstrate a skill is usually referred to as a competency. This chapter will focus on some techniques of using Moodle to define competencies and use them to aid tracking of continual professional development.

Enabling Outcomes in Moodle

Outcomes, Competencies, and Goals are all terms for the same thing in Moodle. Once **Outcomes** are enabled site-wide and within a course, you can set up an activity which has one or more **Outcomes** associated with it and each of these **Outcomes** can have a grade associated with it. Normally, grades for **Outcomes** are created using a custom scale other than numbers.

However, unlike a normal grade, you can allocate an Outcome to a number of activities. This makes it quite powerful for use within building competency maps. So, when you grade an activity, you not only provide an overall grade for the activity, but also for the **Outcome**. Hence, someone could pass a test but display a less than desired level for the **Outcome**. More on this later.

Time for action – enabling Outcomes

Outcomes are an advanced feature of Moodle 2, and as such, only an administrator can enable or disable them.

1. Log in as the initial Moodle administrator or as a user with Administrator role.

2. Look at the **Settings** block.

3. Expand the **Site Administration** tree of options.

4. Click on **Advanced features**. **Advanced features** is the third option, after **Notifications** and **Registration**.

5. The first option on the **Advanced features** page is **Enable outcomes**, which is defaulted to **No**.

6. Tick the box beside **Enable outcomes**.

7. Scroll to the bottom of the page and click on **Save changes**.

What just happened?

Now you have enabled **Outcomes** for your Moodle site. This is just the first step. Now we will need to add some **Outcomes** into the Moodle system so that they can be used in courses and in activities.

However, before we add an Outcome, let's add a custom scale suitable to our needs. For knowledge, we will select a simple proficiency scale of basic, proficient, and advanced. You could come up with many variations, but we will work with this.

Adding a scale

As explained earlier, scales are used when grading **Outcomes**. They are a way of evaluating the learner's performance and by default they are usually numeric. However, it is possible to create custom scales, and that is what we will do now.

Scales can be used for grading an activity and also for rating purposes on some activities including Glossaries and Forums.

Time for action – creating a scale

Moodle already includes some numeric scales and one example non-numeric scale, but we will create our own.

1. Select the **Site administration** tree from the **Settings** block.

2. Click on **Grades** to expand the options available there. You will see **Outcomes** there, but for now, we will focus on **Scales**.

3. Click on **Scales**. This will bring up the scales management page.

4. There are two lists, namely, **Custom scales** and **Standard scales**.

5. Click on **Add a new scale**. As you can see, a scale has a name, the scale information, and a description. You will see that the **Standard scale** option is ticked and cannot be edited. This is because we are adding a scale at the site level for use throughout Moodle.

6. Fill in the **Name** as **knowledge proficiency**.

7. In the **Scale** text box, fill in the following words separated by a comma: **basic, proficient, advanced**. It is important to get the syntax correct or else it will not work. It is also important to list the possible grades from the lowest to highest value.

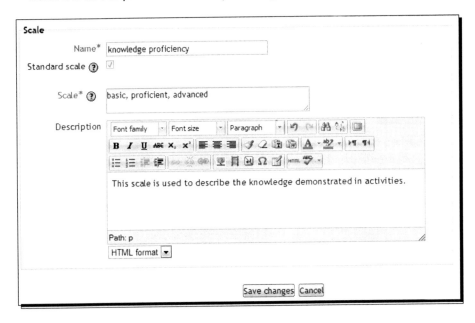

8. Click on **Save changes**.

9. Repeat steps 5 through 8 and add in another scale with the following text: **Disappointing, Not good enough, Average, Good, Very good, Excellent**.

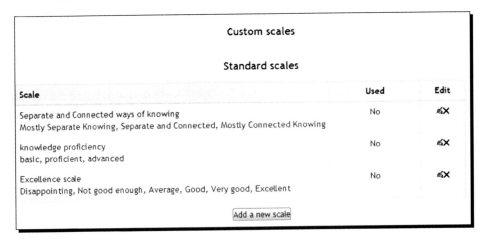

10. Now you can see there are three standard scales set up.

What just happened?

We have set up two extra **scales** that we can use to grade our **Outcomes** which we will now add. You don't need to create extra scales and could use the existing ones, but it is important to consider how you grade an Outcome as much as what Outcome you want to add.

Now we can continue with the **Outcomes** themselves.

Adding an Outcome

There are two types of **Outcomes**—standard outcomes and custom outcomes. The **standard outcomes** are those added site-wide while the **custom outcomes** are those which are added within a course.

Time for action – editing topic summaries

If you recall, you have already seen the **Outcomes** option on the **Site Administration** tree. That is where we are going now.

1. Select the **Site Administration** tree from the **Settings** block.

2. Click on **Grades** to expand the options available there.

3. Click on **Outcomes** to enter into the Outcomes management page. Unless you have added some before, this page will just have the button **Add a new outcome**.

4. Click on **Add a new outcome**. The form has 5 parts. The standard outcome option is locked. All outcomes added through the site administration are standard outcomes. We should fill in the complete form. However, **Description** is not a required field.

5. Type **Mahara Description** into the **Full name** field.

6. Type **Mahara Description** into the **Short name** field.

7. For **Scale**, select **knowledge proficiency** from the drop-down list. If you have added more options, they will appear here. If you have forgotten to add a scale that you want to use, there is a link here which brings you to that page.

8. Ignore the **Description** field for now as it is not required (you can see required fields shown in red with an asterisk beside them).

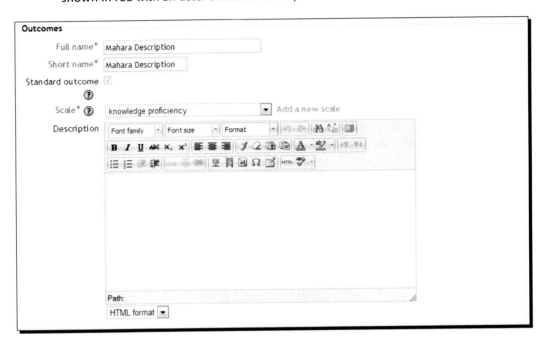

9. Click on **Save changes**.

10. Repeat steps 4 to 9 to add three more Outcomes: **Mahara Benefits**, **Mahara Pricing**, and **Mahara USP**.

11. You will notice that these are displayed in alphabetical order on the **Outcomes** page. This is also the case when you select them for courses and activities.

What just happened?

We just added in four **Outcomes** into the Moodle database. These are all graded by the new **Scale**, which we had entered previously.

You will also notice that these are displayed in alphabetical order on the **Outcomes** page. This is also the case when you select them for **courses** and **activities.**

Adding **Outcomes** one at a time is pretty straightforward. However, if you have hundreds of **Outcomes**, this may become a bit tedious and time consuming. There is another way too.

Adding Outcomes in bulk

Luckily, there is a solution for adding in Outcomes in bulk. You are able to import a CSV file to import Outcomes and their associated **Scales**. As with any CSV import, the format of this file is very important. Any deviation from the format will, at best, break the import and at worst give you some undesired results in the content. A refused import is better than bad content being imported. However, the import will not overwrite any existing **Scales** or **Outcomes** and will stop immediately if it detects invalid data.

There are six field names which the CSV import recognizes. They are:

Required	Field Name	Description
Yes	outcome_name	This is the **Full name** of the Outcome, as mentioned in the form.
Yes	outcome_ shortname	This is the **Short name** of the Outcome, as mentioned in the form.
No	outcome_ description	This is the **Description** of the Outcome, as mentioned in the form.
Yes	scale_name	This is the name of the Scale, as mentioned in the form.
Yes	scale_items	This is the list of entries in a comma separated list.
No	scale_ description	This is the **Description** of the Scale.

Please note that four of these entries are required. The import will not work without these entries.

The following is the sample CSV file data, which would have been used to create the four entries that we did earlier.

```
outcome_name;outcome_shortname;outcome_description;scale_name;
scale_items
Mahara Benefits;"Mahara Benefits";"knowledge proficiency";basic,
proficient,advanced
Mahara Description;"Mahara Description";"knowledge proficiency";basic,
proficient,advanced
Mahara Pricing;"Mahara Pricing";"knowledge proficiency";basic,
proficient,advanced
Mahara USP;"Mahara USP";"knowledge proficiency";basic,proficient,
advanced
```

Reflection

Think about the type of continual development that currently occurs within your organization. Think about the set of competencies or **Outcomes** that you could track for that development. Are there industry led or industry defined competencies that you may want to use within your organization? Who would be best to assist you in creating a competency matrix for a product, a service, or skill sets if none exist? Would it be beneficial or harmful to use competencies to track training and skill development in your organization?

One very good case I recall for competency tracking was related to maintaining a certain skill set within a team at all times. By knowing which members have various competencies, the manager was able to ensure that each core competency was represented during holidays, sick leave, and also from shift-to-shift. This can be especially important for some skills like first aid in certain environments.

Have a go hero – creating more Outcomes

You suddenly are faced with a new product rollout. You need to track the progress of the support staff to know who has the different knowledge related to the product. Draw up a list of **Outcomes** for the product and add them into Moodle for use in training.

You can either use the one-by-one method or the bulk method. Don't forget that you must include all the required fields.

Using Outcomes in a course

Defining and building a set of competencies for your organization is just one step. Importing them into Moodle is the second step, but before you can actually use them for an activity, you need to enable them in the course itself.

You should only add the **Outcomes** that relate to the course goals and objectives so that you don't need to wade through a longer than necessary list when adding to activities.

You will now be thankful for having them in a good alphabetical order.

Time for action – adding an Outcome to a course

So we have already added the Outcomes to the site. Now let's go through the steps required to enable one Outcome for your course.

1. Log in as **admin**, or a **teacher** who has the rights to Mahara Product Course.

2. Using the **Navigation** block, click on the course name to browse to the course.

3. In the **Settings** block, under **Course administration**, click on the **Outcomes** link.

4. You will see that this brings you to a page under **Grade administration**. That is because **Outcomes** are directly related to grading. You should see an image like the following one. There are no **Outcomes** in the left column as we have not yet selected any for the course.

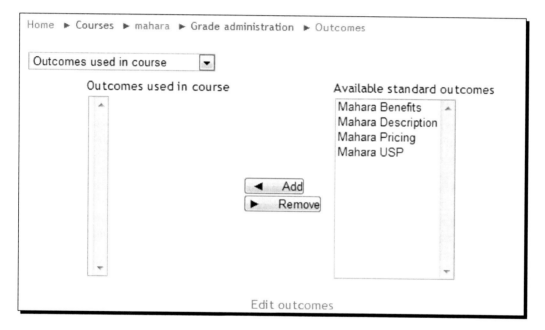

5. Select **Mahara Benefits** from the column **Available standard outcomes**.

6. Click on the **Add** button and this will add the **Mahara Benefits** to the left-hand column. You will also notice that it has **Standard not used** above it to indicate that it has not been used in an activity yet.

7. Select **Mahara Description** from the column **Available standard outcomes**.

8. Click on the **Add button** and this will add the **Mahara Description** to the left-hand column. You will now see in the following image that two Outcomes have been enabled on this course and two Outcomes have not.

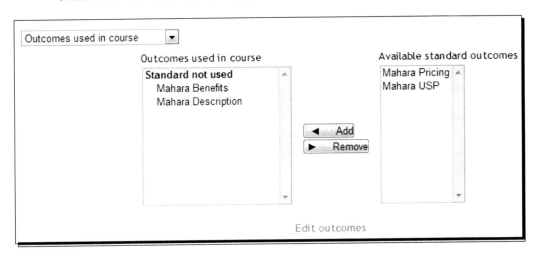

What just happened?

We just enabled two of the site-wide **Outcomes** on our test course. This will allow you to assign either of those two Outcomes to activities. The other two Outcomes are not going to be available to an activity until they are added to the course.

There is also a link to **Edit outcomes** below the two columns. This brings you to an Outcome manager page like the one before, with one exception. Now when you add an Outcome, you can decide if it is a **Standard outcome** or not. If you just want to add an Outcome to the local course that is not relevant site-wide, this is where you add it. This locally added Outcome would be a custom Outcome.

There are probably many reasons that one may want to add a course-level **Outcome**, and one that I have come across is when there is no centralized course design and management and each course creator adds their own **Outcomes** for their own course. This does work in some circumstances, but may lead to duplication of effort if the same Outcome is used in multiple courses.

I do not recommend you using this method to add **Outcomes**. **Outcomes** by their nature should be approached from a site-wide basis and not an individual course basis, if possible.

Have a go hero – adding more Outcomes to the course

While you are rolling out a new product or service, you need a simple and concise course that covers all aspects of the product. Suppose someone has already created the course which includes various resources and activities, and you have been asked to create two **Outcomes**, what should you do?

Should you create the new **Outcomes** site-wide or just within the course? What will influence this decision?

Adding an Outcome to an activity

Some activities work well with **Outcomes** and some don't work at all with **Outcomes**—this is usually related to a design decision for the grading mechanisms of that activity. Some activities allow you to set an Outcome when creating or editing the activity. There are exceptions to this, for example, the Choice activity.

For most of the activities, you grade the **Outcome**(s) at the same time as grading the activity. However, this only works for modules that have inbuilt grading. For those of other activities, you would need to go into the gradebook to grade the Outcome for the activity.

The gradebook is a repository for all the grades attributed to a person in a course. When a grade is awarded on an activity, the activity pushes that grade into the gradebook. It is also possible to edit and award the grades directly in the gradebook. But enough about that for now.

The following table shows which activities can use **Outcomes** and where they need to be graded. If you plan to use any custom activities, you would need to check if they support **Outcomes** or not.

Activity Name	Can use Outcome?	Where to grade
Advanced upload of files	Yes	Activity
Online text	Yes	Activity
Upload a single file	Yes	Activity
Offline activity	Yes	Activity
Chat	Yes	Gradebook
Database	Yes	Gradebook
Forum	Yes	Gradebook
Feedback	No	
Glossary	Yes	Gradebook
Lesson	Yes	Gradebook

Activity Name	Can use Outcome?	Where to grade
Quiz	Yes	Activity/Gradebook
Scorm	Yes	Gradebook
Survey	No	
Wiki	No	
Workshop	Yes	Gradebook

Time for action – adding an Outcome to an online assignment

To help test a learner's knowledge on the product Mahara, we are going to ask them to submit an online assignment. We are also going to select an Outcome which will be graded for this assignment. View your course, and make sure that "editing" is turned on.

1. In the topic area that you want to create the assignment, select the **Add an Activity** drop-down and choose the **Online text** option. This brings you to the setup page for adding a new assignment.

2. As with all names of activities and resources, the name is the call to action that appears on the course. Enter **How much do you know about Mahara?** as the text for the **Assignment name** field.

3. In the **Description** field, this is where you elaborate on your call to action from the name field. Type in the following text into the **Description** field: **Please describe the application Mahara in 50 words or less**.

4. Uncheck both of the dates (**Available from** and **Due Date**) otherwise the assignment cannot be done, except during those dates.

5. The **Grade** options can remain the same. If you have built **Categories** for your grades, you would be able to select it here, but as this is a more advanced usage of the Grade book, I recommend you leave it for the time being.

6. The **Online Text** options enable you control the assignment. Leave these three as **No** for now.

7. If you wanted to allow a user to resubmit his assignment multiple times, you would change the first option in this section to **Yes**. This is usual in cases where you allow a draft submission and provide feedback on it, to enable the learner to make a more comprehensive submission the next time, before grading.

8. If you want to be alerted every time there is a submission, you should change the **Email alerts to teachers** to **Yes**. This helps you with grading by prompting you soon after a submission.

9. The **Comment inline** option can be helpful as it copies the submission into your feedback reply when you grade the submission. This saves time and enables you to add your comments into the learner's text. It is recommended that if you use this option of using a different color for your reply.

10. The next options are **Outcomes**. Tick the **Mahara Description** and leave the other Outcome **Mahara Benefits** unchecked.

11. The **Common modules settings** are the same as outlined before and you can ignore them for this exercise.

12. Click on **Save and display**.

13. It will now display the description page of the assignment.

What just happened?

We just went through the process of adding an **Online Text assignment** and enabling one of the **Outcomes** as a grading option. Only **Outcomes** that are enabled on the course are available for the activity. Should you wish to create an Outcome just for this activity, you will need to do so at course level first.

Grading an Outcome in an assignment

Before you can grade, you need a submission! To do this, we need to first assign a user to the course and then do one of the following options:

1. Log in as the user.
2. Type some text in the online assignment.
3. Log out of user account.
4. Log back in as the admin.

OR

1. Assign user to the course.
2. Log in as the user in a different browser.
3. Type some text in the online assignment.
4. Return to the browser where you are logged in as the admin user.

Once there is a submission of the assignment, you can then grade the assignment. If you have enabled the alert, you will have got an e-mail about the submission. To view the submissions, you need to go into the assignment. As explained earlier, this is not the case for every activity.

Time for action – grading the assignment

Make sure you have returned to your course page by clicking on the short name in the navigation block.

1. Click on the assignment name **How much do you know about Mahara?** to view the assignment page. After a learner submits an entry, there will be an extra link with **View 1 submitted assignments**.

2. Click on **View 1 submitted assignments** (or however many submitted).

3. You will now see the following image. You can see that there is an option to grade the assignment from the user.

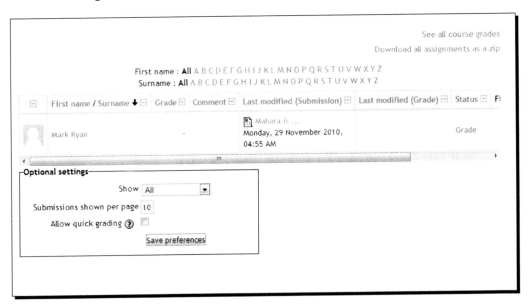

4. Click on the **Grade** link under **Status**. This brings you to the following image, which is the grading page for the **Online text** assignment.

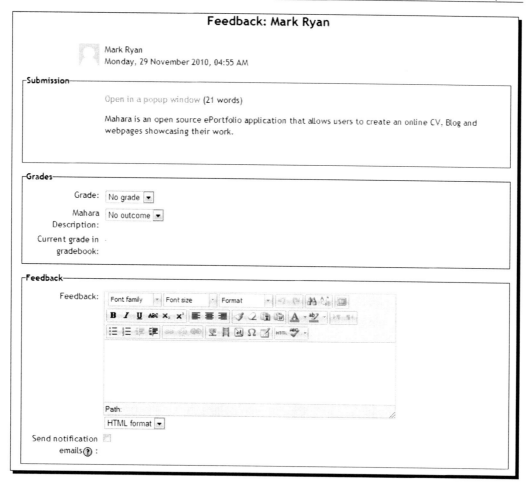

5. To grade the submission, select the **Grade** drop-down where it says **No Grade** and select **100/100**. This will award maximum marks for the assignment.

6. To grade the **Outcome**, select the **Mahara Description** drop-down where it says **No Outcome** and choose **advanced**. This will assign that grade on the **Outcome**.

7. If you have not graded this entry before, the **Current grade in gradebook** will be empty and show a -.

8. You can optionally provide **feedback** here, which is recommended to help give context to the learner and other trainers at a later stage as to why the grade/outcome grading were selected. Enter in a suitable **feedback** like **Excellent work, you really know your stuff**. If you want the user to receive an e-mail once you submit your reply, then tick the **Send notification Emails**. Otherwise, leave it empty.

9. Scroll down and click on **Save changes**. You will now see the submissions overview page for the assignment and the grade, comment, and Outcome information is shown.

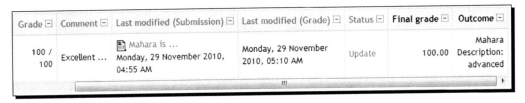

Grade ⊟	Comment ⊟	Last modified (Submission) ⊟	Last modified (Grade) ⊟	Status ⊟	Final grade ⊟	Outcome ⊟
100 / 100	Excellent ...	📄 Mahara is ... Monday, 29 November 2010, 04:55 AM	Monday, 29 November 2010, 05:10 AM	Update	100.00	Mahara Description: advanced

10. If you want to change the grading, you can click on **Update**.

11. If you have a lot of entries, you may want to click on **Allow quick grading** which is under the **optional settings**. This is handy so you don't need to go in and out for every submission.

12. Click on **See all course grades**. This brings up **Grader report** as follows from the gradebook, which provides an instant overview of each learner, their **grades**, and **Outcomes**. It also provides an overall average.

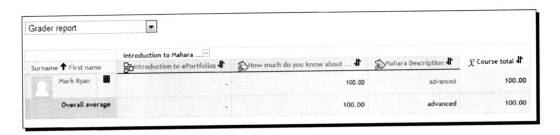

Grader report ▼					
	Introduction to Mahara ... ⊟				
Surname ↑ First name	🔲Introduction to ePortfolios ↓↑	How much do you know about ... ↓↑	Mahara Description ↓↑	X̄ Course total ↓↑
Mark Ryan 🔳		-	100.00	advanced	100.00
Overall average		-	100.00	advanced	100.00

13. To see what the learner views, log in as a user in a separate browser. You will see a similar report in the **gradebook** called the **User report**. This provides the same information, but from the learner's or user's point of view.

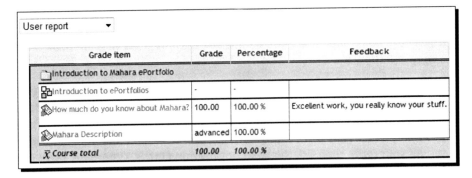

User report ▼			
Grade item	Grade	Percentage	Feedback
🗀Introduction to Mahara ePortfolio			
🔲Introduction to ePortfolios	-	-	
How much do you know about Mahara?	100.00	100.00 %	Excellent work, you really know your stuff.
Mahara Description	advanced	100.00 %	
X̄ Course total	100.00	100.00 %	

What just happened?

Now when we go to grade a submitted assignment, we not only provide a grade on the assignment alone, but also provide a scaled grade on the Outcome. This double grading provides a subjective grading and a numeric grading. This gives more context to the learner and to other trainers when they review the gradebook.

Have a go hero – add more Outcomes in the course

Suppose you have more activities in your course and you want to enable **Outcomes** for them, go ahead and edit them, and turn on **Outcomes** and see what happens.

It would be a good idea to go back to the table that we saw earlier and add a couple of different activities (including one which doesn't require marking in the gradebook). Then have a look at how they appear and work together.

Reflection

Think about the different types of assessments and activities that are available to you in Moodle. Which of them are more suited to Outcome usage? Should more than one activity have the same Outcome? How does this help demonstrate the skill, knowledge, or understanding?

Reporting on Outcomes in a course

One of the more powerful parts of Moodle is the **gradebook**. This holds a lot of information regarding the users, their activities within the course, their **grades**, **Outcomes**, and **comments** or feedback from trainers.

For learners or trainers, access to the **gradebook** is through the **Course administration** in the **Settings** block.

Users get access to two reports: An **Overview report** which lists the course and the actual overall grade, and the more detailed course **User report**. This second report provides the activity-by-activity grading and outcome information.

Time for action – viewing reports

To view the **gradebook** reports in a course, you need to go to the **Course administration**.

1. Make sure you are logged in as the admin or a teacher who has rights to the course.

2. Using the **Settings** block, click on the **Course administration**.

3. Under **Course administration**, click on the **Grades** link.

4. This brings you, by default, to the **Grader report**. While viewing **Outcomes** as part of the overall **Grader report** is useful, it is quite a lot of information for one screen. You often end up with a significant scroll across all the activities that are in the course, as shown in the following image.

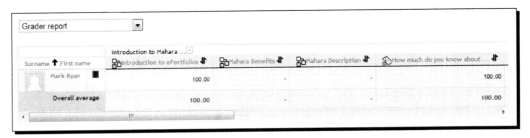

5. In the drop-down list, you will have access to a number of reports. Be sure to check them all later. However, let's continue.

6. Click on the drop-down list which has the **Grader report** and this will show you all the options that are available.

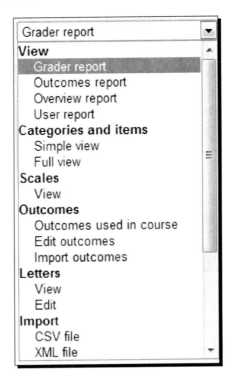

7. Select the **Outcomes report**. Although there are four basic reports, we will look at the **Outcomes report** for now. This report provides you with a fast overview on the **Outcomes** that you had selected for the course.

Outcomes report ▼					
Outcome name	**Course average**	**Site-wide**	**Activities**	**Average**	**Number of grades**
Mahara Description	proficient (2.67)	Yes	Glossary of Product Terminology	proficient (2)	1
			Course announcements	advanced (3)	1
			How much do you know about Mahara?	advanced (3)	1
Mahara Benefits	basic (0)	Yes	-	-	0

8. As you can see, this provides a simple, six column report on **Outcomes**. For each Outcome, you get a **Course average** which shows the average scores given to students for this Outcome in this course. Please note that this is not site-wide and only displays grades from within this course.

9. You also get a list of the activities which use the Outcome in this course. To help you navigate to that activity, the name is a direct link to that page.

10. Where earlier we got the **Course average**, you also get the activity **Average** in the fifth column. This is very useful to compare between the various activities, and between the activity and the **Course average** itself.

11. The last column shows the **Number of grades** given to students for each of the activities, which have the Outcome enabled.

What just happened?

We just had a brief look at the **Outcomes report** in the **gradebook**. This report is a good summary of Outcome results across all activities and students. To get a more detailed view on a specific student, you would need to use one of the other reports called the **User report**. The following is an example of the **User report**:

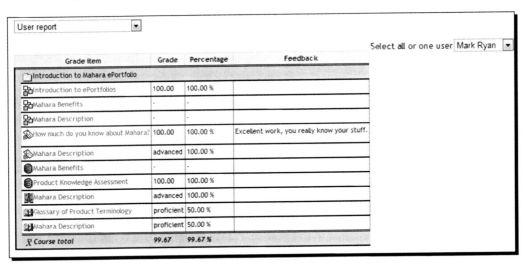

This report is the same as the one the user can see in his/her **Grades** area of the **Course administration** and lists the **Grade Item**, the **Grade**, **Percentage**, and the **feedback** for the learner.

The **gradebook** area of Moodle does have a lot of options, different reports, and ways of customizing the output. At some point, you will need to become more accustomed with these features, but as with many aspects of Moodle, you can focus on those parts when you need them.

Have a go hero – customizing the grader report

In the drop-down of the grading area, you may have seen an option called **My Preferences** with Grader report under it. This allows you to customize how the **Grader report** looks.

Spend a bit of time trying each of the options and see how they work and influence the interface. Don't worry, it just specifies what the defaults are, so you can easily recover the original report options.

Case study – National Health Institute, Italy

Since 1989, the External Relations Office (ERO) of the Italian National Health Institute (NHI) has been a WHO Reference Centre for active learning.

The External Relations Office is staffed by doctors, researchers from a variety of disciplines and other professionals with specific skills in the areas of public health, health management and training.

What was the business problem(s) for which Moodle was chosen as the solution?

Since 1989, the External Relations Office (ERO) of the Italian National Health Institute (NHI) has been a WHO Reference Centre for active learning. Since 2004, the ERO has been providing distance training in Public Health for professionals, experimenting, innovative learning methods based on the integration of active learning methodologies such as Problem Based Learning (PBL), which were originally devised for classroom learning, with e-learning tools. PBL is a methodology that challenges participants to "learn to learn" by working in small groups to solve real-world problems that mirror their working context, with the goal of developing life-long learning skills. This way, the process of working towards the understanding or solving of a problem leads to the participants' learning. The aim of ERO's work group as to e-learning development consists of finding innovative models to reproduce PBL in the e-learning context through the best available web tools. Moodle was chosen in 2005.

What was the solution and how did they arrive at the solution?

Following a first experience with a commercial platform in 2004, which was not adequate to support either the high number of participants, nor ERO's teaching methodology, a series of accurate evaluations began, in order to select a new platform able to respond to such needs. Moreover, there was the necessity to choose an open source platform, compliant with W3C guidelines and with Italian law on accessibility. Usability, stability, and security were crucial features, too. At the time of the evaluations, Moodle was suitable for becoming accessible and its availability of tools met ERO's methodology needs. Thanks to the NHI's will and financial support and with the Italian Moodle partner's active support, an accessible version was released in 2007 for the entire Moodle Community. At the same time, ERO's work group was strongly involved in the development of an e-learning model that increasingly adhered to PBL. After providing training for five years andby using experimenting progressive interaction pattern both, among and between participants and the facilitator of the learning process (as defined by PBL methodology), in 2009, a six month training course on Continuity of Care had been carried out, as the online phase of a Master's degree in Clinical Governance for Internal Medicine. Actually, this training experience has represented, so far, the highest level of ERO's learning model.

Why did they choose Moodle?

In comparison with other e-learning courses previously provided, this project was characterized by high-interaction among participants, facilitation in small groups, virtual classroom activities, and required various web features for its implementation. Ultimately, all the essential requirements to start the experimentation, such as platform usability, flexibility, tools availability, and the possibility to develop a module for integrating an appropriate virtual classroom system, were included in Moodle. The entire PBL cycle has been set up using Moodle 1.9 tools such as forum, database, workshop, feedback, consultation (see the following table for a comparison between traditional PBL steps and the corresponding activities in platform). Moreover, the Moodle grouping function allowed the ERO's work group to assign a facilitator to each group (as suggested in PBL). Finally, the constructivist approach characterizing Moodle matched with ERO's active learning methodology.

PBL Steps	Rendering in Moodle platform tools
Analyse the problem with the facilitator's active support. Define problem's focus, activation of prior knowledge, sharing opinions among the group	Forum and Virtual classroom
Formulate learning issues for self-directed learning	Forum, Virtual classroom and Feedback
Collect and share learning materials in order to fill the knowledge's gaps	Database, Feedback
Write the individual problem's solution and submit it to the group. Discussion among the group on each individual solution in order to compose a shared one	Wokshop and Virtual classroom
Write the group problem's solution, integrating the most significants points from each individual solution	Forum and Virtual classroom
Facilitator and expert's feedback	Forum

Was the project a success?

The training path was successfully completed, thanks to the innovative method of providing the course based on a high level of interactivity and to the low number of participants (n = 33), who were divided into small groups (5-7), with the active presence of a facilitator. Pre and post-test, composed by using the quiz tool, showed a significant knowledge improvement (22 percent). The final Customer Satisfaction Questionnaire, composed by using the feedback tool, showed a high level of satisfaction among participants, mainly as to the innovative learning method and the platform usability.

What were the benefits gained?

This experience represents an important basis for future improvements and experimentations. Thanks to the distance learning, this crucial phase of the Master's degree reached participants coming from all the regions of Italy. The participants, all specialists in internal medicine, despite the strict timetable planned and their job commitment, were able to carry on the activities during after-work hours, all day long. The participants referred to an improvement in their computer based skills and in the ability of working collaboratively in groups. On the basis of such results, the institutions involved in the Master's degree decided to replicate the training course and asked ERO's work group to collaborate in implementing further learning experiences.

What lessons were learned

This experience showed that high interaction leads to high levels of satisfaction among participants.

Actually, although large numbers of participants could be reached through e-learning, high interaction is possible only for courses with limited number of participants, as each small group requires the presence of a facilitator. Meetings in a virtual classroom, crucial for a good interaction during the key phases of PBL, require small groups as well. Furthermore, thanks to its flexibility, Moodle can be used for purposes other than learning, such as communication system, project activities, and documents sharing. Indeed, ERO is currently using Moodle for the communication between experts and staff developing curriculum for a medical college in Liberia, in the framework of another project that the ERO's staff is implementing.

What advice does National Health Institute, Italy, have for businesses that plan to implement Moodle?

It should be considered that the implementation of a learning project requires considerable planning. In order to create an accessible learning project, particular attention should be paid to documents accessibility. High involvement of an adequate staff endowed with different skills (technology, planning, communication, web writing, and training methodology) is also necessary. Furthermore, it must be considered that a high interaction among participants necessarily requires a low number of enrollments. Infact, the higher the chosen level of interaction is, the lower the number of participants needs to be.

Some thoughts

Moodle 2.0 version will allow the ERO's workgroup to improve the preceding model with new tools and features. Indeed, the availability of conditional activities could be an important tool in order to schedule activities according to certain conditions, such as previous activity completion, as set in the course timetable. Moreover, blended learning should be considered as a possible way to facilitate interaction among participants and to robustly reproduce the PBL cycle on the platform.

Case study – Gulf Agency Company

The Gulf Agency Company (GAC) was established in 1956 and is now one of the world's leading global providers of shipping, logistics, marine, and related services. The company employs more than 8,000 staff and has close to 300 offices globally. Its corporate head office is located in Dubai, with four regional offices in Houston, Cairo, Dubai, and Singapore.

What was the business problem(s) for which Moodle was chosen as the solution?

GAC launched the GAC Corporate Academy in 2007 to deliver new training opportunities to staff around the world. GAC Corporate Academy is a fundamental building block of the GAC Group's strategic plan, which recognizes that people and organizational learning are fundamental to GAC's business. A public overview of the GAC Corporate Academy is available at the portal page `http://www.gacacademy.com`.

Courses are available to all staff employed throughout the GAC Group, as well as nominated personnel from GAC Network Agents and cover a variety of topics related to all aspects of GAC business.

What was the solution and how did they arrive at the solution?

From the beginning stages of the Academy, Human Resource Development International and HRDNZ, (a Moodle Partner in New Zealand) have played a key support role. HRD worked with GAC to develop and facilitate courses such as Business Communication in the Information Age, Introduction to the GAC World, Personal and Professional Development, Customer Services Excellence, Shipping Agency Operations, and Microsoft Office Tune-up. One of the most popular courses is the Global English Programme with more than 350 staff from the global network enrolling for this during 2010. The close relationship between GAC and HRD continues today with the design of tailor-made online courses and the training and mentoring of GAC e-facilitators—the subject matter experts. Almost half of the GAC facilitators have completed the HRD MoodleBites© online courses (`http://www.moodlebites.com`).

Why did they choose Moodle?

In 2006 Damien O'Donoghue—General Manager of GAC—outlined the business, functional, and technical requirements for the Academy's Learning Management System, and considered several options: a commercial LMS, an open source LMS solution, or GAC's in-house LMS.

As part of his exploration, Damien attended the Moodle Moot in Wellington, New Zealand, in June 2006 and met Stuart Mealor (Managing Director of HRD) and discussed the potential benefits of Moodle as the most robust, scalable, and cost-effective solution.

By selecting the free and open source Moodle software as the e-learning platform, GAC was able to spend a higher proportion of the budget on what would ultimately make GAC the success it is today—great course design and facilitation support. The GAC mission is "To deliver specialized, job-based skills and self-development techniques to all GAC individuals, using leading-edge technology and enlightened learning processes."

Although not commonly used in the large corporate sector back in 2006, Damien was keen to use the online collaborative learning opportunities that Moodle enables and encourages.

Was the project a success?

In short, yes. GAC Corporate Academy started off by offering quite generic courses, and has now moved to courses specifically linked to key business objectives. After a less than successful strategy of purchasing off-the-shelf SCORM content, GAC has now moved to developing courses with a combination of internal subject specialists, HRD e-learning consultants, and facilitators. The course content is uploaded into Moodle course pages with GAC-specific assignments and discussion forums added.

There is a clear strategy to ensure that the learner does not simply click through a series of screens without context and interaction. Interaction and collaboration in courses is now a fundamental part of the learning process, with the courses tightly integrating content, tasks, and collaboration.

What were the benefits gained?

With such a diverse professional development requirement, GAC has managed to save many thousands of dollars by using Moodle. A traditional two-day regional workshop would cost US $35K-$40K with the expenses of travel, accommodation, venue, facilitation fees, and so on, and this would only be available for staff within a specific region. An international workshop might be as much as US $50K. By using Moodle, the cost per course has been reduced by around 80 percent to approximately US $10K, and also makes the course available for staff from any region.

What lessons were learned?

GAC are one of the groups of commercial Moodle users that have been able to take the academic best-practice models of online learning, and apply it in a very real way within the business context. Keeping its learning philosophy simple through action based learning, GAC will continue to offer well rounded learning solutions for the business and its support functions. Adjustments are made each year, in terms of course provision, delivery style, facilitation, and the team involved in delivering the service. This constant review of GAC ensures provision remains linked to critical business drivers, and continues to look to the wider Moodle Community and specialists for new and innovative ideas.

Reflection

There are many challenges in developing a competency model for use within your organization. In choosing to use competencies, the organization is letting its staff know that these are the areas that will be measured. Therefore, it is important to ensure that there is a level of buy in and understanding from the staff in both, the areas and levels being measured and in the methodology of assessment.

There may be a temptation to build a comprehensive map of every area, and the competencies related to it, and sub competencies and so on. However, too much detail risks alienating the learners and the trainers who need to match, assess, and justify the tracking. In other words, it can be overkill.

In the example earlier, with the various product-related competencies, different staff would need different competencies. A support staff member would not necessarily need to be able to handle the pricing model or a sales team member would not need to be able to handle the technical setup of the product. So it is important to remember the competencies related to the role of the person being assessed.

In building a set of competencies, or a map, for a specific role, you may want to group them together for ease of reporting and understanding. Such groups could be soft skills, product skills, or technical skills.

One thing to remember about competencies is that for them to be useful today and tomorrow, they need to be updated and kept current. This is where they can fit into tracking the continual professional development of staff.

Summary

In this chapter, we learnt how to apply **Outcomes** to help track user competencies in Moodle. We looked at two case studies, the National Health Institute of Italy and the Gulf Agency Company and their use of Moodle in managing on-going professional development.

Specifically, we covered the following:

◆ You need to select the scale when creating the Outcome. Therefore, when considering **Outcomes**, you need to think about the scales that you want to measure the **Outcomes** with.

◆ Although you can go back and add **Outcomes** one at a time, it is more practical to build a CSV spreadsheet and import the **Outcomes** in bulk.

◆ It is important to align the objectives and **Outcomes** with the course as the **Outcomes** are only available to activities when they have been added to the course first.

◆ It is possible to add a course level Outcome which is not available throughout the site. However, this is not always a wise thing to do. The risk is that someone else may create the same Outcome in another course and they will not be tracked together.

Not all activities can be graded within the activity. This has an impact on where the grading of the Outcome occurs. Familiarity with the gradebook grader report is essential for those using **Outcomes** so that they can edit and override grades as and when required.

We have also discussed the creation of the Outcome or competency maps and frameworks.

Now that we've learnt about using competencies in Moodle to help track skill and talent management, we're ready to move onto the next chapter that covers building communities with Moodle.

6
Communities of Practice in Moodle

In this chapter, we are going to use Moodle to support an informal community of practice within an organization. This is one of the areas where Moodle's social constructivist perspective becomes evident. Moodle was built to support people working together to learn and to teach each other. In the business community, these informal learning groups have become known as "communities of practice".

Communities of practice are "groups of people who share a concern, a set of problems, or a passion about a topic, and who deepen their knowledge and expertise in the area by interacting on an on-going basis".

Communities of practice (CoPs) have become widespread in a number of organizations. Ford Motor Company, Cisco, IBM, and other large organizations have developed communities of practice to help technical specialists working in different branches of the organization come together to trade best practices and collaboratively solve problems.

Research into communities of practice have identified four principle strategic types of communities of practice:

- ◆ Helping communities
- ◆ "Best practice" communities
- ◆ Knowledge sharing communities
- ◆ Innovation communities

Each type of community has different goals and different requirements for support in Moodle. Helping communities may just need a few forums for members to find each other and talk. "Best practice" communities need a way to document best practices and share what they have learned about their application. Knowledge sharing and innovation communities need methods for effectively communicating about problems and their solutions.

Over time, CoP's develop a unique perspective on their topic as well as a body of common knowledge, practices, and approaches. Using the social and collaborative tools in Moodle can help the community both build their perspective and share it with newcomers. Many of the tools, including the wiki and the glossary, can help the community document how it changes over time as well. The main Moodle website, `http\\www.moodle.org`, is an excellent example of a community of practice with many thousands of people working together to understand and use Moodle.

Moodle can effectively support communities of practice through a number of tools. In this chapter, we are going to explore the wiki module, get more in-depth with the database module, modify user roles to make it easier for community members to moderate discussions, and bring in an external news feed to keep community members up to date in their field.

Specifically, in this chapter, we will:

1. Set up a wiki for collaborative community editing.
2. Create a collaborative glossary for community members to build a shared vocabulary.
3. Create a database for the community to build an annotated reference library.
4. Create a new role, Community Moderator, and assign users the ability to edit forums.
5. Create an RSS feed from a forum.
6. Create a block to display an RSS feed from an external source.

So—let's get started!

Creating a wiki for your community

A wiki is a collaboratively edited document users can create together. The most famous example of a wiki, Wikipedia, is a sprawling collection of community developed encyclopedia entries. Anyone in the world can contribute to the collection of knowledge represented by Wikipedia, either by creating new articles or editing existing entries.

Moodle provides users with a more controlled wiki environment. Only people enrolled in a course can contribute to the wiki, so you don't need to worry about external readers or editors. In addition, you can configure the wiki to be editable only by certain people, or provide a wiki for each group.

Time for action - adding a wiki to the community site

To create a wiki in your community site:

1. Log in to Moodle as an administrator. Create a course for your "community of practice" following the instructions from *Chapter 1, Getting Started with Moodle*.

2. **Turn editing on** in your course.

3. Select **Wiki** from the **Add an Activity** menu in the first section.

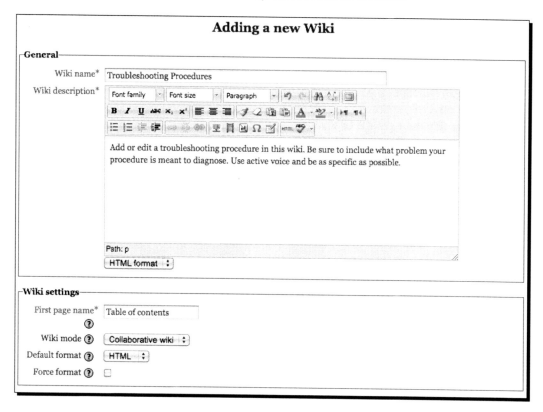

4. On the **Adding a new Wiki** page, give the wiki a name. Give the wiki a descriptive name that explains the purpose of the wiki. For example, call the wiki **Troubleshooting Procedures** rather than something vaguer like **Community Wiki**.

5. Fill in the wiki description area with instructions to the users about the purpose of the wiki and any suggestions for community standards or referencing. Do all of their statements need references? What sort of language is expected? Is the tone of the wiki formal or informal?

6. In the wiki settings area, change the name of the first page. Make the name specific to help your audience understand the purpose of the wiki. For example, call the first page **Table of Contents**, rather than **First page**.

7. For a wiki that everyone in the course can edit, leave the **Wiki Mode** set to **Collaborative Wiki**. Changing the mode to **Individual Wiki** will give each user his/her own wiki. This would be useful if you want everyone to write their own essay, but not as useful for a knowledge sharing site.

8. Leave the **Default format** set to HTML. This will allow the users to stick with the HTML editor, rather than trying to learn the Creole or nWiki markup tags.

9. If you want to prohibit users from using alternative markup, select the **Force format** checkbox.

10. In the **Common module settings**, you will usually leave the **Group mode** set to **No groups**. However, if you have groups in the course, it might be useful to give them their own wiki space. To quickly enable a wiki for each group, set the **Group mode** to either **Separate groups** or **Visible groups**. **Separate groups** prevents group members from seeing another group's wiki area. **Visible groups** enables them to see, but not edit, another group's wiki.

11. If the wiki is ready to go live, then make sure the **Visible** indicator is set to **Show**.

12. For most communities of practice wikis, you don't want to restrict the availability of the wiki. You want it to be available to everyone in the community to collect the ideas of as many people as possible. I would recommend leaving the restrict availability settings as they are.

13. Once you have entered the wiki settings, click the **Save and display** button. The next page will ask you to create the first page in the wiki. The new page title you entered in the settings page will be there. If you haven't forced the markup type in the settings, you can set the markup for the first page here. For the purposes of our example, I'll leave it set to HTML Format.

```
┌─Create Page──────────────────────────────────────────────────────────────┐
│                                                                           │
│   New page title   List of Procedures                                     │
│                    (•)  HTML Format                                        │
│                    ( )  Creole Format                                      │
│                    ( )  NWIKI Format                                       │
│                                                                           │
└───────────────────────────────────────────────────────────────────────┘
```

14. After you select **Create Page**, Moodle will display the editing page for your new wiki page. The tabs across the top present your administration options.

15. The **View** tab displays the page in read-only mode.

16. The **Edit** view gives you the tools to edit or create the page. The comments tab allows users to leave comments on the page rather than edit the page.

17. The **History** tab enables users to see the history of changes to the page, and even revert the page to an earlier version. The **Map** tab displays how the page is linked to other pages.

18. In the **Edit** tab, the General area is for editing the page itself. Add the text for your page to the Content area. You can use the HTML editor as normal on this page.

19. Below the General editing, you can add tags to the page to help other people find what you have written. Tags can be selected from the **Official tags** (tags created at the site level).

20. To create a new page in the wiki, you first need to link to that page from the first page. To create a link with the HTML format, put a double square bracket around the words you want to link to a new page. The link to the new page should look like **[[Link Text]]** in the editor. Once you click on **Save**, the link text will be highlighted. Click the text and you will see the **Create Page** dialog. Click the **Create Page** button and you will be taken to the editing screen for your newly created page.

21. Once you have created your page draft, select **Save** to save the page, or **Preview** to look at what you have done before making it public.

What just happened?

You have now created a wiki and the first page for your community members. The link to the wiki will appear in the topic where you added the activity. Community members can now begin to add new pages and edit each other's contributions to develop a community knowledge base.

Administering your wiki

Once you have created your community wiki, the community will have the ability to add and edit content. You or someone in the community may need to play the role of a wiki moderator to help shape the contributions and ensure that the wiki is useful to the community. There are a few tools in the wiki which you should know in order to help the community members create a useful resource.

Time for action: Revert a wiki page

Occasionally, you will need to change a wiki page back to an earlier version. If a community member accidentally deletes a section of content or makes an inappropriate change, it's easy to revert the page to an earlier version. To revert the page:

1. Select the wiki from the course page.

2. Navigate to the page you want to revert. Select the **History** tab.

3. Every time someone saves a change to the wiki, Moodle creates a new version of the page. You can compare versions by selecting the radio buttons (one on the left and one on the right) for the two page versions you want to compare.

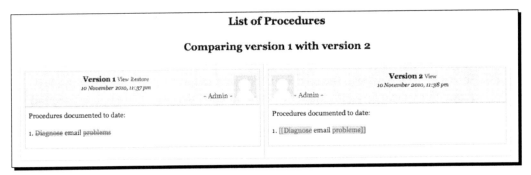

4. The comparison page displays deleted words with a line through them, and additions with a green background.

5. To restore one of the versions you are analyzing in the comparison screen, select the **Restore** link next to the name of the page.

What just happened?

You've now restored a previous version of a page and hidden the changes made since that last version. The page now looks like it did at a point in the past and is available for regular editing by the community.

Avoiding Reversion Wars

Be careful about using this procedure as it can cause confusion or conflict within the community. Members may become confused if a series of changes suddenly disappear without warning. Others may feel their contributions have been slighted and may react angrily. On Wikipedia 'reversion wars' occur when two groups continuously revert each other's editorial changes, usually due to a political or religious dispute (although sometimes the science fiction fans can get a little rabid as well). Avoid reversion wars by only using the revert function to bring back pages from catastrophic loss or to avoid liability. Other editorial changes should be agreed by the community and not force reverted.

Managing pages

As the community creates new pages in the wiki, some pages may become orphaned with no direct links to them. You may also want to track contributions to the wiki by date or contributor. Tools to get a view into the activity in a wiki are available through the Map tab.

1. To access the **Map** tab, go to any page in the wiki. Select the **Map** tab.

2. The drop-down menu in the **Map menu** provides a variety of options for managing the wiki pages.

Command	Description
Contributions	This option displays the list of pages you have edited
Links	Displays the pages that link to this page and the outgoing page links for this page.
Orphaned Pages	Lists pages that do not have links from other pages
Page Index	Lists all of the pages in the wiki in a hierarchical view
Page List	Lists all the pages in the wiki alphabetically by page title
Updated Pages	Displays the dates pages in the wiki were updated

3. Select each command once to get a feel for the data and tools available to manage your wiki.

Time for reflection

Managing a wiki can be a time consuming process. If community members have different understandings of the purpose of the wiki, or appropriate standards for contributions, how will you manage this situation? How will you market your wiki within the community to encourage appropriate contributions?

Creating a collaborative glossary

Learning the vocabulary of a community is one of the keys to becoming a member of that group. The Moodle Glossary tool provides the community with a method to collaboratively build a dictionary of terms to help novices understand the vocabulary of the community.

Time for action - creating a glossary

To create a collaborative glossary:

1. Go to the community course and **Turn editing on**.

2. In the section where you want to add the glossary, select **Glossary** from the **Add an Activity** menu.

3. On the adding a new **Glossary** screen, give the glossary a name. You can be a bit more generic with the name in this instance and simply call it **Glossary**.

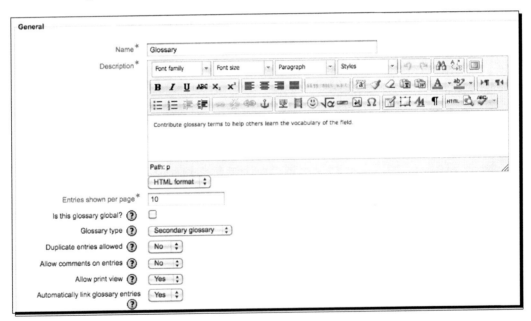

4. In the description field, describe the purpose of the glossary and give special instructions, if any.

5. The entries shown per page can be left at the default **10**, or changed as desired.

6. Only select **Is this glossary global?** if you want the glossary to be available throughout the site. Most glossaries are only used in a given course.

7. Leave the glossary type on **Secondary glossary**, unless you plan on combining glossaries later. Secondary glossaries can be imported into a primary glossary, but there can only be one primary glossary per site.

8. For a community glossary, it might be useful to set the **Duplicate entries allowed** to **Yes**, in order to allow multiple community members to create different definitions of the same term. You can use ratings to allow the members of the community to vote on which definition is more accurate or popular.

9. In a community glossary you should set **Allow comments on entries** to **Yes**, to enable community members to comment on each other's entries.

10. Keep **Allow print view** set to **Yes** in order to allow community members to print the glossary for reference.

11. The **Approved by default** option determines whether a submitted definition must be approved by someone with the **Approve Entry** privilege. In a community site, this should either be set to **Yes** or there should be a group of more experienced community members with this privilege.

12. The next four options determine how the glossary is displayed by default. You can leave these as they are.

13. **Edit always** enables contributors to always go back and edit their contributions. If you set this to **No**, contributors will have 30 minutes to edit their contribution.

14. If you want to enable voting on glossary terms, set the **Aggregate type** in the **Ratings** area to either Average or Sum of ratings. Then set the **Scale** to a numeric value, usually something small like **10**. This will give raters a 10 point scale to rate other contributions.

15. When you have set up the glossary options, select **Save and display** to save your settings and see the glossary.

What just happened?

You've now created a glossary activity for everyone in the community to add terms and definitions. While you may also want to create glossaries that are only editable by course authors, a collaborative glossary can be a great tool for community members to contribute their perspective on the vocabulary of the community. As new terms emerge, the community will probably be faster to recognize and define them than a central editor.

Create a database for an annotated bibliography.

One of the most basic interactions for a community is to share resources with each other. Most corporate communities will want to share intellectual resources like articles and whitepapers. You could simply create a forum to allow users to attach articles and copy URLs but a structured entry format would make the collection much more useful to your end users.

The database module will allow users to add entries, list other users' entries, comment and rate entries, and download resources. It takes a bit of work to get the database set up and look good, but it will make a big difference in the usability of the collection in the long run.

You've had some experience creating a database in *Chapter 3, Rollout Products and Services with Moodle*. This time, we are going to create a slightly more complex database. In the next step, we will look at how to edit the display templates in order to customize the look and make the database more useable.

Time for action - creating the basic database shell

To begin creating a database, we need to set up the basic activity.

1. With the course in editing mode, select **Database** from the **Add an Activity** menu.

2. On the next screen **Adding a new Database to Topic**, enter the name of the database. For now, let's just call it **Annotated Bibliography**.

3. In the **Introduction** area, be sure to tell the community members what the database is for.

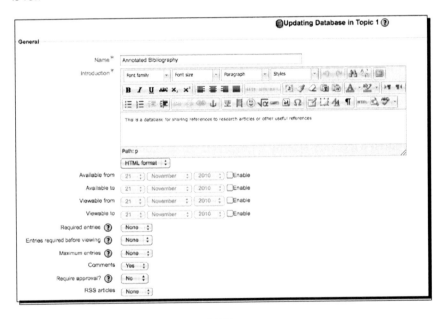

4. The Available and Viewable dates should probably be left disabled for a community shared resource. If you want to restrict availability of the database, you will select the **Enable** checkbox next to the setting, and then select the date.

5. The **Required entries** setting allows you to require community members to submit a certain number of entries before the activity can be considered complete. If you want to formally recognize contributors by checking off the activity when they have contributed a pre-defined level of resources, then you could use this setting. Otherwise, leave it set to **None**.

6. The **Entries required before viewing** setting allows you to require the user to submit one or more entries before being allowed to see other users' entries. This setting is usually used for a graded submission where the user is required to submit their own work before they can see others'. For a community database, leave this set to **None**.

7. If you are opening your database to community members outside of your organization, you can prevent database entry spam by setting a maximum number of entries. Otherwise, you probably want to leave this set to **None** to encourage community members to submit as many resources as possible.

8. Set the **Comments** setting to **Yes**. This will enable community members to comment on each other's entries.

9. If you want the community moderators to approve entries before they are visible to other users, set the **Require approval** to **Yes**.

10. You will need to think carefully about using ratings in your database. Ratings can be useful to allow community members to judge the usefulness of a particular entry, but they can also discourage people from submitting entries that might not get a high rating.

11. If you do decide to use ratings, set the **Aggregate type** on the rating to either **Sum of ratings** or **Average of ratings**. The **Average** rating will probably be more useful for community members looking for the best resources.

12. Set the **Scale** to a numeric rating, most likely somewhere around **5**. This gives raters enough variation to make a judgment without overwhelming them with too many choices.

13. If you are going to allow ratings for a community, do not restrict the ratings to entries with a certain date range. Entries may change in value over time, so a continuous rating will allow the community to signal when a resource has outlived its usefulness.

14. If you are using groups in your community, for example, special interest groups (SIG), then you may want to set the **Group mode** on your database, to enable each SIG to have its own collection. If you are going to set up a group specific database, I would recommend setting up two databases, one for the whole community, and another for the SIGs. Most of the time, you will set the group mode to **Visible groups**, to enable the SIG members to see the resources from other groups.

15. Make sure the **Visible** setting is set to **Show** to enable community members to see the database.

16. For a community database, you will not want to enable any of the settings to restrict availability.

17. When you have adjusted all the settings, click **Save and display**.

What just happened

You now have the empty shell of a database. Over the next few action steps, we will set up the database as an annotated bibliography.

Time for action - Creating the database fields

In the **Fields** tab of the database we created, you can create the fields that will store the data you want your users to enter. For an annotated bibliography, we want to create fields for a resource name, a synopsis, a pointer to the resource (most likely a URL), an area to upload a resource, a time added field, and some topic categories.

1. To create the resource name field, select **Text** from the field drop-down list. Give it a name using the **Field Name** field and set autolink to allow any mention of the resource to be linked back to the original entry.

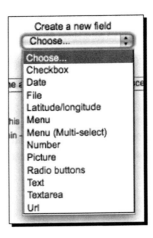

2. The synopsis field will require more space than the resource name. Select text area to create a larger text entry field (like the instruction fields in most Moodle activities).

3. Next, we want to add two fields for the resource itself. We want to add a URL field for a web resource and a file upload field if the user wants to upload the file directly to Moodle.

4. Add a URL field type by selecting **Url** from the dropdown list. Give it a **Field name** like **Link to Resource** and a **Field description** like **The URL of the resource**. To make it easier to layout your display pages, the **Forced name for the link** will make the link text the same for every link. Enter **Link** in the Forced name. Check **Autolink the URL** to link any occurrence of the URL to the database entry.

5. Next, we need to create an area for community members to upload files directly, rather than simply sharing a link to another website. Select **File** from the fields drop-down. Name the field **Upload File** and set the maximum file size to something you think will enable a useful upload without creating long upload or download times. The largest upload size is set by your Moodle administrator.

6. A date added field will enable users to add a date to the resource. Select **Date** from the **Fields** menu.

7. Finally, we want to create a way for users to categorize their entry, to make it easier for other users to find it. There are two methods you can use to do this. First, you can create a list of checkboxes with predefined categories, or you can create a text box for users to enter searchable tags.

8. To create a series of checkboxes with predefined categories, select **Checkbox** from the **Fields** menu. Set the name to **Categories** and enter a field description. In the **Options (one per line)** box, put one option per line. Moodle will create one checkbox for each option.

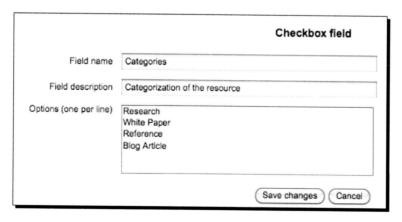

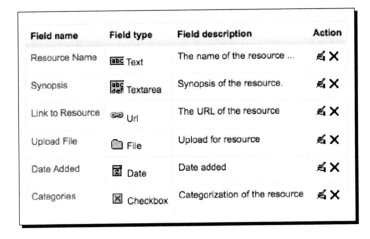

9. Once you have created all of the fields, you will need to save the default templates to see how Moodle is going to arrange your new fields by default. Select the **Templates** tab from the menu. Then select the **List template** from the sub-tabs.

10. At the bottom of the screen, select the **Save template** button. This will save the default template for the list view.

11. Repeat the last two steps for the **Single template** and the **Advanced search template**.

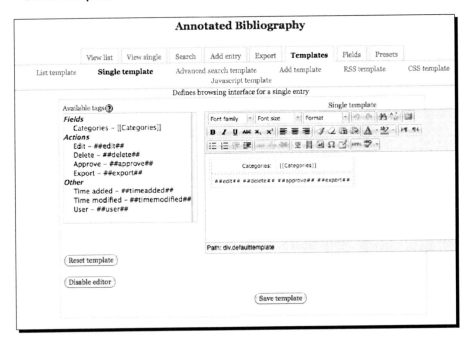

12. You can see how the default display template will look by selecting the **Add entry** tab. This provides a default layout for your fields in the order you created them. In the next section, we will look at how to change the layout template.

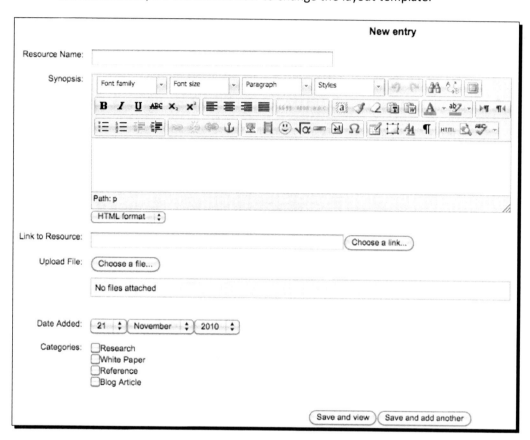

13. Create an entry in the **Add entry** tab, so you can look at the **View list** and **View single** templates.

What just happened?

You have now created the fields for the database. The database fields can hold a wide variety of data and the uses of the database are limited only to your imagination.

Time for action - edit the display template for a database

The default layout for the display templates in Moodle is usually not refined enough to use on a community site. Since the templates are automatically generated, the display is usually too generic. We'll look at how to change the **List template** in this example. Many of the skills we will learn here will enable us to modify other templates.

1. Select your database as a user with editing privileges for the course.

2. From the database page, select the **Templates** tab. From this page, you can edit the display templates for the database.

3. Select the **List template** from the list below the tabs. We'll focus on this template for this example. We would like to create a list view with each resource on one row.

4. The **Header** field displays the header for the page. It is only displayed once, so we'll use it as the header row in our list. We want it to display the name of each field which we will display in the list view. Create a table of one row with five columns. In each column, put the label for the data: **Resource**, **Synopsis**, **Date**, **Categories**, and a column for the Edit and View buttons.

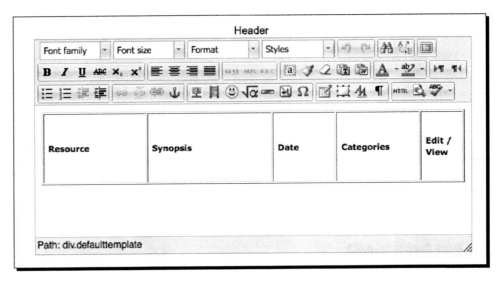

5. If you want finer control over the display of the table, switch to HTML mode by selecting the HTML button. This will switch the editor over to code view. You can then enter the HTML by hand, which enables you finer control and will make it easier to line up the columns in the header and the repeated entry. For this example, I used the following code to display the header table:

```
<div class="defaulttemplate">
 <table style="width: 65%; height: 88px;" border="1"
cellspacing="1" cellpadding="5" align="left">
<tbody>
<tr>
<td width="25%" align="left" valign="middle"> <strong>Resource</
strong></td>
<td width="30%" align="left" valign="middle"> <strong>Synopsis</
strong></td>
<td width="15%" align="left" valign="middle"> <strong>Date</
strong></td>
<td width="20%" align="left" valign="middle"> <strong>Categories</
strong></td>
<td width="10%" align="left" valign="middle"><strong>Edit / View</
strong></td>
</tr>
</tbody>
</table>
</div>
```

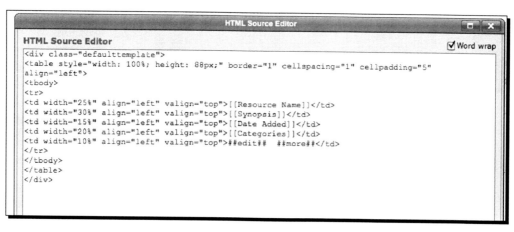

6. Now we need to create the repeating row for each entry. Copy your table from the **Header** area and paste it into the repeated entry to get the basic structure of the table.

7. Now we need to tell Moodle to replace the text in the table cells with the data from the database. Field replacement is designated by double square brackets on both sides of the field name. For example, to replace the text in the **Resource** cell with the actual name of the resource, enter **[[Resource Name]]**. The **Available Tags** window on the left side displays all of the available tags to help you remember what you named your fields.

8. In the **Edit/View** column, we want to display the icons to edit or view the entry in the database. To replace the text with an action button, use a double hash around the command. For example, to place an edit button on the screen, use ##edit## to tell Moodle to display the edit icon, instead of the word "edit". The available action buttons are listed in the **Actions** list in the **Available Tags** window on the left side.

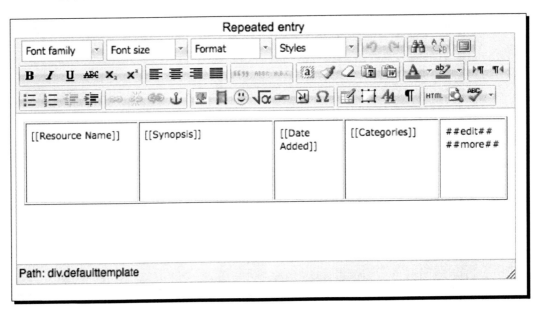

9. Again, you can use the HTML view to gain finer control over the display of the table. The code that I have used in this example is:

```
<div class="defaulttemplate">
<table style="width: 100%; height: 88px;" border="1"
cellspacing="1" cellpadding="5" align="left">
<tbody>
<tr>
<td width="25%" align="left" valign="top">[[Resource Name]]</td>
<td width="30%" align="left" valign="top">[[Synopsis]]</td>
<td width="15%" align="left" valign="top">[[Date Added]]</td>
<td width="20%" align="left" valign="top">[[Categories]]</td>
<td width="10%" align="left" valign="top">##edit##  ##more##</td>
</tr>
</tbody>
</table>
</div>
```

10. Once you have made your changes, be sure to click on **Save template** at the bottom of the screen. It's quite frustrating to make a number of changes to the template only to lose them by selecting the **View List** tab before saving your changes.

11. After you have clicked on the **Save template** button, select the **View List** tab. You should see all of the resources listed in a nice tabular format.

What just happened?

You have just modified the display template for the database list view. Creating a useable, nice looking interface for the database will increase the likelihood of community members engaging with the activity and sharing resources with each other.

Have a go hero

Improve the **View Single** template to make it easier to read. Add a border around the table and alternate the background shading in every other row. See the following image for an example.

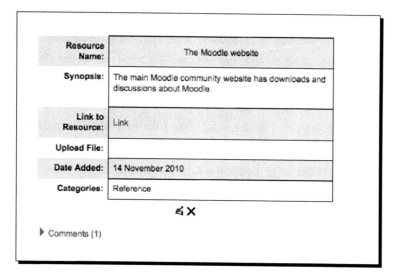

Time for reflection

As you build tools for your community, refer to the framework from *Chapter 1, Getting Started with Moodle*. In your community site, how will you measure the impact of the "community of practice" on your organization? What problems are you hoping to solve by implementing a community of practice?

Creating community moderators

We've spent a bit of time in previous chapters discussing Forums in Moodle. Most "communities of practice" (CoPs) are going to be focused on forums as well as the activities you have just created. Forums are a really good general tool for communication and collaboration. Every online discussion however, requires a bit of care and feeding to maintain a good collaborative atmosphere and provide useful information to its participants. As a system administrator, you probably do not want to have the responsibility of moderating every community forum. Delegating moderation to community members is the easiest way to both promote self-regulation within the community and to alleviate your workload.

Time for action - creating the moderator role

To create a community moderator role, we will create a basic role at the site level, and then assign that role to a participant at the forum level within our "community of practice" course.

1. From the main page on the site, select **Site Administration** from the **Settings** block. Then select **Users | Permissions | Define Roles**.

2. On the **Define Roles** page, select the **Add a new role** button.

3. Moodle will then display the **Adding a new role** page. Name your new role **Community Moderator**.

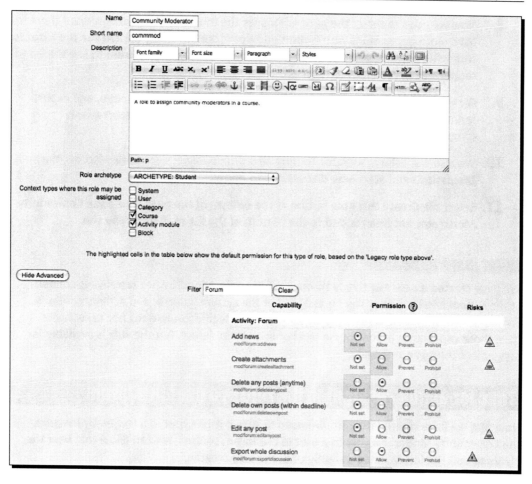

4. The role **Short name** is used to assign the role through external data sources, so you'll want a short name without special characters or even spaces. I've given this role the name of **CommMod**.

5. The **Description** should tell other admins the purpose of the role. In this example, the role is used to assign community moderators in a course.

6. The **Role Archetype** defines the base permission set of the role. This makes it easier to create roles based on existing roles. For this example, we want to use the **Student** role as a base role, and just change the forum related permissions.

7. The context defines where the role can be assigned within the system. For this role, we might want to assign it at the course level or at the individual forum level. So we'll select **Course** and **Activity Module**.

8.   Now we need to select the permissions for the moderator. As we only want them to have more permissions with forums and not other activities, we can use the **Filter** to shrink the list of possible permissions. In the **Filter** box, type **Forum** to see the list of capabilities related only to forums.

9.   For this example, we want the moderator to be able to delete, move, and export forum posts. So select **Allow** for **Delete any posts (anytime)**, **Export whole discussion**, and **Move discussions**.

10. We also want the moderator to start new discussions if necessary. Also, set the **Split Discussions** and **Start new discussions** to **Allow**.

11. Select the **Create this Role** button at the bottom of the page. You'll see **Community Moderator** has been added to the bottom of the list of roles on the site.

What just happened?

We have created a new role to use throughout Moodle. Moodle roles are always created at the system level, but they can be assigned at the system, course, and activity contexts. Someone with the **Community Moderator** role in a specific forum does not necessarily have those capabilities at the course level or in another forum. But the role is available for assignment throughout the site.

Time for action - Assigning the role to a user in a forum

Now that we have created the role, we need to assign it to a user in a forum. By assigning the **Community Moderator** role to a user in the forum context, we can allow that user the ability to edit the forum independently of the course creator.

1.   Go back to the CoP class and click the **Turn editing on** button.

2.   Select **Forum** from the **Add an Activity** menu.

3.   Give the forum a name. I've used **Moderated Forum**.

4.   Set the **Description** of the forum as you've done previously.

5.   For now, leave everything else as a default and click on **Save and display**.

6.   On the main forum page, select **Locally assigned roles** from the **Settings** block on the left.

7.   Select the **Community Moderator** role from the list of roles to assign.

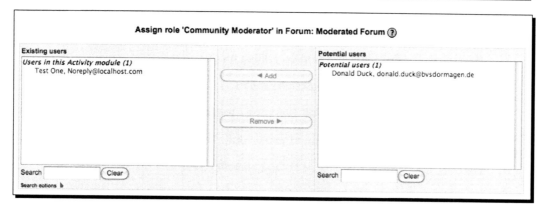

8. You'll then see the list of users enrolled in the course in a pick list on the right side of the screen and the users assigned to the role on the left. Select your community moderators on the right and click **Add** to assign them the **Community Moderator** role on this forum.

9. Select **Locally assigned roles** from the **Settings** block again. You'll then see the list of roles and the number of people assigned to each role.

What just happened?

We assigned the community moderator role to a community member. The user with this role in the forum can edit posts and perform other moderator's duties.

Have a go hero

Moodle manages permissions based on the context where the user has a given role. So anyone assigned **Community Moderator** in this forum doesn't have the moderator privileges throughout the course. If you wanted to allow a user to edit every forum in the community course, how would you assign their role?

Editing privileges for an existing role

We've looked at how to create and assign a new role in a course, but what if we just want everyone in the community to have the ability to moderate a forum? Just as roles can be assigned in a given context, like a specific forum for instance, a role can be modified in a context. Every course and activity in Moodle can interpret the roles assigned to users in a different way. It can get a little confusing, but Moodle 2 has some new tools to help track permission changes. Let's start by assigning moderator level privileges to all of our community members in a forum. Then we'll check their permissions to make sure they are what we want.

Time for action - editing the privileges in a forum

1. Go back to the CoP class and turn on editing mode.

2. Select **Forum** from the **Add an Activity** menu.

3. Give the forum a name. I've used **Everyone Moderates Forum**.

4. Set the **Description** of the forum as you've done before.

5. For now, leave everything else as default and click **Save and display**.

6. From the Forum page, select **Permissions** under **Forum administration** in the **Settings** block.

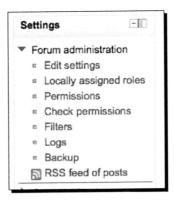

7. The **Permissions** in **Forum** page lists all of the roles and their permissions in the forum. The permission is listed on the left. The icon in the next column indicates the security implications of changing the permission. The third column lists the roles which have that permission. If you've followed the steps to create a role, you'll see the **Community Moderator** role with the editing permissions we created. The fourth column lists the roles that have prohibited that permission.

8. Now we need to give the **Student** role permission to edit the posts. In the **Roles** column for the **Edit Any Post** capability, click on the **+** in the third column under the roles with that capability.

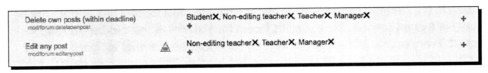

9. You'll then see the "Allow role" page. Select the **Student** role from the **Allow Role** drop-down menu.

10. Click the **Allow** button.

11. Now we need to repeat the process to allow the student role to **Delete Any Posts**, **Move discussions**, **Split discussions**, and **Export posts**. For each capability, click the + symbol in the role column, and select the **Student** role from the drop-down list and click **Allow**.

What just happened?

You have now edited what users with a role can do in a particular forum. By changing the permissions on an activity, you can greatly change how users interact with the particular module instance. Remember the changes you made here do not affect what the user can do in any other forum.

Time for action - checking the users permissions

Now that we've added the permissions, we need to check to see what permissions the users have. This is a useful procedure to know if users report they can't do something they think they should.

1. From the **Settings** menu, select **Check permissions** under **Forum Administration**.

2. From the **Check permissions** page, select a user from the **Select a user** dialog. If there are too many users, you can use the search box underneath the user list to narrow the options.

3. If you want to refine your search, select the **Search options** toggle below the search box. This will reveal the refinements available for your search. The options are:

   - Keep selected users, even if they no longer match the search: With this option, you can select some users, and then change the search criteria and keep the users you have selected.

   - If only one user matches the search, select them automatically: If you know the exact name of the user you want to check, then you can enter it in the search box and Moodle will select it automatically if no one else has the same name.

   - Match the search text anywhere in the user's name: Instead of matching whole strings, Moodle will search for a string anywhere in the user's name.

4. Once you have selected the user you want, select **Show this user's permissions**.

5. The **Check permissions** page will display the permissions for the user you have selected. If you followed the preceding directions and selected a user with student privileges on the course, then you should see **Edit any post** set to **Yes** and green.

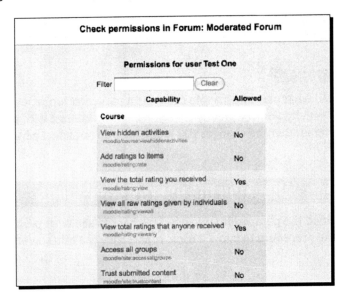

6. If the list is very long, you can filter the list of permissions using the **Filter** text box above the list of permissions. For example, if you just wanted to see permissions with the word "View" in the title, simply type **View** in the filter box.

7. To check another user's permissions, select the **Select another User** from the list below the permissions view.

What just happened

You have now checked a user's permissions on an activity. This is useful if you want to check a given user's role, or if you need to troubleshoot a permissions issue. Unfortunately, the display doesn't indicate where each permission is set (for example, can the user edit posts because of a role at the forum or course level? Is there a permission override somewhere that allows them to edit?). For that you would need to look at the roles assigned to the user at each level of the hierarchy. Start with the most specific context, like the individual forum, and work your way up the hierarchy.

Time for reflection

How will you use roles and permissions to help your implementation plan? Are their special roles you need to define for various groups of users in the community? How will roles be assigned within the community? Will there be a special group of community members with special privileges? Or will everyone in the community be able to moderate?

Using RSS feeds to improve communication

Real Simple Syndication (RSS) is a simple XML protocol for sharing news stories across the web. RSS has been applied in a lot of areas, from simple news readers to audio and video distribution through podcasting. Moodle can both create and consume RSS feeds and we'll explore how to do both in this section.

Creating RSS feeds from a forum

We'll start exploring RSS by creating a news feed from a forum. Although forum subscriptions allow users to receive posts through e-mail, syndicating content through an RSS feed allows users to consume content from the Moodle site through another channel.

Time for action - Enabling RSS

RSS feeds need to be enabled at the site level before you can use them in an activity. So let's do that first.

1.   Log in to your site as the site administrator.

2.   From the front page, find the **Site Administration** area. To search for all RSS related settings, type **RSS** into the search box.

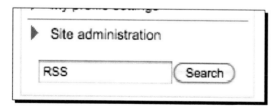

3.   To allow any activity to use RSS, we need to enable it at the site level first. Select the checkbox next to **Enable RSS** feeds in the **Advanced features** box. You will then need to scroll down to the bottom of the screen and **Save changes** before you can enable feeds in specific activities.

4. After you select **Save changes**, the drop-down menus for the **Enable RSS** feeds for **Database**, **Forum**, and **Glossary** should change from **Disabled at server level** to a **No/Yes** selection. For now, let's enable RSS feeds for **Database** and **Forum** activities by setting **Enable RSS feeds** to **Yes**.

5. Scroll down to the bottom of the page and select **Save changes** once again.

6. Each forum and database activity on the site can now generate an RSS feed. However, we need to enable each specific activity to generate a feed.

What just happened

We just enabled RSS feeds across our Moodle site for both Databases and Forums. We now need to go into the individual forums and databases to enable those activities to publish feeds.

Time for action - Enabling RSS in a forum

Now that we have enabled RSS at the site level, we can enable RSS in a forum. By enabling RSS, users can add the news feed from the forum to their preferred RSS reader.

1. Log in as a site admin or course teacher and go to your Community of Practice course.

2. Click on the forum you want to enable for RSS feeds. Then select **Edit settings** from the forum **Settings** menu.

3. If you have enabled RSS feeds at the site level and enabled them for forums, you will see a new area in the settings page labeled **RSS**. There are two options for enabling your RSS feed.

4. Set **RSS feed for this activity** to either **Discussion** or **Posts**. If you set it to Discussion, then each discussion will appear as a news item in your RSS feed. If you want each post to be a news item in the feed, select **Posts** from the drop-down.

5. The **number of RSS recent articles** sets the number of articles to display in the RSS feed. Most often you will set this to a number larger than **5**.

6. Save your changes by selecting **Save and display**.

7. In the **Settings** menu, you should now see a new option, **RSS feed of posts** (or discussions if you selected that option) at the bottom of the **Forum Administration** menu. Select this menu item to see the feed. You may need to wait for the Moodle cron script to run before the feed is updated.

8. The display of the resulting RSS feed will depend on your browser. You can either copy and paste the RSS feed URL into your RSS reader, or use your browser's subscribe features to subscribe to the feed in another application.

What just happened?

We created an RSS feed from a forum. Anyone subscribed to the feed will get topics and discussions in their RSS news reader. The feed can also be used to display the activity in a forum in other places in Moodle through the RSS News block, which we will explore next.

Displaying an RSS feed in a course

While we are on the subject of RSS feeds, lets look at how to bring in an external RSS feed from an outside source to help community members stay up on the latest news from the outside world. In this example, we'll add the **Discovery News** feed as a generic example. Your community will probably have more specific and focused news feeds from organizations in the field, but the process for creating the block is the same, irrespective of the source.

 You will need to have RSS feeds enabled at the system level before you can configure an external RSS feed. Follow the preceding instructions to enable RSS feeds at the system level.

Time for action - creating an RSS feed block

1. From the course home page, turn on editing mode.

2. Find the **Add a block** menu (at the bottom of the right column by default). Select **Remote RSS feeds** from the drop-down list.

3. The new block should now appear just above the **Add a block** menu. By default, it is named **Remote News Feed**.

4. Select the editing icon in the new **Remote News Feed** block.

5. On the **Configuring a Remote News Feed block** page, you need to configure a few options. Let's start by adding the feed to the Moodle news feeds library. Below the **Choose the feeds** menu, select the **Add/Edit Feeds** link.

6. The next screen will enable you to add a new feed to the feed library. Click the **Add a new feed**.

7. The **Add a new feed** page allows you to add a new news feed to the site. Find the feed URL of the news source that you want to add to the site. For the **Discovery News** site, I went to `http//www.news.discovery.com` and found the link for the RSS feed. Copy the URL into the **Feed URL** text box.

8. Each RSS feed supplies its own name for the feed. In this example, the name is **Discovery News—Top Stories**. If you want to replace the name for the feed with one of your own, then put your own name in the **Feed Name** text box. If you leave it blank, Moodle will use the name supplied by the feed itself.

9. If you want to enable other course's authors to use the same news feed, then select **Yes** in the **Shared Feed** option.

10. Click **Add a new feed** to save your feed.

11. Back on the **Manage all my feeds** page, select the course name from the cookie crumbs at the top of the screen.

12. Select the editing button on your **Remote News Feed** block again.

13. Now we can configure the block for the feed we just created. The **Display each link's description?** setting allows you to select whether the description text is displayed along with the news item headline. Setting this to **Yes** will make the block longer, but will provide more information to a reader in deciding whether to select the link or not.

14. The **Max number of entries** to show per block determines how many new entries will be displayed in the block. I would recommend leaving this to the default **5** entries to start with, and then adjust later.

15. In the **Choose the Feed** menu, select the **Discovery News** feed we just created. You can select multiple feeds to display in one block, if you choose to do so. The block will combine them in a sequential order.

16. The **Title** field determines the title of the block on the page. Usually you will want to give the block the same name as the feed itself.

17. The next setting allows you to choose whether to display a link to the feed itself. This displays a **Source Site** link to allow users to go directly to the feed to add it to their own feed readers if they choose. Usually you would set this to **Yes**.

18. The **Channel image** is a branding image provided by the feed to display a logo for the source provider. The logo provides a clear indication of the source of the news feed. Unless company policy prohibits this, I would set this to **Yes**.

19. Now we can set where the block appears. **The Page Contexts** menu has two options. The **Display on Course: Community of Practice only** option will put the block only on the main page. The other option **Display on Course: Community of Practice and any pages within it** will display the block on every page in the course.

20. You can further refine where the block appears with the **Restrict to these page types** menu selection. In this case, the block will display only if the course is set to any one particular topics format, such as any course format, the course page, or any page.

21. The default region sets the default display column for the block. You can choose whether the block displays on the left or right side by default. Course authors or users could move the block if they choose to.

22. The default weight determines the order in which the block will be displayed. The lower the weight, the higher on the page the block will appear. Values range from -10 to +10.

23. Finally, you can set where the block appears on the current page by setting the visibility, region, and weight for the specific page.

24. Select **Save changes** when you have finished configuring your block. The **Discovery News block** with link description, channel link, and channel image is pictured as follows.

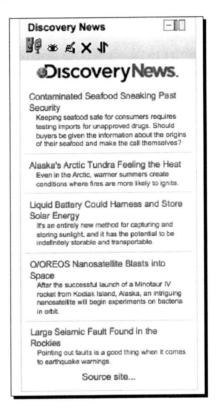

What just happened?

We have created an RSS block to display a news feed from an external news source. Adding external news sources to a community site can help bring in information from outside the community to help members stay current in the field and adopt the best ideas from other places.

Case Study – Adapt

Adapt is an association for international and comparative studies in the field of labor, law, and industrial relations. It has several research centers in Italy and abroad. The company has about 10 employers and about 200 co-workers, mainly PhD students from different research fields (Law, Modern Languages, Human Sciences, Economics, Education, International Relations, and so on).

What was the business problem(s) for which Moodle was chosen as the solution?

Our need was to find a place where we could meet from different parts of the world in order to share materials for our activities, to organize the company, and update the whole group about the different projects.

What was the solution and how did they arrive at the solution?

The solution was our Moodle site, not only for educational purpose (e-Learning), but for managing the company as well. We have just begun opening a "course" where our administration staff could upload documents that were useful for any member of the company. After that, we opened other courses dedicated to different aspects of the organization of the company (for example, we opened a course just for managing every activity related to the placement of our students and combining the request from our partners, about eighty big companies, to the different curricula we had in our database).

Why did they choose Moodle?

It's simple and very adaptable to what we needed. First of all, we needed a tool where we could control access for every user, and with Moodle that is possible for each resource and activity. When you have to work with a lot of people, it could be necessary that in the same course you have to manage several objects (docs, wikis, and so on) showing some parts only to a person, some other parts to a group, and so on.

Was the project a success?

We have been using it since October 2009. At the very beginning, there was only one course for business and managing purpose (3 users); now there are more than ten (about fifty users, but it grows every day). We consider it a success.

What were the benefits gained?

We could manage our activities and saving of data more efficiently and keep it updated. For example, we have interviewed young students in order to suggest them to our partners (about eighty big companies). During the interview, we could immediately see the Curriculum Vitae of the candidate and write about our impression and other notes regarding the candidate on a dedicated wiki. This wiki was open to other co-workers who could share this information with the whole group of people related to the placement activity, just in time.

What were the lessons learned?

Technology is a tool that can help anybody to save time and to organize efficiently, especially for an activity that must be shared with a group of people.

Do you have any advice for future businesses that plan to implement Moodle?

It's useful to begin with the basic functions of Moodle, then add the most peculiar. It's important to have an administrator of the Moodle platform who knows in depth, what the company needs and how it works.

Summary

We learned a lot in this chapter about configuring tools in Moodle to support a "community of practice". Moodle's social constructivist approach makes it easier to support this type of interaction when compared to other LMS systems.

Specifically, we covered:

1. How to create and manage a wiki.
2. How to create a collaborative glossary for development of shared vocabulary.
3. Setting up a database to manage an annotated bibliography.
4. Creating a new Community Moderator role to enable the community to be self-moderating.
5. Creating and consuming RSS feeds in forums and blocks.

This chapter is the last direct business solution chapter in the book. The next three chapters cover more technical issues. The next chapter covers how web conferencing software can be integrated with Moodle. The next chapter covers other open source tools that can add significant functionality to Moodle to expand the number of business problems you can solve with the system.

Web Conferencing with Moodle

7

In other chapters, we have looked at communication tools in Moodle, namely forums and chat. Although the text chat does provide a level of synchronous communication, mostly Moodle alone delivers a strong asynchronous environment which allows time for thought and reflection in responses and interactions. These types of features enable building of communities of practice and knowledge sharing centers. However, sometimes having learners/ participants involved in real-time, synchronous video, chat, and interaction is required.

In addition, as noted by Michelle in the case study at the end of the chapter from Remote-Learner, some people do learn better when given the opportunity to interact with the facilitators and other participants in this real-time environment. By providing the participants with the chance to ask questions with instant responses and enabling them to easily demonstrate the challenge or issue they are facing through screen sharing technology, you can swiftly help them through the problem they encounter. This provides a greater sense of engagement by connecting users with each other.

So what do you do if you want to extend Moodle with video? What features do you need? What features are available? Which products work with Moodle? What will it cost?

In this chapter, we shall learn:

- ◆ Some of the main applications in use
- ◆ The key integration options available
- ◆ The key features which need to be considered

- Technical challenges which you may encounter
- How to configure and use Adobe Connect Pro with Moodle
- How to configure and use BigBlueButton with Moodle

So let's get on with the show.

Some points to keep in mind

As there are many different applications in this area, we cannot handle them all in this chapter. So we focus on the 3 most popular integrations and deal with the following aspects for each:

- Where to get the integration
- The basics of installation
- The configuration options
- Key steps for usage

Most applications will be somewhat similar to those covered. Hence even if you do eventually choose a different web conferencing system, you can have expectations of how it could work.

Don't forget that the sample course outline will be available throughout 2011 for all purchasers of this book on `http://www.moodleforbusiness.com/`.

Background on web conferencing

There are a lot of products available which provide some level of synchronous audio, video, or collaboration and it can be a lot of work going through the process of assessing each one, for features and for integration with Moodle.

The Moodle community website has a forum dedicated to discussions about the various web conferencing plugins, so this is a good place to look for information about what is available and useful.

The community forum is at `http://moodle.org/mod/forum/view.php?id=7797`.

The Moodle community website also has a plugin database of add-ons which is open to download by everyone. If you search through this with a variety of keywords such as conference, meeting, and so on, you will find a range of applications. Some of these are up-to-date and some others have not been updated in over a year. Some of the better known ones are:

- Adobe Connect Pro
- BigBlueButton
- Elluminate Live
- OpenMeetings

The plugin database is found on the Moodle community website at `http://moodle.org/mod/data/view.php?id=6009`.

To help provide some extra and open context for this chapter, I ran a short survey on `www.surveymonkey.com` in mid-2010, asking people three questions:

- Which web conferencing software have you used before?
- Which of the following aspects of integration with LMS (Learning Management System) are important?
- Please rate the following features of web conferencing software with respect to training and education?

Each question provided the user with a selection of options, and an option to add more information.

This survey was run through my PLN (Personal Learning Network) on Twitter, and in a short time I got just over 50 responses from the network of mainly professionals within the training and development arena. The results go some way to answering some of the initial questions that people raise about web conferencing.

If you want to check out the survey it can be found at `http://www.surveymonkey.com/s/BQSKXVR`.

Products

Users were able to select multiple products that they have used. Over 28 different products were mentioned and as expected, the top three mentioned products were WebEx (70%), Adobe Connect (64%), and Elluminate (50%). The top open source product to get voted was DimDim although BigBlueButton did get a mention. However, DimDim has recently been purchased by Salesforce, and so is no longer an option.

Integration

When considering integration with the LMS, the most sought after option was single sign on (81%), where the participant did not have to log into the web conferencing system in addition to having logged into the LMS. The second most important integration option was having the entry to appear in the course calendar (61%). One thing that was clear from the results was that it needed to be simple for the participants to see and access the web conferencing system from the LMS.

Features

With as many applications as you can expect, there are a wide range of features. For the survey, I had included 13 options, and the results were really interesting. The respondents were asked to rate the feature as **Extremely Important, Important, Doesn't Matter Much, Deal Break** or **N/A**. Four features were deemed Extremely Important by 50% or more of the responders. They were:

- Synchronous Audio
- Text Chat
- Desktop Sharing
- Recording for Replay

When considering **Important** as the option, the following four features topped the selections:

- Single Video Feed
- Collaborative Document Creation
- Publication as Video
- Scheduling of Events

Having experienced the most popular tools as presenter and participant, I think these two groups of features are certainly a good representation of what is generally deemed essential.

One point that came across in survey and comments is that quality audio is the key with 95% of people feeling it is important or extremely important. I have been on web conference systems where the audio didn't work well, was cumbersome to configure and manage, or just didn't do what was expected, and it is frustrating as a participant and as a trainer.

So before you start choosing a product, you will need to have considered what level of integration you need with Moodle and which features you deem are "must have" to provide the synchronous environment for your participants.

Using Moodle to connect with synchronous web conferencing systems

Working from home and increasingly distributed workforces have increased the costs in time and money for arranging face-to-face training. Adding synchronous video and web conferencing to Moodle helps provide a deeper real time communication than just chat. In this chapter, we look at web conferencing features and the Moodle integration modules for three well-known systems used today.

We won't be dealing with cost of the respective systems, which is without doubt an important factor. However, there is another aspect to consider, and that is technology.

Technology and web conferencing

Having used a variety of platforms, I have found that there are often some technical hitches, or challenges which need to be solved before using the system. Some of the challenges are not directly related to the web conferencing technology itself, but web conferencing in general.

As with all training, it is important to consider where the training will take place for the end user and how it could impact on their participation.

Audio:

There are some things to consider about how audio will impact your participant. The first is their environment. Do they have speakers or headphones for their computer, and does their computer have a sound card (which some may not have in some workplaces)?

If they are going to be listening to the conference at work, and they don't have a headset, will this impact others around them?

If they may want to talk, or are required to talk during the web conference, do they have a microphone working? Perhaps there is background noise which makes this unusable? If they If they don't have headset or headphones, this may generate a lot of feedback unless the system can disable their speakers while they talk.

Video:

Some systems can deliver just one video stream, where others can deliver multiple video streams. The level of quality and the choice of colour or black and white will impact the user's experience of the training.

If the participant is expected to be on video, do they have a webcam, and are they in a room where using the webcam is okay?

Bandwidth:

Although broadband has become more available over the last few years, bandwidth for usage can still be a challenge. Where someone's office may have enough bandwidth normally, if multiple people are streaming a web conference audio and video, this may change things.

If someone is trying to access the web conference session while travelling from a hotel or Wi-Fi, bandwidth and stability of connection may be an issue.

Especially when considering video, care must be given to the choice of colour over black and white if you are going to use one or more video streams, as these can be bandwidth hogs.

Technologies:

Not all web conferencing systems work for all desktops or laptops equally. Some require the use of Flash or JAVA, some platforms require the configuring of firewall rules, and some just don't work well on Linux or Mac as well as they do on Windows.

Time for reflection

When considering the business needs for deploying a web conferencing solution for Moodle, thought needs to be given to all of these technical challenges. Understanding the participant's limitations from their environment and available technical resources is a key step in selecting the correct platform for you organization.

Using Adobe Connect Pro with Moodle

Adobe Connect is one of the more popular virtual classroom applications in use with Moodle. It is also one I use every week for training, meetings, and webinars. Every virtual classroom application has a unique feature profile, and Adobe Connect is no different.

You will find full information on the product on the Adobe website under the following URL `http://www.adobe.com/education/products/adobeconnect.html`. There is a lot of good information on the website, and notably there are links to the various integrations with a number of LMS, including Moodle.

The page describing the Moodle integration can be found at `http://remote-learner.net/adobeconnectpro` and the actual module for Moodle can be found in the Modules and plugins page on Moodle at `http://moodle.org/mod/data/view.php?d=13&rid=3599`.

For the purpose of the instructions below, you will need to have a fully working Adobe Connect Pro 7 server installation. If you are using the Adobe Connect Pro hosted account, some features such as Single Sign On and external authentication will not work. For more information about any extra ACP installation issues, check with Adobe or look at the Moodle documentation `http://docs.moodle.org/en/Remote_Learner_Adobe_Connect_Pro_Module`.

Time for action – find and install the module

The first thing we are going to do is to download the module to your machine. If you are not the LMS admin or IT manager, you may want them to do this for you as you need access to the Moodle code installation.

1. Open up your web browser and go to the webpage `http://www.moodle.org`.

2. In the top **Menu** you have an option called **Downloads**. Click on this option and select the **Modules and Plugins** option. This brings up the database of modules, and shows the most recent entries in the database.

3. Click on the **Search** tab.

4. Type the word **Adobe Connect Pro** into the **Name** field in the search form and click on **Save settings**. The page will now load with just the Remote-Learner Adobe Connect Pro Module.

5. Click on the name **Remote-Learner Adobe Connect Pro Module**. This brings up the full view of the Module database entry including the type, requirements, status, the name maintainers, and also other information like the description and links to download.

6. It is important to ensure that when you select a custom module from the **Module and Plugins** database, you check that it is for your version of moodle, and that is maintained. Check out any comments for any issues with the Module too. It is also advisable to test all third-party plugins on a non-production site first and before you deploy to the live site. Make sure you or your IT person takes a backup of the site. Don't forget that backing up the site involves the three part OS: Database, moodledata, and the web files themselves.

7. Also check out the actual description of how the module works. It may or may not be what you are looking for, so this will help set expectations. If it is not what you are looking for, then perform the search again and change the search options.

8. Under the description, there are links to **Download the Latest Version**, and **The Moodle 1.9 version** and to the discussion. Click on the link to **Download for Moodle 2.0**.

9. This will prompt you to download and save the file to somewhere accessible on your machine.

What just happened?

We have just gone to the Moodle community site, and searched through the modules and plugins for the Adobe Connect Pro integration. We then checked that the module is the correct one, and that it is for our version of Moodle. We then downloaded the correct version of the integration module to our machine.

You will download most modules and plugins for Moodle the same way. However, sometimes the actual code is stored elsewhere and you will need to follow instructions on how to retrieve it.

Installing the module

Now that you have the file of the module, you need to upload it to the Moodle site. Currently the module is in a ZIP file. So the first thing you need to do is to unpack this ZIP file using an application like WinZip, 7zip, Windows Compressed Folders, or if you are using a non-Windows machine, then by using a similar application. For example, on Linux you may use the "tar" application.

Time for action – unzipping and uploading

Now we have to get the module into our Moodle. You will need to have FTP access to your Moodle site to install the module. If you don't have access, talk to your host who looks after the site for you, or your IT department as required.

1. Unzip the module download file using your available application. This should create a folder called adobeconnect. Inside this folder there are more folders, and lots of files which make up the module.

2. Using your FTP client, connect to your Moodle site host server (I use WinSCP for Windows).

3. Using your FTP client, browse to the mod folder inside your **Moodle** installation.

4. **Select** your adobeconnect folder (not just the files) and upload this to the **mod** folder. You should now see the folder along with the assignment, and any other mods you may have installed. Depending on whether you are using a fast connection or not, it may take some time to upload each part of the module.

5. Once all the files are uploaded, you need to **log into your Moodle site**.

6. Once logged in as admin, you need to click on the **Notifications** link in your **Site administration** block or go to http://yourmoodle.com/admin/index.php. This link triggers the installation of any newly uploaded module. The setup then auto-creates database tables and settings options for the Adobe Connect integration.

7. If all has gone well, it should say **adobeconnect tables have been set up correctly**. Click on the **Continue** button.

8. You will be displayed the new settings options for the Adobe Connect module. There are seven options to edit. I will cover these next.

New settings - Adobe Connect

Host | localhost/api/xml | Default: localhost/api/xml
adobeconnect_host
Where REST calls get sent to

Meeting domain | localhost | Default: localhost
adobeconnect_meethost
Domain where the Adobe server is installed

Port | 80 | Default: 80
adobeconnect_port
Port used to connect to Adobe Connect

Admin Login | admin | Default: admin
adobeconnect_admin_login
Login for main admin account

Admin Password | | ☐ Unmask
adobeconnect_admin_password
Password for main admin account

HTTP Authentication Header | my-user-id | Default: my-user-id
adobeconnect_admin_httpauth
The HTTP_AUTH_HEADER value used in your custom.ini

Email address login ☐ Default: No
adobeconnect_email_login
Check this option only if your Connect Pro server login is set to use email address. Note that toggling this option on/off during regular usage of this activity module can potentially create duplicaed users on the Connect Pro server

In the Host field, you enter the URL of the Adobe Connect Pro Server which accepts the REST calls. For example, if you are using `example.com` as the domain for the Adobe Connect Pro server, then you should use `example.com/api/xml` in the Host field unless you have set up your Adobe Connect Pro differently.

1. The **Meeting domain** field needs the domain name of the host, but without the `/api/xml` included. So if the host was `example.com/api/xml` then the domain would be `example.com`.

2. On most servers the standard **Port** is **80** for running a web application, and in this case you can leave the default **80** in the **Port** field. Change this setting only if you know that Adobe Connect Pro is running on a different port.

3. The Adobe Connect integration requires you to enter in the Adobe Connect Pro server **admin** username and password in the **Admin Login** and **Admin Password** respectively. This account is used to make all the requests to create users and assign roles.

4. To complete the **HTTP Authentication Header** field, you need to consult with your `custom.ini` file belonging to the Adobe Connect Pro server. The file will have a line where it specifies the `HTTP_AUTH_HEADER=something`. You need to copy the text after the = sign. In this example, we have used "something". Put this into the **HTTP Authentication Header** field.

5. The **Email address login** field is only enabled if your server is set up to use the email address as login. This is found under **Administration | Users and Groups | Login and Password Policies** on the Adobe Connect Pro admin site.

6. Once you have entered all the required information on this settings page, click on the **Save changes** button at the bottom of the page.

What just happened?

After we had downloaded the module from the `Moodle.org` site, we had to unpackage it (unzip it) and then upload the files to the Moodle site using an FTP program. We were careful to upload the full folder of the files inside the `moodle/mod` folder on the server. This is because this module is a Moodle mod. Other integrations may be activities, or blocks, and may be uploaded to other locations. Always follow the `README` or documentation for this guidance.

Once uploaded, we logged into our Moodle website, and triggered the installation of the module using the **Notifications** link in the **Site administration** block. This created database tables required to run the module and activate it within Moodle.

We then entered in the key configuration information including the Host, Domain, Port, Admin user login and password, and the **HTTP Authentication Header** value so that the Moodle site could talk to the Adobe Connect Pro server.

Finally, we saved the settings and are now ready to create an Adobe Connect activity within a test Moodle course.

Creating an Adobe Connect activity in Moodle

As mentioned earlier, when you install this module, you give the module the "admin" information so that it can set roles based on Moodle roles. The module created three roles—Adobe Connect Host, Presenter, and Participant within Moodle during installation. Users can be assigned these roles through Moodle and with the single-sign on; they will have the corresponding roles on the Adobe Connect Pro server when they join it.

Time for action – creating an activity

To create an activity, we must first either create a test course, or go into an existing course which you have editing rights on. As always, when planning changes, make sure that editing is turned on to allow you to add activities.

1. In the topic you want to add the Adobe Connect activity, select the **Add an activity** dropdown and select the **Adobe Connect** option. This brings up the **Adding a new Adobe Connect** screen.

2. As normal with activities, the first field is the text which appears on the course page for the link to the activity. Type **Test Adobe Connect Room** in the **Adobe Connect** field.

3. The **Intro** field should hold any guidance information that you want participants to follow when entering the room. This could be information about login (if you are using the hosted account) or a link to the "Acceptable User Guidelines" for interactions in virtual classrooms.

4. The **Meeting URL** is an optional field. If you want to customize the URL of the room you can do so. However, in this case, we won't. So leave it blank. If you want more information on this setting, you can check out the "help" icon which explains how to customise the URL.

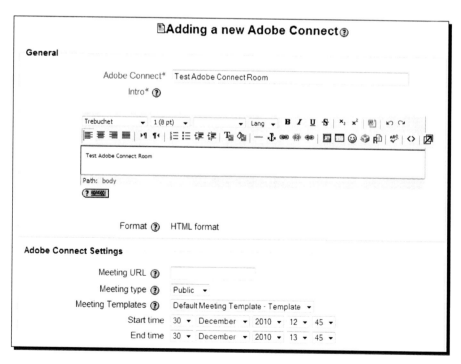

5. The **Meeting type** field allows you to set the meeting type. **Private** will be available to just those with privileges and **Public** will be available to anyone who has the URL of the meeting. For this example, create a **Public** meeting room by leaving the fields to their default information.

6. If there are meeting templates on the server, the **Meeting Templates** drop-down will provide a choice of the type of template to use in creating the meeting.

7. The **Start time** field should be filled in with the information about when the meeting will begin. You should remember that some people would like to be able to join a few minutes early, so take this into account when setting meeting times. If you leave the field with the default information, the meeting will be set to begin immediately.

8. The **End time** option is also set to the same time as the start, by default. If you want the meeting to be one hour long, increase the time field of the **End time**.

9. For this example, you can leave the **Common module settings** to their default values. There is support for Moodle groups in Module which enables us to ensure that only the users who are part of a group can join meetings for their specific group. However, for this example you can leave that setting to its default.

10. Click on **Save and Return to Course**.

11. You will notice the entry **Test Adobe Connect Room** is now displayed in the topic that you added it to.

12. Click on the link **Test Adobe Connect Room** and it will display the summary of the meeting information. This is what the users will see when they click on the link.

What just happened?

We just added an Adobe Connect test room to our course. The default setting options are easy enough to follow, but the available options give you a lot of control over the usage of the meeting room.

We also looked at the basic configuration options and the summary information page for the meeting. There are two options left, either to enable roles on the room using the **Assign roles** button or to **Join Meeting**. Enabling roles can be done when the meeting is set to private. The person who creates the room is automatically assigned the role of **Host** for the Adobe Connect meeting. A public meeting also automatically assigns users the role of a participant unless they are assigned **Host** or **Presenter** in the roles screen.

Joining the Adobe Connect Room

After clicking **Join Meeting**, you will be brought to a new window or tab depending on your browser settings. If you are the presenter and have not been presented with Adobe before, you will be prompted to install the updated Adobe Connect Add-in to share your screen with other users, upload files, and experience the enhanced version of the VOIP. This is advisable to get the most out of the Adobe Connect Pro meeting room, but it's not required. I clicked on **Yes**.

The screen you see that is displayed when you are a participant looks like the the following image. This is the standard meeting layout, with the Share, Video, Attendees, and Chat blocks on the window.

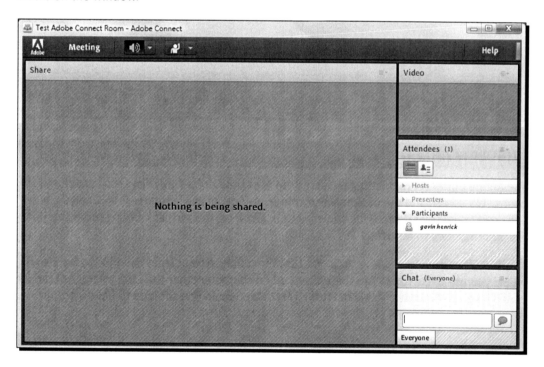

The **Host** and **Presenter** roles are given a different view. There are a lot of extra possibilities in layout and content of the screen. An example of a default layout is shown in the following image. As you can see, as a host, you are prompted if you want to share your screen, documents, or a whiteboard. This is a very user friendly interface.

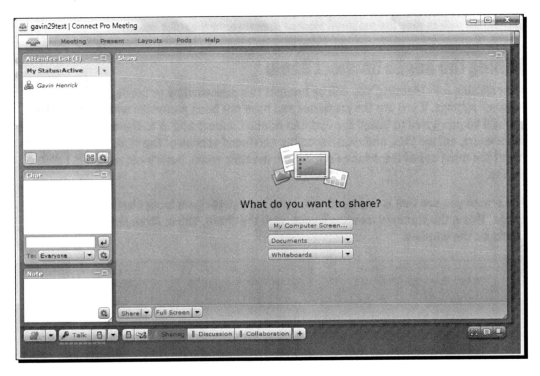

Time for reflection

The Adobe Connect Pro meeting room system uses the Adobe Flash Player to render and control the screen and the camera/microphone. As part of the "requirement" analysis, you will need to consider if everyone can use Flash, and if so, this virtual meeting room solution is a good addition to Moodle.

As shown the module provides options to set the different roles from within Moodle. How would you use these roles? Are there times when someone other than the trainer or teacher would be given Presenter rights or Host rights? How would you set it up to have a group collaborate together on a plan?

Have a go hero – creating more rooms

You are requested to organise a mini in-house training day on a number of different specialist topics which will have attendees from both on-site and remote locations. You need to set up a course which will provide local users access to materials and the ability to interact with other specialists in their area. How would you go about setting up the Moodle course or courses to achieve this? How would the Adobe Connect Meeting module fit into the equation, and what new options does it provide?

Using BigBlueButton with Moodle

BigBlueButton is another virtual classroom solution. BigBlueButton also uses Flash to load the classroom just like Adobe Connect. BigBlueButton is a new product and has features similar to Adobe Connect including the provision of screen sharing, whiteboard, presentation upload, text chat, audio chat, web cam, and some classroom tools. BigBlueButton is built by combining over fourteen open source components to make an integrated solution that runs on Mac, Unix, or Windows computers.

You will find full information about this product on the `http://www.bigbluebutton.org` website. There is a lot of good information on the website, and it provides detailed information on the various components that make up the product and a product feature overview. BigBlueButton has been integrated into a range of open source platforms including Joomla, Wordpress, and Moodle.

You can get the latest version of the BigBlueButton code itself. You can go to the BigBlueButton Google Code page which includes information on installing the platform into virtual machines, Ubuntu, and Debian.

To get the integration code for Moodle, you can either download from the Moodle community website plugin database at `http://moodle.org/mod/data/view.php?d=13&rid=4536` or get it yourself from the BigBlueButton Github account at `https://github.com/blindsidenetworks/bigbluebutton-integrations`.

For more information on the integration, check out the Blindside Networks site: `http://blindsidenetworks.com/integration`.

Time for action – find and install the Module

The first thing we are going to do is to download the module to your machine.

1. Open your web browser and go to the webpage `http://www.moodle.org`.

2. In the top Menu, you have an option **Downloads**. Click on this and select the **Modules and Plugins** option. This brings up the database of modules, and shows the most recent entries in the database.

3. Click on the **Search** tab.

4. Type the word **BigBlueButton** into the **Name** field in the search form and click on **Save Settings**. The page will now load with two options, the **Easy Integration with BigBlueButton** and the **BigBlueButton**. For the purpose of these instructions, we will be using the **Easy Integration with BigBlueButton** created by Fred Dixon (Blindside Networks).

5. Click on the name of the module you need (in my case **Easy Integration with BigBlueButton**). This brings up the full view of the module database entry including the type, requirements, status, names of maintainers and other information like the description and links for download.

6. Under the description, click on the link **Download for Moodle 2.0**.

7. This will prompt you to download and save the file somewhere on your machine. The file will be called **bbb_activity_module_moodle20.zip**.

What just happened?

We have just gone to the Moodle community site, and searched through the modules and plugins for the **BigBlueButton** integration. We then downloaded the correct version of the integration module to our machine.

Installing the Module

Like the Adobe Connect Pro module, this is an Activity Module. So now that you have the file downloaded, you need to unzip it and then upload the mod folder to the mod section of the Moodle site.

Time for action – Unzipping and uploading

Unzip the module download file using your available application. This should create a folder called bbb_activity_module_moodle20. Inside this folder, there is a mod folder which contains the actual bigbluebutton folder of files.

1. Using your FTP client, connect to your Moodle site host server.

2. Using your FTP client, browse to the mod folder inside your Moodle installation and to the mod folder in your bbb_activity_module_moodle20 folder.

3. Select the local mod/bigbluebutton folder and upload this to the mod folder on the Moodle server.

4. Once all the files are uploaded, you need to log into your Moodle site.

5. Once logged in as admin, you will be prompted to upgrade to include the new plugin.

6. Click on the **Upgrade** button at the bottom of the page.

7. If the installation has gone well, the screen will display the name of the mod followed by Success. You then click on the Continue Button.

8. One of the nice things about using this module is that it comes with some test settings already, as shown in the following image:

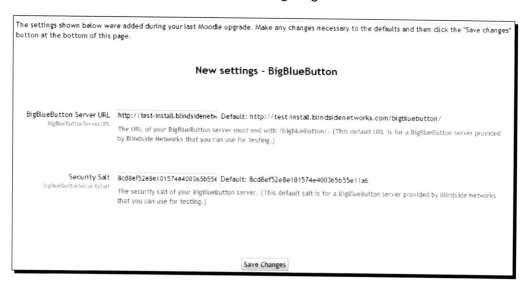

The settings shown below were added during your last Moodle upgrade. Make any changes necessary to the defaults and then click the "Save changes" button at the bottom of this page.

New settings - BigBlueButton

BigBlueButton Server URL
BigBlueButtonServerURL

http://test-install.blindsidenetw   Default: http://test-install.blindsidenetworks.com/bigbluebutton/

The URL of your BigBlueButton server must end with /bigbluebutton/. (This default URL is for a BigBlueButton server provided by Blindside Networks that you can use for testing.)

Security Salt
BigBlueButtonSecuritySalt

8cd8ef52e8e101574e400365b55€   Default: 8cd8ef52e8e101574e400365b55e11a6

The security salt of your BigBlueButton server. (This default salt is for a BigBlueButton server provided by Blindside Networks that you can use for testing.)

Save Changes

However, if you have your own server setup, or a hosted server to which you have the URL and Security Salt settings, you should use them here.

9. Once you have completed all the settings, click on **Save changes**.

What just happened?

After we had downloaded the `BigBlueButton` module from the Moodle website, we had to unpack it (unzip it) and then upload the files (`mod`) to the Moodle site with FTP.

Once uploaded, we logged into our Moodle website as administrator and triggered the installation of the module using the **Upgrade** button. This created any database tables required to run the module and then enabled the block by activating it within Moodle.

We then entered in the key configuration information which we would have got from the BigBlueButton Server Administrator or chosen to leave the test settings as they were.

Finally, we saved the settings and are now ready to create a BigBlueButton activity within our Moodle course.

Creating a BigBlueButton activity in Moodle

The BigBlueButton Meeting Module has some different features from the Adobe Connect Pro Module. This is a very simple integration. There are other more complex integrations available, and you may want to assess the other ones at some other time.

The BigBlueButton Module interacts with the BigBlueButton server over web services allowing an admin or teacher to schedule a meeting as a Moodle activity. The user management takes place with Moodle so that students do not require a second login. Students will join the virtual classroom as a viewer, and the admins or teachers on Moodle will join as moderators.

Time for action – creating a BigBlueButton activity

As always, make sure that you are in a test course, or go into an existing course which you have editing rights on. Make sure that Editing is turned on to allow you to add activities and let's begin.

1. Scroll to the topic that you want to include the **BigBlueButton** Meeting activity in.

2. Select the **Add an activity** drop down and choose the **BigBlueButton** option. This brings up the **Adding a new BigBlueButton to Topic 1** screen.

3. Type **Test BigBlueButton** in the **Virtual classroom name** field.

4. If you want to force the students to wait until a moderator joins, you can select that here. It is selected by default. For now, leave it ticked.

5. Click on **Save and Return to course** and your **BigBlueButton** meeting will now be set up.

6. If you click on the link **Test BigBlueButton**, then it will auto-forward you to the BigBlueButton meeting room.

7. Once you have finished this, you can return to course. Your meeting is now ready configured with times, grades, and users.

What just happened?

We just created a BigBlueButton meeting room in our course.

Joining the BigBlueButton virtual classroom

After you click on the link **Test BigBlueButton**, it will auto-forward you to the BigBlueButton meeting room.

Once loaded, you are presented with a screen like the following one. There are a number of boxes including:

- Users
- Listeners
- Chat box
- Presentation

There are also controls at the top left for your microphone, video, and desktop sharing.

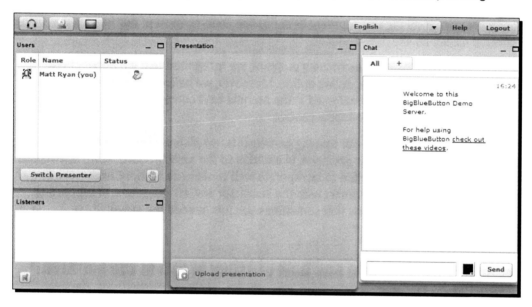

One thing I really like about the BigBlueButton room is the simplicity and ease of use. The UI for student/participant interaction is direct, accessible, and the chat provides some of the best controls I have seen.

Time for reflection

The **BigBlueButton** meeting room integration is very straightforward and offers the basic set of options to the end user and the participant in the training. It is important to consider which features are more important to your training when assessing which application to use.

Have a go hero – creating more rooms

You are needed to run a training session on one of your products. Come up with a whiteboard activity which helps support the e-learning in Moodle. One such option could be to create images of the product with empty labels and have the participants on the course add them in with the whiteboard feature.

Case study—Remote-Learner

What was the business problem(s) for which Moodle and Web Conferencing was chosen as the solution?

Remote-Learner needed an online version of their Moodle training program for teachers and course creators. Until the development of our online courses, most of our training was being delivered mainly on-site (face-to-face).

In deciding to develop an online training program, we recognized that a number of our clients wanted a more flexible, online option. Moreover, we believed our clients would benefit significantly by being immersed in the Moodle environment as a learner while they learned to develop their own Moodle courses.

To help ensure the success of our training participants, we planned to offer a facilitated course with a strong instructor presence. In addition to the asynchronous forum discussions and activity feedback, we wanted to incorporate web conference sessions each week to allow course participants to connect with the instructor and ask questions. In supporting clients previously, we also knew that sometimes you just needed the power of screen sharing!

What was the solution and how did they arrive at the solution?

Today, we offer a Foundations and Intermediate course for course creators as well as a course for Moodle Administrators, with yet another course in development. In their current iteration, our online courses each extend over a period of four weeks with participants spending approximately 4-6 hours each week completing various activities. The course is primarily asynchronous, with one week or unit being revealed at a time. Learners can complete the course activities for a given week any time during that week.

In addition to the asynchronous activities, we also offer weekly synchronous sessions using Elluminate (soon to be Adobe Connect). These web conference sessions are designed to supplement and extend the material that is delivered in the course and to give participants an opportunity to connect with the facilitator and ask questions. We encourage participants to attend the weekly web conference sessions, but for those unable to attend, all sessions are recorded and made available after the fact.

From the start, we knew we wanted to have regular web conference sessions with our learners. The ability level of our learners varied and some needed the option for immediate feedback and screen sharing that the web conference sessions could provide. In previous experiences of teaching online courses, we also found that the synchronous sessions provided opportunities for the learners to get to know each other and connect in ways that are more difficult through text in asynchronous discussion forums. Learners will sometimes ask questions in the web conference sessions that they wouldn't take the time to add to a discussion forum. Plus, having a voice to go with the names and pictures you see in Moodle is great!

Why did they choose Moodle with these web conferencing platforms?

For us, offering the student perspective for our training participants is the key to our training philosophy. Even in our synchronous or face-to-face training sessions, we strive to make sure the participants have an opportunity to see and experience a tool from the student or learner perspective before they ever open the settings page.

In researching the various web conferencing tools, Elluminate and Adobe Connect were generally accepted as "best of breed" for delivering online training. There are many other web conferencing programs available, but I've yet to find any that offer the full range of tools that you'll find in Elluminate and Adobe Connect. If you're simply delivering lectures or webinars (web seminars) another tool might suffice, but we wanted the ability to deliver engaging, interactive training through web conference and these tools fit the bill.

Today, we are in the process of moving to Adobe Connect for the delivery of our web conference sessions. We recently developed the Adobe Connect integration for Moodle and have partnered with them as well.

Was the project a success?

Yes, the feedback has been positive and having the online training option has helped us reach more of our clients so we can better help them to be successful.

The sessions are valuable and needed for a significant subset of our course participants. Specifically, we find that the web conference sessions are popular in our introductory level Foundations course and even more so for the participants just beginning to use Moodle. A broader set of our participants seem to take advantage of the session recordings.

What were the benefits gained?

The primary benefit is that we have been able to expand our training options. With the addition of our online courses, our clients can basically choose the training delivery mode that works best for them, whether that's face-to-face, online, or through web conference.

The materials we've created for our online courses have been useful in other settings as well. We've shared videos from the courses with clients, used explanations in the course to help address client questions elsewhere, and utilized the online courses in our own internal training programs.

Our online courses and more specifically, the web conference sessions, have also enhanced our relationships with our clients. A client may not pick up the phone or submit a ticket to report what they see as a small issue, but in a conversation in a web conference session, it's easy for them to slip in that sort of thing. In some cases, the issue has been a point of irritation for some time and, in the web conference session, we solve it in minutes!

The web conference sessions are a great place to learn more about our clients and their Moodle implementations. This information then carries over in terms of on-going support.

What lessons were learned?

First, our clients were more successful in shorter courses with a flexible, minimal time requirement. Most of our participants are not provided with release time to complete training, and therefore, it's important that the course not be time intensive and inflexible. As a result, we regularly schedule the weekly web conference sessions for the evening and our facilitators can be found online at all times of the day, every day.

The second lesson we learned is that our participants were more successful when we started providing them sample content with which to develop. We knew from the start that we needed to provide participants an opportunity to actually build in Moodle, and providing just the information about how to do it isn't enough.

For the web conference sessions, we found that participants wanted more substance and structure than just a live question and answer session. The time to ask questions is important and necessary, but it should not comprise the bulk of the session. Participants also want the session material to provide more than just a summary of what's in the course content. They're looking for new information and activities.

Finally, since we have a variety of facilitators, we identified a need for a detailed course facilitator's guide. Like other elements of our course, this guide has evolved and become much more detailed over time. The guide includes information about scheduling the course orientation session, sample responses for common questions, text for the weekly announcements, and details regarding who to contact for help. The more detailed the guide, the more successful and less stressed is the facilitator.

What advice does Remote-Learner have for businesses that plan to implement Web Conferencing with Moodle?

Branch out! Take advantage of the more interactive, collaborative features Moodle has to offer and engage your learners. If you really, truly want learning to take place, you have to offer more than a lecture equivalent. The same is true when talking about your web conferencing software! The capabilities are tremendous and you can do so much more than just deliver slides and lecture.

You don't need to go it alone. I know it can be tough to resist the urge to figure it all out on your own, but you can save yourself a lot of time and have a much better result in the long run if you take advantage of the experience and skills of others.

Specifically, you can try the following:

◆ Get Moodle training and/or read the book. If you're coming from another LMS, the learning curve will likely be less steep, but you'll still need help. Every LMS has its own quirks, protocols, features, and training should help you discover a few of those.

◆ Take advantage of all the Moodle community has to offer. Moodle website and the Moodle Docs at `http:\\docs.moodle.org` have tons to offer—for free! An Internet search will reveal tons of tutorials and resources and YouTube has a collection of Moodle videos as well.

◆ Invest in developing effective synchronous learning. There are companies who specialize in the development and delivery of effective synchronous learning. These organizations can provide training, support, and development services so that your synchronous sessions are as effective as possible. At Remote-Learner, we received training from InSync Training (`http://insynctraining.com`). Their team was experienced with several different web conference tools and was willing to deliver the training on the system of our choice.

Some thoughts

Although it's great to just jump in and implement synchronous tools to extend Moodle based training, emphasis should be placed on sourcing good training on the adopted system and on the effective use of synchronous tools. Remote-Learner works hard to ensure their web conference sessions are highly interactive. The choice of the platform and techniques are important in delivering a successful session.

Reflection

The addition of a synchronous application to Moodle based training provides some neat features which can be leveraged to improve the response time and quality of the knowledge.

Think about how you would use a whiteboard in your training. Would it be useful? How could you promote interactivity on it, and avoid just presenting PowerPoint slides?

Think about the voting tools—how would you use these? When in the meeting/session would you use these and why?

Most web conferencing systems enable the creation of break-out rooms to have focused group-work. Would you see a fit for this type of feature in your training?

Think about the one feature which seems to make web conferencing a must for inclusion in your training and then test it out. Does it work like you expected?

Summary

In this chapter, we learnt about virtual web meeting solutions which can be used to extend our training with Moodle. We looked at the background to web conferencing, some of the main features and at some of the integration options.

We looked at two case studies, BP and Remote-Learner, in their use of Moodle and synchronous interactivity of participants. Each company had their own approach to enable students and each had their own process.

Specifically, we covered:

- The main applications available for virtual meetings and Moodle
- What types of integration are wanted and what are possible
- We looked at key features and what was a must have, and what was an also-ran
- We walked through the setup and configuration of the two more popular applications

Interaction can be central to a Moodle course. Therefore, a provision for synchronous and asynchronous chat, audio, and video has been kept to enhance the student experience.

8
Integrating Moodle with Other Systems

Moodle 2.0 includes two important new points of integration with other open source products. The Repository integration allows admins to set up external content management systems and use them to complement Moodle's own file management system. Using this integration you can now manage content outside of Moodle and publish it to the system once the document or other content is ready. The Portfolio integration enables users to store their Moodle content in an external e-portfolio system to share with evaluators, peers, and others.

In this chapter, we will focus on both an open source solution and a Google Docs solution for both repositories and portfolios. Alfresco is an open source content management system that integrates well with Moodle and can act as Moodle's content repository. Mahara is an open source e-portfolio system which has been tightly integrated with Moodle 2.0. Google Docs is a cloud-based office suite which is available for free from Google. You can get a personal account for free, or your organization can sign up for a Google Enterprise account.

In this chapter, we will:

- ◆ Set up an Alfresco content repository and tie it in with Moodle
- ◆ Integrate Moodle with Google Docs to act as both a repository and a portfolio
- ◆ Link Moodle with Mahara, an open source e-portfolio system

Managing content in repositories

The repository system of Moodle 2 allows you to store and manipulate content outside of Moodle and easily add it to courses. By managing content outside of Moodle, you can provide users with a more robust editing experience. Many organizations utilize workflows and approval processes to ensure the accuracy of the content used in the LMS. A content repository can help you manage that process, and then make the content available on Moodle when it is ready for final publication.

We'll take a look at Alfresco first, then we will explore using Google Docs to manage content for publishing in Moodle.

Using Alfresco to manage content

Alfresco is an open source, enterprise content management system, similar in many ways to Microsoft Sharepoint or EMC's Documentum. Alfresco has seen widespread adoption over the last few years as more people begin to recognize the advantages of open source software. We will start by installing Alfresco, then look at how to link it to Moodle and add content to a Moodle site. At the end of this section, we'll take a look at Alfresco's content conversion services as a tool to ensure content is reliably converted to web friendly formats.

Time for action – installing Alfresco on your test site

To get us started, we'll install Alfresco on our test system to experiment with the integration. Alfresco runs on a different architecture than Moodle. Alfresco requires a Java application server instead of PHP. Fortunately, there are installers available on the Alfresco site that include everything we will need to develop a test system on your local computer.

To install Alfresco, run through the following steps:

1. Open your browser and go to `http:\\www.alfresco.com`. Go to the **Downloads** tab and select the **Download Now** button for **Alfresco Document Management** in the **Community Edition** column.

2. Select the installer for your operating system and download it to your computer.

3. Double-click on the installer (it may take a moment to get started).

4. Select your language for the installer.

5. Choose the database option you want to use. Use the included database, unless you have a good reason not to.

6. When prompted, enter a database password. Be sure to write it down somewhere.

7. The next screen will prompt you for an Alfresco admin password. Definitely write this down.

8. The final screen will prompt you to choose the packages you want to install. Choose the defaults and click on **Next**. For the examples below, you will need to make sure that you have the OpenOffice component installed.

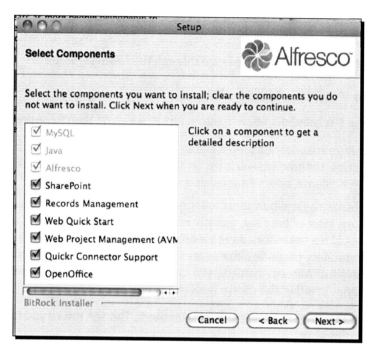

9. The installer will begin to run. This will probably take a while, so it may be time to go and get a cup of tea.

10. Once the installer is complete, select **Launch**. This will take a while as well, so a second cup of tea might be in order.

11. Once Alfresco has launched, you can configure the interface with Moodle.

What just happened

You now have a full-functioning open source enterprise content management system installed on your personal computer. Alfresco has a lot of power for manipulating and sharing documents, but we will only focus on a few features for now. There are a lot of books available to help you learn how to use the more advanced features in Alfresco (a few of them from this publisher as well).

Time for action - add a repository plugin to Moodle

To allow users to access your new Alfresco repository, you will need to configure Moodle to allow access to the repository. The new repository architecture of Moodle 2 enables developers to create plugins to connect Moodle with other systems. Each system will have its own type of plugin to allow a direct connection between Moodle and the system. To enable Moodle to talk to an external repository, we need to enable the plugin and any associated options.

To enable the Alfresco repository plug-in, go through the following steps:

1. Login to Moodle as a Moodle admin.

2. From the **Site administration** menu, select **Plugins** and then **Repositories**.

3. The **Manage repositories** screen allows you to select from all of the available plugin repositories. For now, we will focus on the **Alfresco repository**. From the menu in the **Active** column, select **Enabled and visible**.

   The Alfresco plugin allows users in Moodle to add multiple instances of the repository. Most of the time, you will not want to allow users to add additional instances of the repository. As the admin, you can create a single site-wide instance of the repository plugin to allow users to link to Alfresco files. However, if you have more than one Alfresco instance, you can allow multiple users to create additional repositories at either the course level or the user level.

4. Click the **Save** button to save the initial settings. This will return you to the **Manage repositories** page.

5. Click on **Settings** under the **Settings** column to the right of the Alfresco repository row.

6. This will take you back to the Alfresco settings page, but will provide an additional ability to add a repository instance at the site level.

7. Click the **Create a repository instance** button at the bottom of the page.

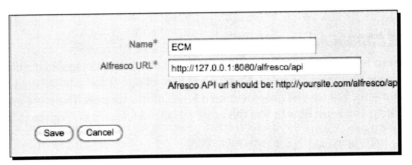

8. Give the name of your Alfresco instance. If this is an institutional repository, give it the same name as you commonly use. For example, if you commonly refer to your Alfresco instance as the "ECM" (for Enterprise Content Management), name the Alfresco instance ECM.

9. Add the URL of your Alfresco site. Be sure to point to the Alfresco Explorer, not the Share application. You will also need to add the API pointer at the end of the string. For example, if you are pointing to the locally installed Alfresco which we described in the preceding case, the URL should be `http://127.0.0.1:8080/alfresco/api`.

10. Click on **Save**. You will now have an instance of Alfresco available for users to add content to their courses.

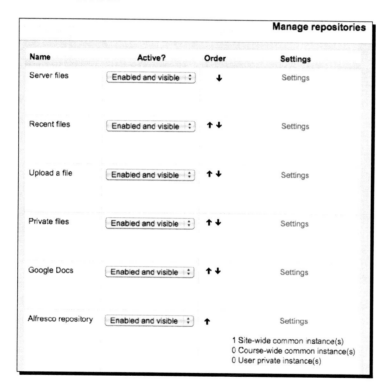

If you get the following error: **Notice SOAP extension must be enabled for Alfresco plugin**, then make sure that the SOAP library is enabled in your `php.ini` file. The location of the file will vary depending on the system you are using. Find the `php.ini` file and un-comment the `extension=php_soap.dll` line. Then restart Moodle and this should solve the error.

What just happened

You have just configured the Alfresco repository plugin to enable Moodle to talk to Alfresco. When you bring up the file picker in a course or at the site level, you should now see the Alfresco repository as an option.

Have a go hero

Later in this chapter, we will configure the Google Docs plugin for Moodle, but there are a number of other plugins. Picasa and Flickr are two photo repositories on the web where many people share their photos. Wikimedia and YouTube are two very popular sources of media as well. Enable one or two of these additional plugins to practice configuring Moodle on your own.

Time for action - adding content to Alfresco

In Moodle 2, repository integrations are read-only. The Moodle design team decided the repository integration should only read from repositories, and the portfolio integration should save content to portfolio repositories. So you can't add content directly to Alfresco with the default plugin. To add content to the repository, we need to use the repository's own interface, then we can add it to Moodle. With Alfresco, that interface is either the Alfresco Explorer or Alfresco Share.

To add content to the repository using Share, run through the following steps:

1. Go to your Alfresco share interface, found at `http://<your Alfresco server>/share`. If your Alfresco is on your local machine with the default install, go to `http://127.0.0.1:8080/share`.

2. Login with your username and password.

3. Select the **Repository** link from the top of the page. This will display the folder structure for the default Alfresco repository.

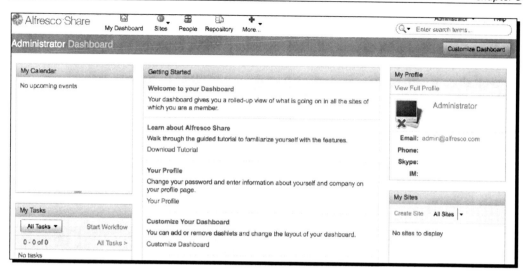

4. Select **User Homes** and then select your user space.

5. From the menu above the file browser, select **Upload**.

6. Click on the **Select file(s) to upload** button at the top of the **Upload Files** screen.

7. Browse to find your file and then click on the **Upload File(s)** button.

8. The file you selected should now appear in the file browser.

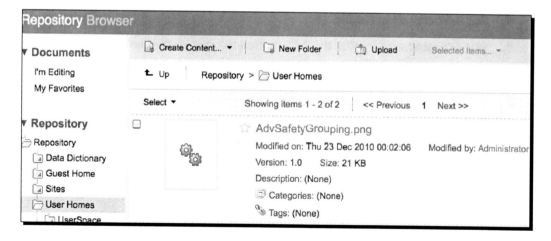

What just happened

You have now added a file to your Alfresco repository. We've explored a very simple example of adding a single file with no workflow or approval needed. You can use Share to create content, share it with colleagues, and use versioning and other features to manage the content creation process.

Have a go hero

Now that you've added a simple file to Alfresco Share, try some of the other features. Check out a file for editing, change it and check it back in for others to use, or create some content directly in Share.

Time for action - adding content from Alfresco to Moodle

Now that you've added some content into Alfresco, it's time to add that content to your Moodle course.

1. Login to Moodle as a user with course editing privileges.

2. Turn on **Editing Mode** and select **File** from the **Add a resource..** menu in the course section where you want the link to appear.

3. Give the file a name. Remember the name will be the link the user selects to get the file, so be descriptive.

4. Add a description of the file.

5. In the **Content** section, click the **Add..** button to bring up the file browser.

6. Select the Alfresco repository you previously created.

7. Login to Alfresco using your Alfresco username and password.

8. Browse through the available Alfresco spaces to find your user folder and the file you want to add.

9. Select the file by clicking on the link.

10. On the next screen, you can rename the file to save it locally, edit the author name, and select a copyright license for the file.

11. Click on **Select this File**.

12. The options for the file are the same as we reviewed in *Chapter 1, Getting Started with Moodle*. You can choose a display option, whether the file appears in a pop-up window, and who can view the file and when.

A note about the Alfresco plugin

When you link to a file in Alfresco, Moodle makes a copy of the file and stores it locally. This increases system reliability as Moodle does not require the Alfresco server to be available to run. However, once the document has been copied to Moodle, it isn't updated if the copy on Alfresco is edited.

What just happened

You have now copied your file from Alfresco to Moodle for use in your course. You can now download or view the file as you would do normally.

Now we are going to explore one of the features of Alfresco—content conversion services. Alfresco has a number of powerful features that are beyond the scope of this book, but we thought we'd give you some basics to help you explore some of the features of Alfresco. For web publishing in Moodle, you can use Alfresco to automatically convert content to web friendly formats in a regular format.

Time for action - creating a content conversion space

To start, we need a place to store the converted files. An Alfresco Space is the equivalent of a file folder on your desktop, but it can have attached rules and workflows. We need to create a Space in our user area to start the process and we'll need to use the Alfresco Explorer to set that up and create the rule.

1. Login to the Alfresco Explorer interface. The URL for Explorer is: `http://<Your Alfresco URL>/alfresco`.

2. Navigate to your user home space by clicking on **My Home** on the left hand side.

3. Create a Space in your home folder by selecting the **Create menu** and selecting **Create Space**.

4. Give your new Space a name. I like to use descriptive names like Word, PDF, and HTML.

5. Next, provide a title for your space. The title will be displayed in the place of the name.

6. Fill in the description field with a useful description.

7. Select the icon you want to use for your space.

8. Click on the **Create Space** button on the right.

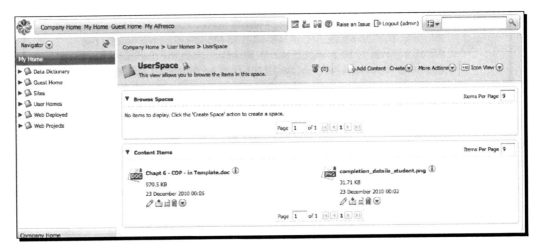

What just happened?

You have now created a space in Alfresco for the content conversion rule to store the converted content. You can use Spaces as content organizers, much like folders on your desktop. In this case, we are using it for Alfresco, but there's nothing to keep us from using it as a regular folder as well.

Time for action - adding a content rule to a space

Once you've created your space, you need to add a place to put your converted content and a content rule to tell Alfresco how to convert your content.

1. From within Alfresco Explorer, click on your newly created space.

2. Select **Create Space** from the **Create menu**. We are now going to create a space to hold the transformed files.

3. Name your new Space PDFs, add a description, and choose an icon.

4. Select **Create Space**.

5. You will now see the Word to PDF space with the new PDFs Space.

6. From the **More Actions** menu, choose **Manage Content Rules**.

7. Select the **Create Rule** button at the top of the screen.

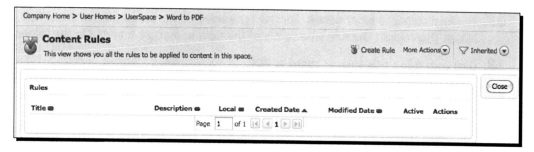

8. On the next page, you will set the conditions that will trigger the rule. For this rule, set the **Select Condition** to **Content of mimetype**. This will trigger the rule if content of a certain type is added to the space.

9. Next, select the **Set Values** and click on the **Add** button to set the file type. On the **Set Values** page, select **Microsoft Word** from the **Set Condition Values** list.

10. Click on **Ok** to save the conditions. You will then see the condition added to the rule. You can add multiple conditions to help better filter your search.

11. Click on **Next** to go to the **Actions** page.

12. From the **Select Action** menu, select **Transform and copy content**.

13. Select the **Set Values** and **Add** to set the target file type.

14. In the **Set action values** form, select **Adobe PDF** as the required format.

15. Set the transformed files destination by selecting the **Click here** to select the destination link.

16. Navigate to the PDFs space you just created. Click the green **+** to the right of the PDF folder to add it to the rule. Click on **Ok** on the **Set action values** page. Then click on **Next**.

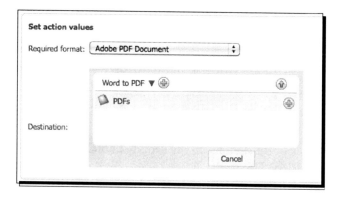

17. The final step is to enter details. For the **Type** select Items are created or enter this folder. This triggers the rule when a file of the right mimetype is added to the folder.

18. Give your rule a title such as **Word to PDF**.

19. There are three options in the **Other Options** section below. For this example, we will leave all the checkboxes blank, but it's useful to know what they mean.

20. The **Apply rule to sub spaces** will apply the rule to subfolders in the `Word to PDF` folder. So if you create a new folder, the same rule will convert any new Word files to PDF.

21. The **Run rule in background** option will run the rule as a background process and create the PDF file when it is ready. Running in the background can speed up the user interface, but may cause confusion as the PDF will not be immediately available.

22. The final option, **Disable Rule**, will allow you to turn off the rule if you need to disable it, without deleting the rule.

23. Click on **Next**.

24. The final screen shows you the rule summary. Review the summary to make sure everything looks right and click on **Finish**.

What just happened?

You have now created a rule in Alfresco that will automatically convert Word files into PDF. When a new Word file is added to the space, Alfresco will automatically make a copy and convert it to PDF. Test your new rule.

Time for action – testing your new rule

Now that you have created a rule, we should test it to make sure it is working.

1. Open the **Word to PDF** space in the Alfresco Explorer.

2. Click on the **Add Content** button in the upper-right area of the explorer.

3. Browse and find a Word file you want to convert.

4. Click on **OK**.

5. You can leave all of the options on the **Modify Content Properties** page at their defaults and click on **OK**.

6. Your Word file should now be added to the Word to PDF space. If you look in the PDF space, you should see the PDF version of the Word file.

What just happened

You have just tested your new rule for converting Word files to PDF. Moving forward, you should be able to simply add Word files to the folder and then link to the PDF version within Moodle.

Have a go hero

There are a number of conversion services available in Alfresco. You can convert a number of different Office files to a variety of formats, including PDF and HTML. You can also convert images loaded on to the system into a standard web friendly format. Try to create a new rule in Alfresco to convert images to PNG files of standard size.

Using Google Docs as a repository for Moodle

A growing number of organizations are using Google Docs as their primary office suite. Moodle allows you to add Google Docs as a repository so your course authors can link to word processing, spreadsheet, and presentation and form documents on Google Docs.

Time for action - configuring the Google Docs plugin

To use Google Docs as a repository for Moodle, we first need to configure the plugin like we did with Alfresco.

1. Login to Moodle as a site administrator.

2. From the **Site Administration** menu, select **Plugins** and then **Repositories**.

3. Select **Manage Repositories** from the **Repositories** menu.

4. Next to the Google Docs plugin, select **Enabled and Visible from the Active menu**.

5. On the **Configure Google Docs plugin** page, give the plugin a different name if you refer to Google Docs as something different in your organization.

6. Click on **Save**.

What just happened

You have now set up the Google Docs repository plugin. Each user will have access to their Google Docs account when they add content to Moodle.

Time for action - adding a Google Doc to your Moodle course

After you have configured the Google Docs plugin, you can add Google Docs to your course.

1. Login to Moodle as a user with course editing privileges.

2. Turn on the editing mode and select **File** from the **Add a resource..** menu in the course section where you want the link to appear.

3. Give the file a name. Remember the name will be the link the user selects to get the file, so be descriptive.

4. Add a description of the file.

5. In the Content section, click the **Add..** button to bring up the file browser.

6. Click the Google Docs plugin in the File Picker pop-up window.

7. The first time you access Google Docs from Moodle, you will see a login button on the screen.

8. Click the button and Moodle will take you to the Google Docs login page.

9. Login to Google Docs. Docs will now display a security warning, letting you know an external application (Moodle) is trying to access your file repository. Click on the **Grant Access** button at the bottom of the screen.

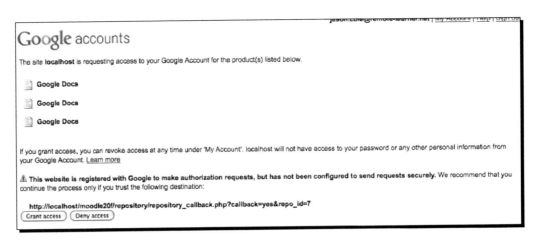

10. Now you will be taken back to the **File Picker**. Select the file you want to link to your course.

11. If you want to rename the document when it is linked to Moodle, rename it in the **Save As** text box.

12. Then edit the **Author** field if necessary and choose a copyright license.

13. Click on **Select this file**.

14. Select the other options for the file as described in *Chapter 1, Getting Started with Moodle*.

15. Click on **Save** and return to course.

What just happened

You have now added a Google Doc to your Moodle course. You can add any of the Google Doc types to your course and share them with Moodle users.

Google Docs File Formats

The Moodle Google Docs plugin makes a copy of the document in a standard office format (rtf, xls, or ppt). When you save the file, any edits to the document after you save it to Moodle will not be displayed.

Have a go hero

Try importing the other Google Docs file formats into your Moodle course and test the download.

Time for reflection

Using Alfresco or Google Docs effectively requires clear goals, planning, integration with organizational workflows, and training. If you want to link Moodle with an external content repository, how will you ensure the implementation is successful? What business processes could you automate by using one of these content services?

Exporting content to e-portfolios

Now that we've integrated Moodle with external content repositories it's time to turn our attention to exporting content from Moodle. The Moodle 2 portfolio system allows users to export Moodle content in standard formats, so they can share their work with other people outside of Moodle, or organize their work into portfolios aimed at a variety of audiences. In a corporate environment, portfolios can be used to demonstrate competency for promotion or performance measurement. They can also be used as a directory of expertise within a company, so others can find people they need for special projects.

One of the more popular open source portfolio systems is called Mahara. Mahara is a dedicated e-portfolio system for creating collections of work and then creating multiple views on those collections for specific audiences. It also includes a blogging platform, resume builder, and social networking tools. In recent versions, Mahara has begun to incorporate social networking features to enable users to find others with similar interests or specific skill sets.

To start, we'll briefly look at installing Mahara, then work through the integration of Moodle with Mahara. Once we've got the two systems talking to each other, we can look at how to export content from Moodle to Mahara and then display it in an e-portfolio.

Time for action – installing Mahara

Mahara is a PHP and MySQL application like Moodle. Mahara and Moodle share a very similar architecture, and are designed to be complementary in many respects.

You can use the same server setup we've already created for Moodle in *Chapter 1, Getting Started with Moodle*. However, we need to create a new database to house the Mahara data as well as ensure Mahara has its own space to operate.

1. Go to `http://mahara.org`. There is a Download link on the right side of the screen. Download the latest stable version (version 1.3 as of this writing). You will need version 1.3 or later to fully integrate with Moodle 2.

2. For the best results, follow the instructions on the Installing Mahara wiki page, `http://wiki.mahara.org/System_Administrator%27s_Guide/Installing_Mahara`.

3. If you are installing Mahara on the same personal machine as Moodle, be sure to put the `Mahara` folder at your web server's root level and keep it separate from Moodle. Your URL for Mahara should be similar to your URL for Moodle.

What just happened?

You have now installed Mahara on your test system. Once you have Mahara up and running on your test server, you can begin to integrate Mahara with Moodle.

Time for action – configuring the networking and SSO

To begin the process of configuring Moodle and Mahara to work together, we need to enable Moodle Networking. You will need to make sure you have `xmlrpc`, `curl`, and `openssl` installed and configured in your PHP build. Networking allows Moodle to share users and authentication with another system. In this case, we are configuring Moodle to allow Moodle users to automatically login to Mahara when they login to Moodle. This will create a more seamless experience for the users and enable them to move back and forth between the systems.

The steps to configure the Mahara portfolio plugin are as follows:

1. From the **Site administration** menu, select **Advanced features**. Find the **Networking** option and set it to **On**. Select **Save changes**.

2. The Networking option will then appear in the site admin menu. Select **Networking**, then **Manage Peers**.

3. In the **Add a new host** form, copy the URL of your Mahara site into the hostname field and then select **Mahara** as the server type.

4. Open a new window and login to your Mahara site as the site admin. Select the **Site Admin** tab.

5. On your Mahara site, select **Configure Site**. Then select **Networking**.

6. Copy the public key from the **BEGIN** tag to the **END CERTIFICATE** and paste it into the Public Key field in the Moodle networking form.

7. On the resulting page, select the **Services** tab to set up the services necessary to integrate the portfolio.

8. You will now need to configure the **SSO** services. Moodle and Mahara can make the following services available for the other system to consume.

Moodle/Mahara Services Descriptions

Remote enrollment service:

Publish: If you **Publish** the Remote Enrollment Service, Mahara admins will be able to enroll students in Moodle courses. To enable this, you must also publish to the Single Sign On Service Provider service.

Subscribe: **Subscribe** allows you to remotely enroll students in courses on the remote server. It doesn't apply in the context of Mahara.

Portfolio Services:

You must enable both Publish and Subscribe to allow users to send content to Mahara.

SSO: (Identity Provider)

If you **Publish** the SSO service, users can go from Moodle to Mahara without having to login again.

If you **Subscribe** to this service, users can go from Mahara to Moodle without having to login again.

SSO: (Service Provider)

This is the converse of Identity Provider service. If you enabled **Publish** previously, you must enable **Subscribe** here. If you enabled **Subscribe** previously, you must enable **Publish** here.

9. Click on **Save changes**.

What just happened

You have just enabled Single Sign-On between Moodle and Mahara. We are now halfway through the setup and now we can configure the Mahara to listen for Moodle users.

Have a go hero

Moodle Networking is also used to enable Moodle servers to communicate with each other. The Moodle Hub system is designed on top of Moodle networking to enable teachers to share courses with each other, and enable multiple Moodle servers to share users. How could you use this feature to spread Moodle within your organization? Could you create an internal and an external facing Moodle and have them talk to each other? Could different departments each use a Moodle and share access to courses using Moodle networking?

For your "have a go hero" activity, design a plan to use Moodle networking within your organization.

Time for action - enabling Mahara portfolio plugin

Now that you've enabled the basic Moodle networking to enable SSO, we need to enable the Mahara portfolio plugin. Like the repository system, the portfolio system is designed as a plugin architecture. Each system capable of being a portfolio system will have its own plugin. You need to enable it to make it available for users.

 The Mahara plugin is a little different than many of the portfolio plugins. You cannot activate it until you've finished the preceding networking configuration.

1. Login to Moodle as an administrator.

2. From the **Site administration** menu, select **Advanced features**. Then select the **Enable Portfolios** checkbox.

3. Then select **Plugins** and **Authentication** from the **Site administration** menu. Select the Manage Authentication page.

4. Click on the **Enable** button next to the the **MNet Authentication** plugin.

5. From the **Site administration** menu, select **Plugins** and then select **Portfolios**.

6. Select **Manage Portfolios**.

7. In the Manage portfolios page, set the **Mahara** plugin to **Enabled and Visible**.

8. You'll then be taken to the **Configure portfolio** plugin page.

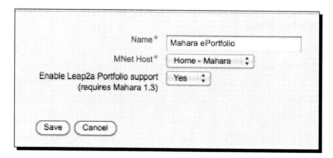

9. Begin the configuration by giving the instance of the portfolio a name. The name will be used to identify the portfolio system to users.

10. In the **MNet Host** option, choose the Mahara networking peer you created in the previous step.

11. If you have Mahara 1.3, you can enable **Leap2a Portfolio** support. Leap2a is a portfolio interoperation protocol which allows systems to easily share portfolio data. If you are using Mahara 1.3, you should enable this protocol.

12. Click on **Save**.

What just happened

You have now enabled the Mahara portfolio plugin on your Moodle site. Between the Networking configuration and the plugin, you should now have your Moodle site fully configured. Next, we need to configure Mahara to listen to Moodle.

Time for action - enabling Mahara to listen to Moodle

Once you've configured Moodle for Mahara networking, you must also enable Mahara to listen for Moodle users. There are two steps to this process. First, we need to enable networking at the site level. Then, we need to create an institution for the Moodle users in Mahara.

1. Login to Mahara as a site admin.

2. In the menu at the top of the page, click **Site administration**.

3. From the **Admin** home page, select the **Configure Site** tab. Then select the **Networking** sub-tab.

4. Set **Enable networking** to **Yes**.

5. Be very careful if you decide to enable **Auto-register all hosts**. This will allow anyone who has a Moodle site and knows the URL of your Mahara instance to connect their Moodle to your Mahara.

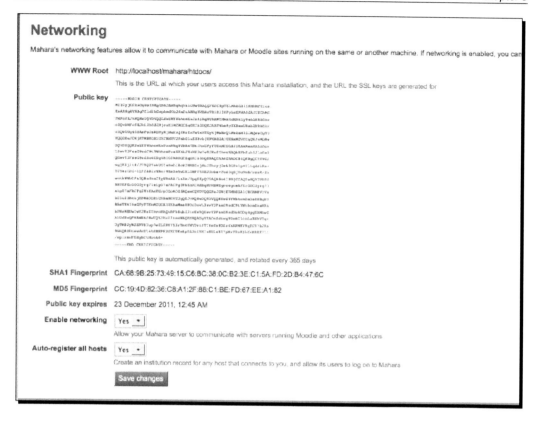

6. Click on **Save changes**.

7. Now we need to create a new institution for your Moodle site. Institutions in Mahara are like sub-sites, with their own collection of users and peer groups. To start the process, click on the **Institutions** tab.

8. From the **Administer Institutions** page, click the **Add Institution** button.

9. Set the institution name to the name of your Moodle website. Set the display name to a shorter but understandable version of the name.

10. Leave the **institution expiry** date set at **Not specified**.

11. Uncheck the **Registration allowed** button. This will disable the manual registration for this institution and force all user accounts to be created through Moodle.

12. Leave the **Default Membership Period**, **Theme**, and **Maximum User Accounts** blank.

13. Click on **Submit**. Mahara will take you to the editing screen for your new institution.

14. Now we have a base institution but we need to associate this institution with Moodle. We will use an authentication plugin to enable Mahara to communicate with Moodle. From the **Authentication plugin** menu, choose **XMLRPC – Authenticate by SSO from an external application** and click **Add**.

15. The **Add an Authority** window will pop up. The Authority we are adding is your Moodle server. The **Authority Name** should be something to help you identify the server later. Use "Moodle" or something similar.

16. Copy the base URL for your Moodle server into the **WWW root** field.

17. The **Site name** is a display field to help users identify from which site they have come to Mahara.

18. Set the **Application** menu to **Moodle**.

19. If your Moodle site is running on a different port than the standard port **80**, enter the port here.

20. If you set a **Parent authority**, users will be able to log in using that login method as well as the Moodle SSO. If you want users to directly log in to Mahara as well as come through Moodle, set this to **Internal**.

21. If you don't set the **Parent Authority**, and users have the URL for the Mahara login, then you will need to add a login error message to the text area below the parent authority. Be sure to include the link to your Moodle login with the error message.

22. The **SSO direction** sets the direction of the authentication. To enable Moodle users to login to Mahara, leave this set to **They SSO in**.

23. Set the checkbox for **Update user info on login**. This will enable Moodle to update any user profile information that may have changed between logins.

24. The **We auto-create users** enables Mahara to automatically create users who come from Moodle but don't have accounts in Mahara. You will usually want to set this to **Yes**.

25. The **We import content** option will allow your users to export content from Moodle and save it in Mahara. Check this box.

26. Click on **Submit**.

27. You will now be taken back to the **Administer Institutions** page. Click on **Submit** again.

What just happened

You have now configured Mahara to accept Moodle user logins. Once a user decides to save a forum post or an assignment from Moodle to their portfolio, Mahara will accept their authentication from Moodle and create a user account for them if they don't have one already.

Time for action - creating a Mahara portfolio

A full discussion of the features and uses of Mahara is beyond the scope of this book. There are a few titles available for a fuller coverage of Mahara's features. To get us started with Mahara and explore the Mahara/Moodle integration, we'll explore creating a simple portfolio.

Each portfolio in Mahara is called a view. You can create a view for different audiences, organizing your files and other information tailored to each group of readers. You can also set access controls on each view, providing you with the ability to share information with select groups of users.

To create a new view:

1. Login to Moodle and go to Mahara using the SSO we configured previously. (Alternatively, login to Mahara as a user).

2. Select the **My Portfolio** tab at the top of the screen. This will take you to the **My Views** sub-tab as well.

3. To create a new view, click the **Create View** button in the upper-right corner of the **My Views** area. This will take you to the **Edit Content and Layout** screen.

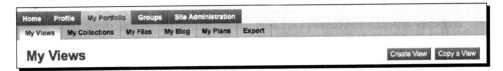

4. The **Edit Content and Layout** screen has three main sections. Below the heading are the tabs for the various view widgets which you can add to your view. Below the tabs are the widgets you can drag into the layout area. To add a widget to your view, simply drag it from the widget display box to the layout area.

5. To add content saved from Moodle, click on the **Files, images, and video** tab. To allow the user to see a single Moodle posting or other activity, drag an HTML widget to the layout. In the **Configure** pop-up window, navigate to the file from Moodle at the bottom of the screen in the **Home** files browser. Click on the **Select** button to choose the file, then click on **Save**.

6. To allow users to view all of the content from Moodle, you can add a folder to your view. Drag the **A Folder** widget into your layout. In the **Configure** pop-up, navigate to the folder with your Moodle content and click on **Select**. Click on **Save** to return to the layout view. The folder widget will list all of the files in the folder you selected.

7. Add other widgets, including any profile information or information from your resume.

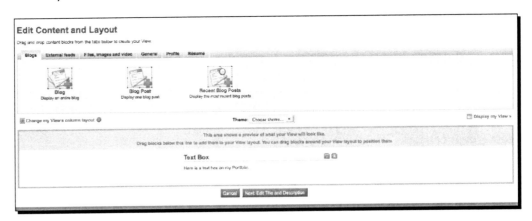

8. When you have added all of the widgets you want on your layout, click on the **Next** button.

9. On the **Edit Title and Description** screen, give your view a title. Make sure that the title is descriptive for your intended audience.

10. In the **View Description** box, provide a brief description for the view.

11. If you want to add meta tags to your view, add them to the tag's text field. Separate each tag with a comma.

12. In the **Name Display Format**, choose how you want your name to be displayed in this view.

13. Once you have finished on this screen, click on the **Next: Edit Access** button.

14. The **Edit Access** screen allows you to set a number of view options for your view. **Allow Comments** allows users to leave comments on your view. This is not a recommended option for views available to the public.

15. Checking **Moderate Comments** is recommended to ensure you can control the comments in your view.

16. **Allow Copying** will allow other users to make copies of your view, including files or folders.

17. The next section determines who can access your portfolio. To add a group, click the **Add** button next to the group name. The default groups include:

  ❏ **Public:** Allows anyone to view your profile

  ❏ **Logged in users:** Your view will be available to anyone with an account and logged into the system.

  ❏ **Friends:** Only people you have identified as **Friends** in Mahara will have access to your view.

  ❏ **Secret URL:** This option makes your portfolio visible only to people who know a special URL. While this option prevents people from randomly guessing the URL of your view, it does not provide any security.

  ❏ Overriding Start/Stop Dates allows you to set start and stop dates for views of your profile, irrespective of the level of other access you may have granted them.

18. Make your selections and click on **Save**.

19. Once you click on **Save**, you will return to the **My Views** screen. The synopsis of your new view will be listed there. If you want to share a particular view with an audience, you can copy and paste the URL from your **My Views** list and they will be able to go directly to your view.

What just happened

You have now created a view of your work in Mahara. This is the basic function of Mahara, to present views of collections of work for viewing and evaluation by others. Mahara has many more features, but they are beyond what we can cover in these pages.

Using Google Docs as a repository

While Mahara is a very well featured, dedicated e-portfolio system, it may not be suitable for all businesses. As we discussed with repositories, Google Docs may provide a simple solution for exporting content from Moodle for sharing with other audiences. For example, if someone in a community of practice has posted a solution for a problem in a forum, you may want them to export their post to Google Docs for final editing and sharing as a best practice.

Time for action - setting up the Google Docs portfolio plugin

1. Login to Moodle as an administrator.

2. From the **Site administration** menu, select **Plugins** and then select **Portfolios**.

3. Select **Manage Portfolios**.

4. In the Manage portfolios page, set the Google Docs plugin to Enabled and Visible

5. You'll then be taken to the **Configure** portfolio plugin page. Here you can rename the Google Docs portfolio plugin if you choose to.

6. Click on **Save**.

What just happened

You have now configured the Google Docs portfolio plugin for Moodle. Your users can now use Google Docs to export their Moodle activities for additional editing and sharing.

Time for Action - exporting from a forum to Google Docs

So now we have allowed users to export their materials from Moodle to Google Docs. Next let's look at how a user would take a forum post and export it to Moodle.

A word about Google Docs accounts in Moodle

Google Docs logins are stored by Moodle, the first time a user uses either the repository or the portfolio plugins. If they are already logged into Google Docs when they access these plugins for the first time, they will only see the security warning as described previously. If they have already accepted the security warning, they will be able to use the plugins without any further action on their part. You should note that Moodle will use whatever account they have logged into when they access either function the first time. So if they are logged into a personal account when they should be using their work account, they will link their Moodle Account to the wrong Google Account. As of this writing, changing that account required accessing the Moodle database.

To export a forum from Moodle to Google Docs:

1. Login to the Moodle site as a user.

2. Navigate to a course with a forum where you have permission to post.

3. Create a new discussion topic or reply to a forum posting. Click on **Save**.

4. Go back to the forum and view your posting. There will now be an **Export to portfolio** link at the bottom of the forum.

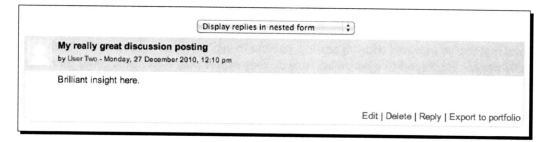

5. When you click the link, you will see the portfolio export complete page. The page will display two links. The **Return to where you were** link will take you back to the forum. The **Continue to your portfolio** link will take you to Google Docs.

6. If you export a forum posting, it will appear in your Google Docs list as an HTML page, with a single table.

7. If you are a teacher in a course, you will have the option to export the entire discussion to Google Docs. Each posting in the discussion will appear as a row in a table on the HTML page.

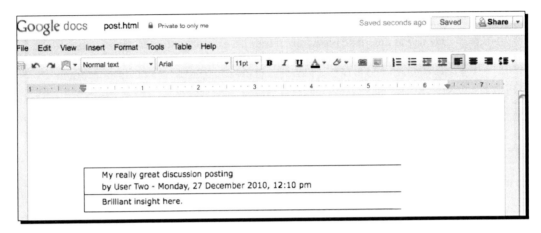

What just happened

You've just exported a forum posting from Moodle to Google Docs. While Google Docs is not a standard portfolio system, you can use it to export content from Moodle for further editing and sharing outside of the Moodle system.

Have a go hero

Now that you've exported a forum posting, its time to explore other activities. What other activities can you export to a portfolio? How do they export their data? How could your users take advantage of this additional functionality?

Time for reflection

Creating a portfolio system can enable users to demonstrate competency and share their expertise with others in the company. If you were to implement a portfolio system integrated with Moodle, how would you measure its success? How would you work to ensure people updated their portfolios with their latest work?

Case study

The Texas Association of School Boards (TASB) provides continuing education courses, on-site seminars, and regional conferences for elected school board members. In an effort to enhance the delivery mechanisms for training, TASB sought alternative modes for providing training to its members through an online Learning Management System (LMS).

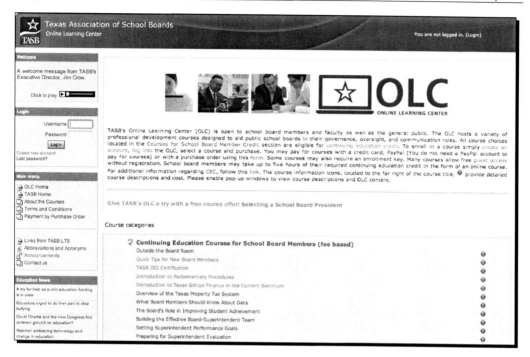

Why did you choose Moodle?

After conducting research on LMS applications with the greatest market share among organizations of size similar to TASB, we decided that Moodle met our requirements best.

The decision to implement Moodle as the LMS to house online content considered many factors: Low cost and no licensing fee, a wide range of features and flexibility, the large network of Moodle users, ability to incorporate "add-on" modules to enhance functionality, interest among other state school board associations to develop a similar solution on the same platform, and the availability of a third-party vendor (Remote-Learner) to provide hosting, site customization, and technical support.

Was the project a success?

Yes, but the Association is still challenged with growing an audience. The TASB Online Learning Center has been met with great fanfare. However, in the two years since its inception, only 10% of the user base is making use of the resources within the Online Learning Center (OLC).

What benefits did TASB and its audience realize from the adoption of Moodle?

Ease of access to timely information for our members and the ability for a school board member to view relevant content anytime, anywhere. The capacity to deliver important and up-to-date information to a large membership base quickly through our LMS system has proved quite useful.

What lessons did you learn if you had to do it again?

Production of content proved a bit more challenging than originally anticipated. Course creation within the organization requires the collaboration of many different people, subject matter experts, LMS administrators, media experts, and approval of final course materials/content by department managers. The process itself is not prohibitive, it's the time required for each party to complete required work on a course that can burden the cycle from inception to launch.

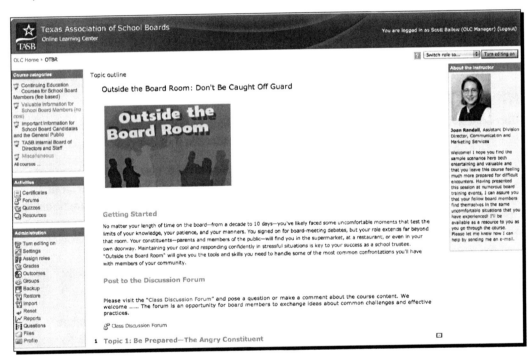

Do you have any advice for future businesses who plan to implement Moodle?

Start small. Moodle is a very big universe. Every installation of Moodle is different and each serves a unique purpose. Pay close attention to reporting needs. Student transcripts are not a native function of Moodle and might require the installation of a secondary application (JasperSoft) for thorough reporting.

Summary

We've covered a lot of fairly technical ground in this chapter. Managing repositories and portfolios requires some technical configuration, but the benefits of both systems can far outweigh the initial effort required. Once you have the systems set up, you usually don't have to worry about the configuration unless something in your system changes.

In this chapter:

- We set up Alfresco and Google Docs to act as file repositories for Moodle

- We practiced adding content to Alfresco and linking that to Moodle

- We also looked at setting up Alfresco to help automate some of the content conversion services

- We practiced setting up your Google Docs account and linking to content from Google Docs

- On the portfolio side, we practiced setting up a basic Mahara instance, as well as linking the Portfolio system to Google Docs

- We set up a Mahara view to share content from Moodle

- We exported forum content to Google Docs for editing and sharing

There is a lot more to learn about Alfresco, Mahara and integrating them with Moodle. The integrations will continue to evolve and some Moodle partners offer alternative integrations with different features sets. This is an area where we will see a lot of growth over the next few years.

Next, we will cover transitioning to Moodle by integrating Moodle with backend data systems and configuring the theme.

9
Integrating Moodle into Enterprise

We've covered a lot of different ways to use Moodle in your business, but to make the move to Moodle a success you need to integrate Moodle with your other business systems. Enabling users to use their existing corporate usernames and passwords will make it easier for them to use your Moodle solution. Automating enrollment will reduce your maintenance overhead and enable you to focus on the development of your learning solution. You will also want Moodle to have a similar look and feel to your other corporate systems. The more familiar and easy to use, the more likely it is that users will adopt the system. In this final chapter, we will cover enrollment and authentication plugins and how to customize a theme for your corporate Moodle site.

In this chapter, we shall:

- Learn about the authentication plugins available in Moodle 2.0
- Take two of the authentication plugins and provide detailed examples of how to implement them
- Learn about the standard enrollment plugins in Moodle 2.0
- Take two of the enrollment plugins and provide detailed examples of how to implement them
- Learn about the existing themes in Moodle 2.0
- Learn how to use the theme selector
- Learn how to add header and footer images to your theme

Learn how to customize the language pack.

Integrating Moodle with other business systems can improve the chances of success for any Moodle project. In this chapter, you will learn how to utilize single sign-on, automate enrollment, and how to customize your Moodle theme.

So let's get on with it...

Authentication plugins available in Moodle

So you have decided to implement Moodle for in your organization. However, how are you going to provide usernames and passwords for all of your users? Is it important to have a single sign-on for all your corporate systems? It is important to determine the answers to these questions before you go live with your Moodle website. Moodle offers several authentication plugins and before we dive into a couple examples, let's briefly cover the different authentication plugins. There are two general authentication types available to you: Internal and external. Internal authentication stores user information locally in the Moodle database. External authentication does not require the user information to be stored locally, but instead uses an external server which you may already be using for your other business systems.

Internal authentication methods

♦ Manual Accounts: This requires the site administrator to manually create all user accounts.

♦ E-mail-based self registration: This allows users to create their own accounts. A confirmation e-mail is then sent to the e-mail they used to register.

External authentication methods

♦ CAS (Central Authentication Service) server (SSO): This method uses a CAS server to authenticate a single sign-on. If CAS authenticates the username and password, then a user account is created in Moodle with the same username and password.

♦ External database: This method uses an external database to check if a username and password is valid. This can also be used to fill other user profile fields from the fields in the external database.

♦ FirstClass, IMAP, NNTP, POP3, and RADIUS servers: This method uses an external server to check if a username and password are valid. If valid, a user account with the same username and password is created in Moodle.

- LDAP server: This method uses an external LDAP server to authenticate the username and password. If valid, a user account with the same username and password is created in Moodle. This module can also use attributes from LDAP to fill other user profile fields in Moodle.

- MNet (Moodle Network) authentication: This enables the sharing of resources between Moodle websites with a single sign-on. This can be set up in your Moodle Network settings and authenticates users according to the web of trust defined in your Moodle Network settings.

- No authentication: This allows users to create their own accounts with no authentication provided by an external server and no e-mail confirmation. This option is not recommended for use due to security and administration risks.

- PAM (Pluggable Authentication Modules): This allows you to use the same Unix user database to authenticate user accounts on several different systems. You need to have the Linux PAM or SUN PAM module installed in order for this to work.

- Shibboleth: It is an open-source software that allows single sign on within an organization or across organizations. Moodle provides README instructions on how to set up Moodle with Shibboleth.

- Web services authentication: This allows an external program to authenticate users via web services. You need to have web services enabled in Moodle for this plugin to work.

If your organization uses an authentication method not mentioned in the preceding list, then consider having a custom authentication plugin developed. Moodle's pluggable architecture makes developing new plugins relatively easy.

Now that we have covered the variety of authentication methods available in Moodle 2.0, let's take two authentication plugins from the list above and go into more detail on how to implement them.

Time for action – enabling the LDAP plugin

You've decided that a single sign-on for all your internal corporate systems is imperative for the success of Moodle in your company. You know several institutions that have had success with an LDAP server and you also want the ability to import other user information into the Moodle user profile fields.

 You must have the LDAP extension for PHP installed and enabled on your server prior to enabling the LDAP plugin.

The first step is to enable the LDAP authentication plugin:

- Log in as the administrator
- Go to the **Site administration** menu
- Select **Plugins** from the menu
- Select **Authentication** and then select **Manage authentication**

You will now be on the Manage authentication page. You will see a list of available authentication plugins. To enable the LDAP server plugin, scroll down the list to the LDAP server under the **Name** column and then click on the eye to the right of LDAP server. When the eye is open, the plugin is enabled.

You will notice that once you have enabled a plugin, it moves to the top of the list with all the other enabled plugins. Next, click on the **Settings** link to the right of the LDAP server. You will be brought to the following LDAP server screen.

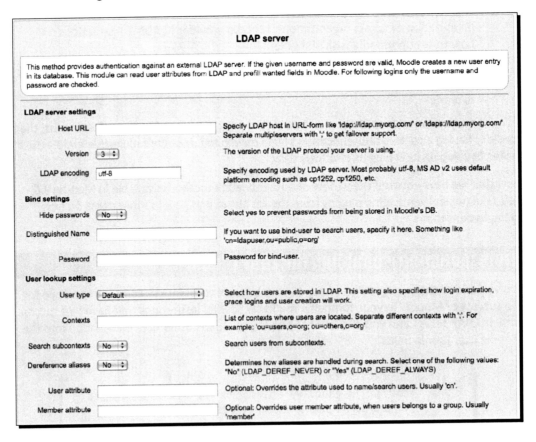

Begin by specifying the URL of your LDAP server in the **Host URL** setting. If you have multiple LDAP servers for failover, separate the URLs with a ;.

Next, select whether your LDAP server is using version 2 or 3 of the LDAP protocol from the **Version** drop down menu. The MS Active Directory supports both LDAP 2 and 3 and so does OpenLDAP (the open source Linux LDAP server).

The **LDAP encoding** setting tells Moodle how your LDAP server encodes characters. Most modern LDAP servers use utf-8. Hence, unless your system administrator tells you otherwise, leave this as the default.

The **Hide Passwords** setting will determine whether Moodle stores passwords locally, or always needs to check the user password against the LDAP server. Setting this to **No** will make your system more robust by reducing the number of round trips Moodle needs to make to log in a user. Also, if your LDAP server goes down, Moodle can use the locally stored password instead of trying to connect to the LDAP server.

The next two settings are used to set the "user" that Moodle will use to log in to the LDAP server. The **bind user** should have limited access, that is, access to only those parts of the server to which Moodle needs to authenticate users. The **Distinguished Name** is the path through the LDAP tree to the Canonical Name (CN) of the user that Moodle should use to log in.

The **Password** in the **Bind Settings** sets the password for the Moodle user.

The **User lookup settings** will determine how Moodle looks for users in your LDAP server. The first option, **User type**, is to select the schema used to store users in your system. For most OpenLDAP systems and Mac OS X, you will use the **posixAccount (rfc2307)** schema. If you are using Novell eDirectory or MS ActiveDirectory, then choose those options.

Next we need to list the LDAP **Contexts** where users for Moodle are located. You may not want everyone in your LDAP directory to have an account on Moodle, especially in the early days. For example, if your first rollout is targeted at the HR department, you may want to restrict your users to just the HR LDAP context.

The next option tells Moodle whether it should **Search sub-contexts** in the LDAP directory. If your HR department has a Benefits Office and a Hiring Office as HR sub-contexts, then you'll want to set this to **Yes** assuming that you want all of the HR users to be included.

If your LDAP schema uses alias entries, you may want to set the **Dereference aliases** option to **Yes**, to allow Moodle to follow the alias to find those users.

If your LDAP schema uses a different attribute for users other than the default CN, put it in the **User attribute** option. Usually, you will leave this blank to use the default CN.

If your LDAP schema uses a different attribute for a user's membership in a group other than the default 'member' attribute, put it in the **Member attribute** option. Usually, you will leave this blank to use the default 'member'.

You can also override the defaults to reflect how your LDAP schema handles membership. If your member attribute uses the dn attribute, leave this blank. Otherwise put in a **0** or **1** to override the dn value.

You will probably leave the **Object class** blank, unless you have a very customized LDAP setup and need to change the code used to search users on your LDAP.

Now that Moodle has searched the LDAP tree for users, we need to tell Moodle how to handle their passwords. The first option allows you to force users to change their LDAP password when they log in to Moodle the first time. Unless Moodle is the primary LDAP password management system for your users, leave this set to **No**. You usually don't want users to need to change their corporate SSO password when they log in to Moodle for the first time.

If you want to allow users to change their passwords using the Moodle interface, set the **Use standard page for changing password** to **Yes**. This will present the user with the Moodle change password page if they are either forced or choose to change their password. If you set this to **No**, you will need to set **Password-change URL** to redirect the user to your corporate "change password" page.

The next setting determines how a password is encrypted before it is sent to the LDAP server, if the user has changed their password in Moodle. MS ActiveDirectory uses plain text, but other systems use encryption to accept changed passwords.

The next field lets you set the **Password-change URL** to redirect users to change their password.

The **Expiration** settings here only work with Novell eDirectory and MS ActiveDirectory. So if you are not using one of those servers, leave this set to **No** and skip to the **Enable User Creation** settings. Otherwise, choose whether you want Moodle to check the LDAP server for password expiration.

If you set the password **Expiration** to **Yes**, set the **Expiration Warning** to tell Moodle when to warn the users that their password is about to expire.

If your LDAP schema is non-standard, set the LDAP attribute where the expiration time is stored here. Usually, you will not change this.

The next setting, **Grace logins**, is specific to Novell eDirectory, which allows a grace login. The grace login allows the user a certain number of logins after their password has expired.

Ignore the Grace login attribute. This isn't actually used in the code anywhere.

So far we've searched the LDAP for users, added them to Moodle, and told Moodle how to handle their passwords. Now we need to tell Moodle whether it can create new users in the LDAP server. In most corporate settings, you will want to leave **Create users externally** set to **No**, as the IT department will have policies and procedures for adding users to the LDAP. However, in certain cases you may want to add users to your LDAP tree if you are selling courses and want to give users access to other systems, like a portal.

If you do choose to create new users, be sure to specify a context to keep them separate from other users and keep your site secure.

The **Creators** option allows you to specify contexts and groups of users which are allowed to create new courses.

The next setting, **Remove ext user**, determines what happens when your Moodle cron runs and does a mass synchronization. If users are removed from the LDAP tree, Moodle has three options. If you leave it at **Keep internal**, Moodle will keep the user active. This would allow the user to continue to log in if the **Hide Passwords** setting is set to **No**. The second option is for Moodle to **Suspend internal**. Moodle will keep the users, but make them inactive. The user will not be able to log in, but their account will not be deleted. If the user reappears in a later LDAP sync, their account will be reactivated. The final option, **Full delete internal**, will delete the user if they do not appear in an LDAP sync. Moodle will remove them from the database and if they reappear later, they will have a new user account. The safest option here is to use the **Suspend internal** option, in case the user has been accidentally removed from the context that Moodle is searching for users.

The next four options deal with **NTLM SSO**, or Windows internal SSO. If you are using a Windows network with NTLM authentication (see `http://docs.moodle.org/en/NTLM_authentication` for details on setting up your Moodle server to use NTLM), Moodle will try to pass the user's Windows authentication to the LDAP server. So if a user logs in to his/her desktop with his/her ActiveDirectory password, the user will automatically be logged in to Moodle, if this is enabled.

The **Subnet** will restrict authentication with NTLM to certain ranges of IP addresses.

If the user has Internet Explorer, you can enable **MS IE fast path** to improve the speed of the SSO.

For most of the cases, you will leave the **Authentication Type** set to **NTLM**.

Now that we have the users, their passwords, and other details set up, we can tell Moodle how to handle the profile information stored in the LDAP server. The **Data Mapping** section lists all of the standard Moodle profile fields and allows you to map those to LDAP fields. For each Profile Field, set the corresponding LDAP field. See the image below for the data mapping settings.

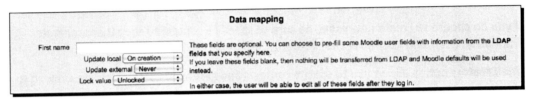

For each field, you can choose when Moodle's local data is updated with the **Update local** setting. You can set the field to update only on account creation (when the user is first added to Moodle) or you can set it to update every time the user logs in. Setting this to update on login will ensure more accurate data but will increase the load on your LDAP server and the speed of the login.

The **Update external** setting determines whether Moodle can pass data back to the LDAP. If the LDAP is the canonical source of data owned by HR and IT, you will probably want to set this to **Never**. If you want users to be able to maintain their LDAP data in Moodle, set this to **On update** and Moodle will send any changes back to the LDAP server when the user saves the change in their profile.

If you want to always maintain user profile data in Moodle as it appears in the LDAP server, set the **Lock value** to **Locked**. If the field is locked, then no one can make changes. If you have set the **Update external** to **On update**, be sure to unlock the field.

Once you have set all of your profile fields, click **Save changes**. Be sure to test your new LDAP authentication by logging in to Moodle as an LDAP user.

What just happened

We have now set up LDAP authentication so users can use their LDAP accounts to log in to Moodle. If your organization has an LDAP server, integrating Moodle with LDAP will make it easier for your users to stay engaged.

Time for action – enabling the external database plugin

Moodle's database authentication plugin allows Moodle to use a table in an external database to check a user's name and password. The external table enables you to use the usernames and passwords in an application like Peoplesoft or a portal system like Drupal. The plugin is relatively simple, but very flexible. All you need is a database table with your usernames, passwords and any profile fields you want to import into Moodle. Give Moodle access to the table (it can be read-only access to ensure the table can only be changed by your external authority) and your users can use their passwords from your other application to log in to Moodle.

To set up Moodle's database authentication plugin:

1. Login to your Moodle as an administrator.

2. From the **Site administration** menu, select **Plugins**. Then select **Authentication**.

3. You will now be on the **Manage authentication** page. You will see a list of available authentication plugins. To enable the Database server plugin, scroll down the list to **Database** under the **Name** column and then click on the eye to the right. When the eye is open, the plugin is enabled. You will now be on the settings page for **External database**. See the following figure.

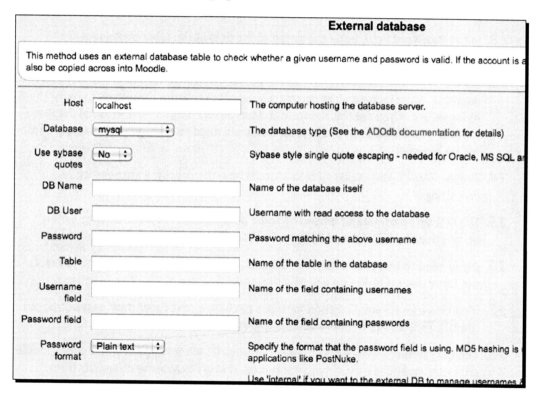

4. Now we need to configure the plugin to use the table that you have set up. Start by providing the URL for the computer hosting the database you want to use in the **Host** field.

5. Next, select the type of database hosting the table from the **Database** drop down menu. Check with your IT person and select the right database type here.

6. If your database type above is Oracle, MS SQL, or a few other types, set the **Use Sybase Quotes** to **Yes**.

7. Set **DB Name** to the name of the database with the user's table.

8. The **DB User** field should be set to the username Moodle will use to log in to the database.

9. Set the **Password** field to the password for the user in the preceding field.

10. The **Table** field stores the name of the table with the Moodle usernames and passwords in the database you set in step 4.

11. In the **Username field**, put the name of the field in the table containing the usernames.

12. In the **Password field**, enter the name of the field in the table containing the passwords for your Moodle users.

13. Set the **Password Format** option to the password storage format in the external database. Most web-services use **MD5** encryption to store passwords to make them more secure. If you set this to **Internal**, Moodle will only use the external database for user information, not passwords. Users will need to manage their password from within Moodle.

14. The `External db encoding` tells Moodle how the database encodes its text strings.

15. The **SQL setup command** is used by some databases to set the encoding. This is usually used by MS SQL and Postgre databases.

16. If you need to test your database connection later, set the `Debug ADOdb` to **Yes**. Do not leave this set to **Yes** on a production site.

17. If you have an external location for users to change or recover their passwords, put the URL for that site in the **Password-change URL** field.

18. The next setting, `Removed ext user`, determines what happens when your Moodle cron runs and does a mass synchronization. If users in Moodle disappear from the database when Moodle checks, Moodle has three options. If you leave this option at **Keep Internal**, Moodle will keep the user active. This would allow the user to continue to log in if the **Hide Passwords** setting is set to **No**. With the second option, **Suspend Internal**, Moodle will keep the users, but make them inactive. The user will not be able to log in, but their account will not be deleted. If the user reappears

in a later database synchronization, their account will be reactivated. Selecting **Full delete Internal** will delete the user if they do not appear in the database. Moodle will remove them from the database and if they reappear later, Moodle will create a new user account. The safest option here is to **Suspend Internal** in case users have been accidentally removed from the database and you need to add them back later.

19. In the **Data mapping** section, you can tell Moodle how to handle user profile information stored in the external database. For each field, you can choose when Moodle's local data is updated. You can set the field to update only on account creation (when the user is first added to Moodle) or you can set it to update every time the user logs in. Setting this to update on login will ensure more accurate data but will increase the load on your database server and the impact speed of the login.

20. The **Update external** setting determines whether Moodle can pass data back to the database table. If the table is the canonical source of data owned by HR and IT, you will probably want to set this to **Never**. If you want users to be able to maintain their data in Moodle, set this to **On Update** and Moodle will send any changes back to the database when the user saves the change in their profile.

21. If you want to always maintain user profile data in Moodle as it appears in the external table, set the **Lock Value** to **Locked**. If the field is locked, then no one can make changes. If you have set the **Update external** to **On Update**, be sure to unlock the field.

22. Once you have set all of your profile fields, click on **Save changes**. Be sure to test your new database authentication by logging in to Moodle as a user with an account in the external table.

What just happened?

You now know about the different authentication options available to you in Moodle and how to set up two of those options, LDAP and external database.

If your organization provides single sign-on through LDAP, then use the Moodle plugin to look up and confirm user login information.

The other method we explored was using an external database to confirm user login information. This is a good option if you want to integrate with a human resource management system such as PeopleSoft or a content management system such as Drupal.

Time for reflection

What other systems does your company use? Is your company currently using a human resource management system, a content management system, a project management system? After you've made a list of all the existing systems your company uses, think about which authentication method would work best for your company and then design a project plan for implementation.

Enrollment plugins available in Moodle 2.0

You've figured out how you are going to authenticate users in Moodle and have learned how to set up two authentication plugins. We now need to consider how you are going to enroll users in courses. You may choose several different methods depending on the course and the purpose of the course. In *Chapter 2, Moodle in Hiring and Interviewing* we set up a course to manage the hiring process for a new position and we enabled self-enrollment so the applicant could enroll in a course that corresponded to the position they were interested in. This is one way to enroll users in a course.

You can also enroll users in courses manually. Teachers and Moodle administrators in a course can assign users a role and thereby enroll them in the course. At the end of *Chapter 2, Moodle in Hiring and Interviewing*, you also learned how to assign roles, and so we won't bother going into that again. However, there may be some instances where you want to automate course enrollment. For example, your company's HR system includes a talent management system and you want to use this information to auto-enroll users in the appropriate training courses. Moodle has several enrollment plugins which will allow you to automate the enrollment process.

Similar to what we did previously with the authentication plugins, we will first briefly describe the enrollment plugins available and then choose two among them for more detailed examples.

Enrollment plugins

♦ Cohort sync: If you are using cohorts, then this will synchronize course enrollment with cohort members.

♦ External database: Like the database authentication plug-in, an external database can be used to look up enrollments. The database would need to contain, at a minimum, fields for a course ID and user ID.

♦ Flat file (CSV): This allows you to import user enrollment data using a specially formatted text file. The file is a comma separated file usually consisting of four or six fields.

◆ IMS Enterprise file: This allows you to import enrollment data using a specially formatted XML file. The file must follow the IMS Enterprise file format.

◆ LDAP enrollments: This allows you to manage enrollment using an external LDAP server in addition to managing authentication. The LDAP tree will need to contain groups that map to courses and entries containing unique identifiers that map to students.

◆ MNet remote enrollments: This allows remote enrollments between Moodle sites in the Moodle Network.

◆ PayPal: It allows you to set up paid courses. Students trying to enroll will be given the option to make a payment to enter. You have the option of setting a site-wide cost or individual course cost.

So let's get into some more detailed examples with the flat file and external database enrollment plugins.

Time for action – automating enrollment with flat file

Enrolling users with a flat file is the easiest way to automate enrollment. For this example we are going to assume you are the Director of Training for your company and you are responsible for making sure employees are enrolled in the appropriate compliance training. We will use the course we created in *Chapter 4* for safety training. You need to make sure that all new hires are enrolled in the safety training course. You have five new hires this week. They have already been given user accounts in Moodle, you just need to enroll them in the safety course.

The first step is to enable the flat file enrollment plugin.

1. Log in to your Moodle site as the administrator.

2. Go to the **Site Administration** menu, select **Plugins**, then select **Enrollments**.

3. From the **Enrollments** menu, select **Manage enrol plugins**.

4. From the list of Available course enrollment plugins, select the eye under the enable column next to Flat file (CSV). The open eye means it is enabled.

Click on the **Settings** link to the right of the Flat file (CSV).

What just happened

We have now enabled the flat file plugin for enrollment. Now we need to create the file to add and enroll users.

Creating an enrollment flat file

Before we edit the settings for the Flat file (CSV) plugin, we need to create the file. You will see on the settings page for Flat file (CSV) that Moodle provides you with guidelines for the formatting of your text file. See the following screenshot.

```
                        Flat file (CSV)


This method will repeatedly check for and process a specially-formatted text file in the location that you specify. The
file is a comma separated file assumed to have four or six fields per line:

  *  operation, role, idnumber(user), idnumber(course) [, starttime, endtime]
where:
  *  operation         = add | del
  *  role              = student | teacher | teacheredit
  *  idnumber(user)    = idnumber in the user table NB not id
  *  idnumber(course)  = idnumber in the course table NB not id
  *  starttime         = start time (in seconds since epoch) - optional
  *  endtime           = end time (in seconds since epoch) - optional

It could look something like this:

    add, student, 5, CF101
    add, teacher, 6, CF101
    add, teacheredit, 7, CF101
    del, student, 8, CF101
    del, student, 17, CF101
    add, student, 21, CF101, 1091115000, 1091215000
```

A flat file, or CSV file, refers to a text file with comma separated values. You can easily create a CSV file by creating an Excel file and saving it in the csv format. This saves the Excel file in a text format where each cell is separated by a comma and each row appears in its own line. I usually create my flat files in Excel or Open Office and save it as a csv file.

The flat file that you will use in Moodle for enrollments will either consist of four or six fields per line as shown in the preceding figure. The four fields you will definitely use are: Operation, role, idnumber (user), and idnumber (course). The operation field is used to add or delete a user from a course. The role field is the role you want to assign to the user in the course. The roles you can assign are mapped out on the settings page, but the three main roles you will probably be applying are student, editing teacher, and non-editing teacher. The user idnumber is a unique identifier for the user. The course idnumber is a unique identifier for the course.

The other two fields, starttime and endtime, are used when you want to restrict enrollment to a specific time period. For our example, we are going to assume that we do not require a specific time period for enrollment. Our training courses are self-paced and employees can take as long as they like to complete a training course.

Time for action – creating an enrollment flat file

So let's create our flat file to enroll the five new hires in the safety course.

1. Open up a new spreadsheet in Excel or Open Office.

2. Since this is a self-paced course, we are only going to create a four field flat file. The first column will be for the operation. The second column will be for the role you are assigning the user. Make sure you use the roles that are located in the Flat file mapping section of the Flat file settings. The third column will be for the user id number. The fourth column will be for the course id number. Do not include a header row in your spreadsheet. Only include the enrollment information.

3. The two values that can be entered in the operation column are **add**, to add a user, or **del**, to delete a user. For the first five rows under the first column, enter **add** because we are adding five new users to the course.

4. The roles that can be assigned with the flat file plugin are defined at the bottom of the settings page. We are going to keep the default role mapping in the Flat file settings page. For the first five rows under the second column, enter student because all the new hires will need to take the course as a student and will not be given access to teacher resources in the course.

5. You may have the user `idnumbers` from an external database or server, but for this example, we are going to look in the user profile field for this number. For our example I created five new users in Moodle to represent the new hires. To look up their ID numbers, we will go to the **Site administration** menu, select **Users**, then select **Accounts**. Further, select **Browse list of users**, and then select the **Edit** link next to the user. You will now see the user's profile. Scroll down toward the optional fields, to the ID number field, for the user ID number. ID number is an optional field in Moodle. For business purposes you will probably have the person's employee number in the field. Enter the five unique user ID numbers, for the users you want to enroll in the course, in the five rows under the third column.

6. To obtain the course ID number, from the **Site administration** menu, select **Courses**, and then select **Add/edit courses**. You will then see the Course categories page. Select the category your course is under, then select the edit icon next to the course. You will now be on the **Edit course settings** page. The fourth line down is the **Course ID number**. Remember **Course ID number** is not a required field, but it is one you will want to use when creating courses because it comes in handy when automating enrollment. Copy the **Course ID number** and paste it in the first five rows under column four, since we are adding all the users to the same course in our example.

7. Finally, save the spreadsheet with the title `enrollments` in CSV format. Your `enrollments.csv` file for this example should look like the following image:

```
add,student,501,12345
add,student,502,12345
add,student,503,12345
add,student,504,12345
add,student,505,12345
```

What just happened

You have now created a file to enroll users in a course with a specific role. Enrollment flat files can be created manually, or as an automated export from an HR system.

Time for action – editing flat file enrollment plugin settings

You've enabled the flat file enrollment plugin and created your enrollment flat file. Now it's time to edit the plugin settings and enroll the new hires in the safety training course.

1. Go back to the settings page for the flat file plugin. In **Site administration** menu, select **Plugins**, select **Enrollments**, select **Manage enrol plugins**, and click on **Settings** to the right of **Flat file (CSV)**.

2. The first setting is for **File location**. This is where you enter the full path to the `enrollment.csv` file on your server. I am running Moodle on my local machine so I will enter `/Applications/MAMP/htdocs/enrollments.csv` for this setting.

3. The next three settings allow you to notify students, teachers, or administrators by e-mail when they have been enrolled in a course. We are going to check the box to the right of **Notify students by email** so that the new hires know when they have been enrolled and can begin the training course.

4. The last section is **Flat file mapping**. This is where you map the role names if you want to change them. As mentioned previously, we are going to leave all the default settings.

5. Finally click on **Save Changes** at the bottom of the page. The figure below shows the Flat file settings we entered previously.

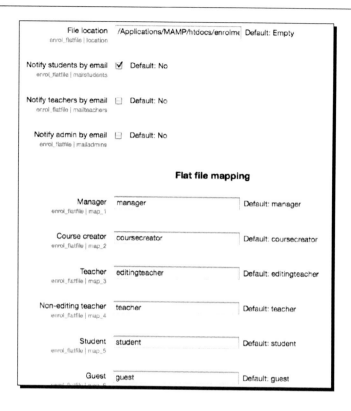

6. Finally, you need to make sure that cron is configured properly so that when Moodle's cron script runs, it will look for and run any new enrollment files in the location specified. Cron configuration is beyond the scope of this book, but your IT department will be able to set this up for you.

7. Once you have set up the enrollment, it is always a good idea to run cron manually and look at the output. This will tell you if it has successfully run the enrollment file. To run cron manually, simply go to your Moodle home page and in the URL, add **admin/cron.php** to the end of the URL, and hit enter. Have a look at the output screen. For our example, you should see text as shown in the following screenshot if it has run properly.

```
Running cron for enrol_flatfile...
Friday, 31 December 2010, 11:12 am
Flatfile enrol cron found file: /Applications/MAMP/htdocs/enrolments.csv

1: add student 501 12345 :OK
2: add student 502 12345 :OK
3: add student 503 12345 :OK
4: add student 504 12345 :OK
5: add student 505 12345 :OK
```

What just happened

We have now uploaded and tested an enrollment file to give students access to courses. If you automate the process by taking a regular CSV extract from your HR system, you can save a lot of manual work.

Time for action – automating enrollment with external database plugin

A more robust method for automating enrollments is the external database enrollment plugin. The external database enrollment plugin is similar to the external database authentication plugin, which we discussed earlier in this chapter. Moodle can use a table in an external database to assign users to courses with the proper role. You or your IT department can create the table from a number of sources, including HR, portal, or e-commerce systems. The table can be relatively simple, with just a few columns with the necessary data.

Using a database table has a few advantages over using a flat file. While the flat file is easy to create, database enrollment is usually easier to manage. Adding or removing a user can be done with a simple SQL command, instead of editing a text file. The database plugin can also create new courses if the course in the enrollment table doesn't already exist in Moodle.

To configure the database plugin:

1. Log in to Moodle as a system administrator.

2. In the **Site Administration** menu, select **Plugins** and then select **Enrollments**.

3. On the **Manage Enroll Plugins**, click on the eye icon in the **Enable** column of the **External Database** row to set the eye to "open".

4. Open the plugin settings page by clicking on the **Settings** link in the **External Database** row. You will now be on the settings page for the external database enrollment plugin. See the following figure.

You can use an external database (of nearly any kind) to control your enrolments. It is assumed your external database contains at least a field containing a course ID, and a field containing a user ID. These are compared against fields that you choose in the local course and user tables.

External database connection

Database driver
enrol_database | dbtype
[‡] Default: Empty
ADOdb database driver name, type of the external database engine.

Database host
enrol_database | dbhost
[localhost   ] Default: localhost
Type database server IP address or host name

Database user
enrol_database | dbuser
[   ] Default: Empty

Database password
enrol_database | dbpass
[   ] ☐ Unmask

Database name
enrol_database | dbname
[   ] Default: Empty

Database encoding
enrol_database | dbencoding
[utf-8   ] Default: utf-8

5. We will begin configuring the plugin by telling Moodle how to connect to the external database. Begin by selecting the database type from the **Database driver** drop-down menu.

6. In the **Database Host** field, enter the URL for the database server hosting your external database.

7. In the **Database User** field, enter the username for the user Moodle should use to log in to your external database. In the **Database Password** field, enter the password for this user.

8. The **Database Encoding** field should be set to the string encoding scheme for the database. Most modern databases use utf-8, so you can probably leave this at the default.

9. Some database systems need a special command to set up the encoding for the communication between Moodle and the database. If your system needs a command, enter the SQL statement in the **Database setup command**. If you don't know what this is, consult your IT department.

10. Oracle, MS SQL, and a few other database systems use Sybase quote escaping for handling quotes in strings (like apostrophes in names). If you are using one of these systems, check the **Use sybase quotes** box, otherwise leave it unchecked.

11. The **Debug ADOdb** option will print debug messages to help you troubleshoot your connection to the external database. Do not leave this on after you have finished debugging the connection.

12. Now that we have Moodle talking to the external database, we need to tell Moodle how to use the data in the external database. The **Local Field Mapping** section lets us select which Moodle fields we will use to match up the database to Moodle's internal systems. In each of the three settings below, we will set the field which Moodle will use to match the reference to a user, course, or role in the external database to an entity in Moodle's database. The system creating the external database will need to have access to the data we plan to use as the key. In most instances, the ID Number can be used if the external system is also used for creating users and courses.

13. The **Local Course Field** drop-down menu determines which field in the course settings we will use as the key to find the course in which the user should be enrolled. The **ID** option will match the data in your database to Moodle's internal ID number for the course (you can find this number by navigating to a course and looking at the URL. At the end of the URL, you will see `course/view.php?id=<some number>`. The number at the end of the string is Moodle's internal course ID for identifying the course). The **ID Number** option is the ID Number stored in the **ID Number** field in the course settings. This is a much more convenient field to use as you can set it when you create the course and don't have to rely on Moodle's internal ID number. As this is the default, you should probably not change it unless you have a good reason. The final option is to use the **Course Short Name** as found in the course settings page. The short name is not guaranteed to be unique, so unless you have good controls as part of the course creation process, this may not be the best option.

14. The options for matching up users in the **Local user field** are similar to the **Local course field**. **ID** is the internal Moodle id number for the user. This information will be difficult for an external system to extract from Moodle. The **ID Number**, again the default, is probably the best choice, as you can add the **ID Number** when the user is created. The user's **email** is another useful key to use as Moodle requires each user to have a unique e-mail address. Of course, your external database system will need to have the same e-mail address for the user as Moodle. The final option, **Username**, will use the user's login to match users.

15. When a user is enrolled in a course, we need to give them a role. The options for the key (using which the external database can tell Moodle which role the user should have) include—**ID**, **shortname** and **fullname**. The ID number is the number of the role. You can find the ID number by going to the role definition page and checking the URL. At the end of the URL string, you will see `roleid=<some number>`. The number at the end is the role ID. The role `shortname` and the role `fullname` both appear on the role definition page. Usually, the shortname is the best option as it tends to contain fewer special characters and it's easier to have a unique shortname.

16. The **Remote Enrollment Sync** section tells Moodle how to match up the data in the external table to the internal data we specified in the **Local Field Mapping** section. Start by entering the name of the table containing the enrollment information (in the remote database), in the **Remote user enrollment table** field.

17. The **Remote course field** tells Moodle which column the external database uses to store the course key.

18. In the **Remote user field**, set the external database field where the user key is stored.

19. The **Remote role field** determines which field Moodle will check for the role the user should have in the course.

20. If your table doesn't always specify a role, set the **Default role** to the role you want users to have, if there is no other role specified.

21. You will usually leave the **Ignore hidden courses** unchecked to allow the system to set up users in courses before they are available. It's usually a good idea to pre-populate courses before users have access.

22. The **External unenrol action** determines what Moodle will do if a user enrollment disappears from the enrollment table. The **Unenrol user from course** option will remove the user from the course. This could result in the loss of some user-data specific to the course. A better option, **Disable course enrollment**, will prevent the user from accessing the course and also ensure that the data is not deleted. The **Disable course enrollment and remove role** will disable the user's enrollment and remove their role in the course. This is useful for users whose role would otherwise enable them to ignore the disabled enrollment.

23. The final section of the configuration allows us to specify a table to create new courses. Specify the table containing the course information in the **Remote new courses table**.

24. The **New course full name field**, **New course shortname field**, and the **New course ID number field** all determine where Moodle will look for the required course information in the table.

25. The **New course category ID field** sets the category for the course when it is created. The **Default new course category** will determine the category if one is not set in the database.

26. The **New course template** allows you to use a course in Moodle as a template to be copied every time a new course is created by the database. Enter the course shortname here to enable this feature.

27. Click on **Save Changes** at the bottom of the screen.

Run the cron script as specified at the end of the **Flat file** (CSV) **Enrollment** section to test your new enrollment plugin configuration.

What just happened?

Now you know of the different enrollment options available in Moodle. You have also learned how to automate enrollment with the Flat file (CSV) and External database enrollment plugins.

Depending on where your data is coming from, you may select to use one of the enrollment plugins instead of another. Some systems may be difficult to tie directly to a database or your IT department might not be able to support the tables Moodle needs for database enrollment. In this case, you may decide the flat file enrollment plugin will suit your needs better. However, if you're using a system that supports the ability to create a table that Moodle can use for enrollment, the external database enrollment plugin is usually a more manageable and robust option.

Time for reflection

Enrollment management is one of the keys to the long-term sustainability of your Moodle solution. After the first one or two courses, manually managing enrollment across your Moodle site can become very time consuming. Planning to implement enrollment management will usually require cooperation from multiple stakeholders across your organization. Deciding how users will be assigned to courses who manage the data sources, and how they interact with Moodle are all critical decisions that need input from multiple stakeholders. For this reflection, decide who from your organization needs to be involved in these decisions, how you will gain their buy-in, and how your group will decide the best approach.

Customizing the look of your Moodle site

You've now learned how to automate authentication and enrollment, and integrate Moodle with other company systems. What about the look and feel of your Moodle site? Do you have a company logo, website header, or custom theme that you want to apply to your Moodle site to make it similar to the look of your company's other systems?

Moodle has several themes available out-of-the-box. Some of these themes have forms that allow you to customize them even more. If you have a very customized corporate theme, and nothing out-of-the-box will do, then you will want to create a custom theme.

In this section, we will cover the different themes Moodle offers, ways to customize them, and the different theme settings.

Applying one of the available existing themes

As mentioned above, Moodle offers many different themes out-of-the-box. Some of these themes also allow for a few customizations. In this section, we will cover how to apply the existing Moodle themes.

Time for action – applying standard themes

To view the existing themes offered by Moodle and apply one of them to your site, carry out the following the instructions:

1. Log in to the Moodle website as the administrator.

2. Go to the **Site administration** menu.

3. From the menu, select **Appearance**, then select **Themes**.

4. From the list select **Theme selector**. You will then be brought to the **Themes** page. You will notice that there are 16 different themes available out-of-the-box.

5. To apply one of these themes to your website, click on the button **Use for modern browsers** or **Use for old browsers** next to the theme you want to apply.

6. For our example, let's apply the **Splash** theme. Scroll down towards the bottom of the page, to the Splash theme, and click on the **Use for modern browsers** button. I'm using modern browsers so I'm not going to bother with the **Use for old browsers** button. When your screen refreshes the Splash screen will be applied. The following screenshot shows our new theme.

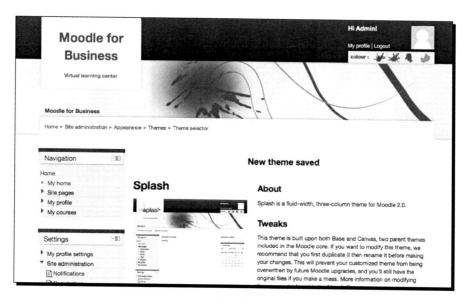

What just happened

We have now changed the look and feel of our Moodle website by applying a new theme. Now we can customize the theme through the theme customization forms.

Time for action – customizing themes with theme customization forms

Several of the themes offered by Moodle have forms that give the user options for different settings in the theme. None of the forms are the same. Different themes give you control over different settings. You will need to spend some time and explore your options. The Splash theme has a setting form for it, so let's take that as our example.

1. To view the themes with setting forms, go to the **Site administration** menu, select **Appearance**, and then select **Themes**.

2. In the menu under **Themes**, below **Theme settings** and **Theme selector**, you will see the list of the themes that offer forms which give the user a few more options to customize the theme. See the following image.

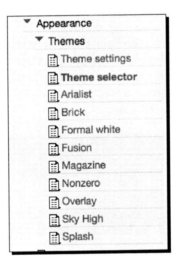

3. For our example, let's stick with the Splash theme. Select **Splash** from the menu.

4. You will now be on the Splash settings page. You will see that you have several options for customization here. You can link to a logo image, create a tagline, add a footnote, or add any custom CSS that will be added to every page.

5. Let's enter an image for the logo. First, we need to upload the logo image to the server. Then copy the URL to the image and paste it in the **Logo** area at the top of the screen. Refer to the following figure.

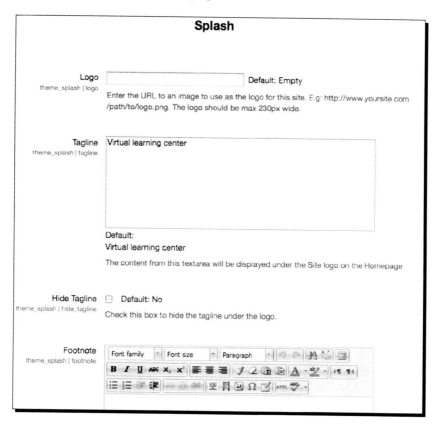

6. If you want a tagline under your logo in the header, enter that text in the **Tagline** area. The default tagline is **Virtual learning center**.

7. If you want to show the default tagline or a custom tagline, leave the checkbox next to **Hide Tagline** unchecked.

8. Next is the **Footnote**. Whatever you would like to display in the footer can be entered here. A footer might contain contact information, copyright information, or links to the privacy policy, frequently asked questions, or terms of use. For our example, we will enter a business location: 1 Main Street, Anytown, CO, USA. Don't forget any formatting you want to do to the text in the footnote also needs to be done in this box. At the top of the box are several formatting icons, and there is also an HTML editor button.

9. The last option on the form is the **Custom CSS** area. You would probably only use this if there was a minor change you wanted to make to the CSS. If you want to make several changes to the theme your best option is to copy the existing theme and create a new custom version of it.

10. After you have added all your customizations, click on the **Save changes** button located at the bottom of the page. Your changes will be applied as soon as you save the changes.

What just happened

We have now customized a base standard theme through a theme customization form. Some forms allow for a wide range of options based on the settings the developer enabled in the form.

Time for action – changing the site header

One of the most visible changes you can make to your theme is changing the header. The header appears across the top of every page and is one of the first things your users will see on your website. If you can, make your Moodle header reflect your corporate website's look and feel, it's a quick and easy way to make your Moodle solution seem more integrated into your corporate network.

Changing the header in one of the standard Moodle themes is relatively straightforward. Moodle themes are stored on the server in the Theme folder. To change the header, you will need access to the Moodle folder in your web server's root directory. Of course, if you are working on a copy of Moodle on your laptop, this is usually not an issue.

To change the site header:

1. Go to the `Moodle` folder on your web server. If you are not working directly on your laptop, you will usually need to use FTP or SSH to log into the server.

2. From the Moodle folder, select the **Theme** folder. Then select the folder with the name of the theme that you want to change.

3. If your theme uses a background image for the header, you will find it in the `pix` folder. The name of the background image can change from theme to theme. For example, the `binarius` theme's background image is called `header.gif`, while the `non-zero` theme uses `n1.gif`.

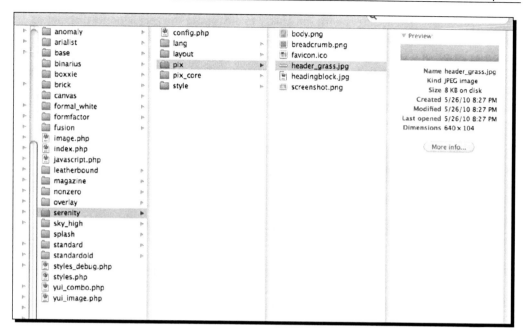

4. Beyond editing the background image, you can change the style of the header by editing the header section in the `core.css` file. All of the theme CSS files are found in the style folder in your theme.

It's as easy as that. Editing your header is one of the easiest and fastest ways to customize the look and feel of your Moodle website. Your corporation probably already has a header image for the existing corporate systems, so all you need to do is to add that to your Moodle theme.

What just happened

We have now changed the header for our Moodle website by changing the background image and header style.

Time for action – editing language strings

One of the greatest complaints that corporations have regarding Moodle, is its school centric language. With a little bit of effort, you can change Moodle from a school centric LMS to a corporate LMS.

Moodle provides administrators with the ability to customize the text Moodle displays as part of its interface. Everything Moodle displays to the user is either entered by a user or stored as a part of a language pack. This system makes it easier for translators to translate Moodle into different languages, and it also makes it easy to customize the terms Moodle uses to describe courses, activities, resources, and settings. For example, if you want to change the word from 'course' to 'community' throughout the website, you can use the language pack to change it.

Moodle provides an interface to search for labels and change them. To change a language string, have a look at the following steps:

1. Log in to Moodle as an administrator.

2. In the **Site administration** menu, select **Language**, and then select **Language Customization**.

3. On the "Language customization" page, select the language pack you would like to customize from the pick-list (refer to the following figure). If you have more than one language available on your Moodle website, choose the language you want to start customizing.

4. Once you pick a language, the **Check out strings into translator** button will appear. Click the button and Moodle will prepare the language pack for you to customize.

5. The next screen, **Filter strings**, allows you to search for the strings you would like to customize. Select one or more of the PHP files in the **Show strings of these components** menu. If you want to change every instance of a word on the website, hold down the shift key and select all of the files.

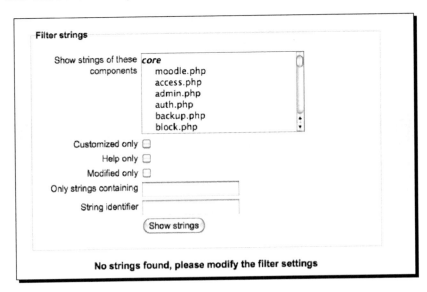

6. The next three checkboxes, **Customized only**, **Help only**, and **Modified only**, allow you to restrict the search further. If you select **Customized only**, Moodle will only display strings you have already customized. The **Help only** option will limit the results set to just the help files. **Modified only** are strings you have modified but haven't saved back to the server yet.

7. If you want to search for a specific word in the language packs, enter it into the **Only strings containing** field. For example, if you wanted to change the word "course" throughout your website, you would select all of the components in the **Show the strings of these components** list and then enter "course" in the **Only strings containing** field.

8. If you know how the string is represented in the code, you can search for that representation using the **String identifier** field. After you run your search, you can see the string identifier in the **String** column of your search results.

9. Once you have your language strings selected, you can look through the strings and make your changes in the **Local customization** field next to the string.

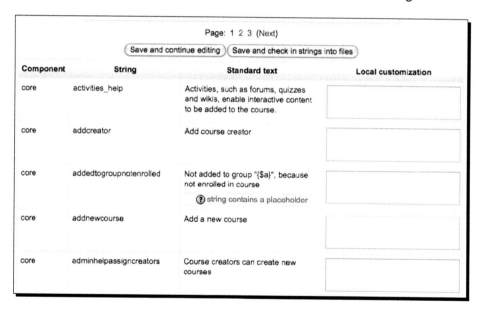

Since there are a lot of strings in Moodle, your search results will probably span several pages. As you make your changes and you want to move between pages, use the **Save and continue editing** button to save your changes. As we discussed previously, you can filter your search results and find changes that you have saved but not checked-in by selecting **Modified only** in the search options. The changes you make will not be displayed in Moodle until you check-in your changes by following the steps given here.

10. Once you have made your changes and are ready to commit them back to the server, select the **Save and check in strings to files** button.

11. Once you check in the strings, you will see a warning asking you if you want to commit your changes. Click on **Continue** to check-in your changes.

What just happened

We have now customized our Moodle's language strings to reflect our internal terminology. Changing terminology can make it easier for our users to understand the various Moodle components and roles.

Have a go hero – adding a custom footer to your Moodle site

Previously in this section, you learned how to apply a custom header to your Moodle website. How about a custom footer? Most corporate sites will have custom information in their header and footer, so go on and add a custom footer to your Moodle website.

Case study – Raiffeisen International Fund Advisory

Raiffeisen International Fund Advisory (RIFA) is the Advisory company operating in Italy for the Austrian Raiffeisen Capital Management (RCM).

RIFA had the need to create a specific "bottom-up" strategy for the retail financial market in order to involve and commit Italian Personal Financial Planners to sell Raiffeisen Capital Management investment funds.

What was the business problem(s) for which Moodle was chosen as the solution?

The strategy required approaching as many financial planners as possible all over Italy, but the RIFA Italian office could rely only on a few of their staff. RIFA needed both to create brand awareness around RCM funds and to make people understand technical and qualitative characteristics of those financial products, but it was impossible to follow Personal Financial Planners networks "physically".

What was the solution and how did they arrive at the solution?

RIFA needed an effective tool in order to communicate, share, inform, teach, and promote any useful resource to make Italian Financial planners understand the numerous advantages of RCM Investment funds and to make them able and motivated to distribute those products. RIFA understood that in the target segment there was still a lack of knowledge in the specific financial field and so decided to offer both qualified information and learning resources in order to stimulate interest and participation among potential users.

Why did they choose Moodle?

RIFA looked for a community solution which was able to support both, informative and learning purposes. It needed an easy and scalable tool which was affordable and fast to develop and which could be modified according to ongoing results. Moodle had all these characteristics and was highly personalized, also in the graphic aspects in order to meet the specific needs of the target. Moodle was not only "technical" solution managed by Austrian IT department, but a practical tool that every member of the Italian commercial staff could use according to the predefined roles. Moodle was directly chosen by the staff who had to use it and was not a top-down choice by the central Wien board.

Was the project a success?

With about two years of effective work, the Italian RIFA team reached the expected goals both in terms of user redemption and brand image awareness, getting a high level of confidence in the use of the whole system (Moodle plus other integrated tools).

Besides, the goals achieved were also in part, reflected in the commercial results of the Italian branch. They were quite good, in spite of uneasy conjunctures.

What were the benefits gained?

In order to cope with the goal, Moodle was integrated with other services: Web-conference, e-mail marketing, online rich media editing and delivering solutions, and authoring tools for multimedia content developing. A total of 25,000 potential user database was approached on weekly/monthly basis by mail, in order to inform them about RIFA activities. In this way, some thousands of financial planners logged in the RIFA Academy becoming regular users of the portal or at least visited the public area on the homepage where a lot of Moodle resources were stored.

Besides, Moodle was also used to book and manage website events, both for registered users and for external guests, wrapping up all the staff operational activities and enhancing all the results of the Italian team.

What were the lessons learned?

One of the key points of the project was the possibility to segment the audience (Salesforce) in several ways: Companies of the financial planners (potential or actual), hierarchical levels in the network of each company, specific needs of the companies, account manager of the Italian team. In this way, it was possible to create a tailored system respecting the different points of view of the users.

Do you have any advice for future businesses which plan to implement Moodle?

According to this experience, the modular approach was a key to success in the project, considering the actual fast evolution of each kind of the market. In our opinion, it is highly recommended to maintain a flexible way in order to avoid very large investments in monolithic technologies which can result in a failure simply due to fast changes in the market that can not be managed with such approaches.

Do you have any other thoughts or comments on Moodle?

Due to its huge flexibility, Moodle can be adopted for various functions inside a corporate context, especially in a modern sales force environment where formal and informal training, learning, and information merge in a complex community. This community is continuously changing and evolving through different tools and social media.

Summary

We learned a lot about integrating and customizing your Moodle website to make it more integrated with your corporate environment. We covered this last, but this does not make it the less important. Integration with the corporate environment is the key to successful Moodle adoption.

We covered several ways to integrate and customize Moodle:

- We learned how to tie Moodle with external authentication systems
- We brought enrollment data in from external systems using external flat files or databases
- We learned how to change the look and feel of Moodle by editing the theme and language strings

Case study credits

Chapter 1: OpenText

Organization	OpenText
Contact Development	Rahmat Costas, Senior Manager—Online Learning
Website	`http://www.opentext.com`
Moodle Partner	Remote-Learner
Contact	Mike Churchward, `mike@remote-learner.net`
Website	`http://www.remote-learner.net/`

Chapter 2: A&L Goodbody

Company	A&L Goodbody
Contact	Hazel Mullan, Assistant Director of Training
Website	`http://www.algoodbody.com`
Moodle Partner	Enovation Solutions Moodle Partner
Contact	Gary Mahon, gary.mahon@enovation.ie
Website	`http://www.enovation.ie/`

Chapter 3: AA Ireland

Company	AA Ireland
Contact	Mary Dempsey, Training Manager
Website	`http://www.aaireland.com`
Moodle Partner	Enovation Solutions Moodle Partner
Contact	Gary Mahon, gary.mahon@enovation.ie
Website	`http://www.enovation.ie/`

Chapter 4: Aer Lingus

Company	Aer Lingus
Contact	Davina Pratt, Director Flight Operations
Website	`http://www.aerlingus.com`
Moodle Partner	Enovation Solutions Moodle Partner
Contact	Gary Mahon, gary.mahon@enovation.ie
Website	`http://www.enovation.ie/`

Chapter 5: ISS

Company	National Health Institute (Istituto Superiore di Sanità), Rome, Italy
Contact	Donatella Barbina, Manila Bonciani, Debora Guerrera, Alfonso Mazzaccara, Ranieri Guerra. External Relations Office (Ufficio Relazioni Esterne)
Website	`http://www.issit.org/`
Moodle Partner	MediaTouch 2000 Srl
Contact	Andrea Bicciolo, `a.bicciolo@mediatouch.it`
Website	`http://www.mediatouch.it`

Chapter 5: GAC

Company	Gulf Agency Company
Contact	Damien O'Donoghue
Website	`http://www.gacacademy.com`
Moodle Partner	Human Resource Development International
Contact	Stuart Mealor, `stuart@hrdnz.com`
Website	`http://www.hrdnz.com`

Chapter 6: ADAPT

Company	ADAPT, Association for international and comparative studies
Contact	Tomaso Tiraboschi, ADAPT Researcher and e-Learning Officer
Website	`http://www.adapt.it/`
Moodle Partner	MediaTouch 2000 Srl
Contact	Andrea Bicciolo, `a.bicciolo@mediatouch.it`
Website	`http://www.mediatouch.it`

Chapter 7: Remote-Learner

Moodle Partner	Remote-Learner
Contact	Michelle Moore, Chief Learning Officer, `michelle@remote-learner.net`
Website	`http://www.remote-learner.net/`

Chapter 8: Texas Association of School Boards

Organization	Texas Association of School Boards
Contact	Scott Ballew, Online Learning Center Manager
Website	`http://www.tasb.org`
Moodle Partner	Remote-Learner
Contact	David Williams, Western Region Manager, `david@remote-learner.net`
Website	`http://www.remote-learner.net/`

Chapter 9: RIFA

Company	Raiffeisen International Fund Advisory
Website	`http://retail.rifaitalia.it`
Moodle Partner	MediaTouch 2000 Srl
Contact	Andrea Bicciolo, `a.bicciolo@mediatouch.it`
Website	`http://www.mediatouch.it`

Index

Enterprise Content Management. *See* ECM
entries
    adding, to database 101, 102
Evaluate phase 28
existing role
    privileges, editing for 191, 193
experimentation
    Moodle, installing for 11
external authentication methods, Moodle
    about 260
    external database 260
    FirstClass server 260
    IMAP server 260
    LDAP authentication plugin, enabling 261-266
    LDAP server 261
    MNet authentication 261
    NNTP server 260
    no authentication 261
    PAM 261
    POP3 server 260
    Shibboleth 261
    web services authentication 261
external database plugin
    about 260
    configuring 276-279
    enabling 266-269
    enrollment, automating with 276-279
External Relations Office (ERO) 161

F

field
    adding, to database 99-101
FirstClass server 260
flashcards
    creating 86, 118
Flat file (CSV) plugin 272
flat file enrollment plugin
    about 270
    creating 272
    enabling 271
    enrollment, automating with 271
    settings, editing 274, 276
Forrester survey 10
forums
    about 22
    creating 22-25

exporting, from Moodle to Google
    Docs 253, 254
privileges, editing in 193
RSS, enabling in 196
RSS feeds, creating from 195, 196

G

General Public License. *See* GPL
glossary
    about 90
    breaking up, into categories 88, 89
    creating 83, 84, 176-178
    random glossary entry block 86, 88
    terms, adding to 84, 85
Google Docs accounts 253
Google Docs plugin
    using, as repository 252
Google Docs portfolio plugin
    setting up 252
GPL 9
gradebook 157
gradebook reports
    viewing 157-160
Grade options section 110
grader report
    customizing 160
groupings
    about 119
    activity access, filtering 124
    creating, in course 122-124
    enabling, in course 121, 122
group mode
    enabling, in course 122
groups
    about 119
    creating 119, 121
    creating, in course 120, 121
    users, adding to 125, 126
Gulf Agency Company
    URL 293
Gulf Agency Company, case study 164-166

H

hiring manager
    about 42
    submitted resumes, screening 42, 43

HRDNZ 164
Human Resource Development International 164
human resources manager 108

I

IMAP server 260
Implement phase 27
IMS Enterprise file 271
installation, Moodle
  for experimentation 11
  on Mac 12, 13
installing
  Moodle, for experimentation 11
  Moodle, on Mac 12, 13
internal authentication methods, Moodle
  e-mail-based self registration 260
  manual accounts 260
interview process 60
interview style 60
Italian National Health Institute (NHI), case
     study 161-163

J

JBoss 10

K

K-12 schools 8

L

labels
  adding, to topics 80, 82
language strings
  editing, in Moodle site 285-288
LDAP authentication plugin
  about 261
  enabling 261-266
LDAP enrollments 271
learning ideas, Moodle 8
Learning Management System. *See* LMS
learning objectives, course 73
lesson module
  content page, creating for 113-115
  creating 108-113
  page jumps, creating 117

question page, creating for 115-117
testing 117, 118
using, as training tool 108
lesson objectives
  adding 80, 82
LMS 8, 205

M

Mac
  Moodle, installing on 12, 13
Mahara
  about 73, 140
  Moodle networking, enabling 246-249
  URL 73
Mahara Description 141
Mahara portfolio
  creating 249, 251
Mahara portfolio plugin
  enabling 246
MAMP 12, 13
manual accounts 260
Map tab 175
Measure phase 27
MNet remote enrollments 271
moderator role
  creating 188-190
Moodle
  about 7
  Adobe Connect activity, creating in 21-215
  Alfresco repository plug-in, adding to 230, 231
  assignment, creating for resumes
     submission 34, 36
  authentication plugins 260
  BigBlueButton activity, creating in 220
  chat settings 93, 94
  choice module, creating to schedule
     interviews 57-59
  communities of practice (CoPs) 169, 170
  competency tests, creating with quiz
     module 44-51
  completion tracking 126
  completion tracking, enabling on site 127, 128
  compliance training, managing 108
  connecting, with synchronous web conferencing
     systems 206
  content, adding from Alfresco 234, 235

virtual classroom applications, Moodle
Adobe Connect Pro 208, 209
BigBlueButton 217-219
VOIP 215

W

web conferencing
about 204
features 206
integration 205
products 205
web conferencing and technology
about 207
audio 207
bandwidth 207
technologies 208
video 207

web services authentication 261
wiki
about 170
adding, to community site 171-173
administering 173
creating, for community 171-173
pages, managing in 175
reversion wars, avoiding 175
wiki page
reverting 174
Wikipedia 170
WYSIWYG editor 101

X

XAMPP 12

Thank you for buying
Moodle 2.0 for Business Beginner's Guide

About Packt Publishing

Packt, pronounced 'packed', published its first book "*Mastering phpMyAdmin for Effective MySQL Management*" in April 2004 and subsequently continued to specialize in publishing highly focused books on specific technologies and solutions.

Our books and publications share the experiences of your fellow IT professionals in adapting and customizing today's systems, applications, and frameworks. Our solution based books give you the knowledge and power to customize the software and technologies you're using to get the job done. Packt books are more specific and less general than the IT books you have seen in the past. Our unique business model allows us to bring you more focused information, giving you more of what you need to know, and less of what you don't.

Packt is a modern, yet unique publishing company, which focuses on producing quality, cutting-edge books for communities of developers, administrators, and newbies alike. For more information, please visit our website: www.packtpub.com.

About Packt Open Source

In 2010, Packt launched two new brands, Packt Open Source and Packt Enterprise, in order to continue its focus on specialization. This book is part of the Packt Open Source brand, home to books published on software built around Open Source licences, and offering information to anybody from advanced developers to budding web designers. The Open Source brand also runs Packt's Open Source Royalty Scheme, by which Packt gives a royalty to each Open Source project about whose software a book is sold.

Writing for Packt

We welcome all inquiries from people who are interested in authoring. Book proposals should be sent to author@packtpub.com. If your book idea is still at an early stage and you would like to discuss it first before writing a formal book proposal, contact us; one of our commissioning editors will get in touch with you.

We're not just looking for published authors; if you have strong technical skills but no writing experience, our experienced editors can help you develop a writing career, or simply get some additional reward for your expertise.

Moodle 2.0 First Look

ISBN: 978-1-849511-94-0   Paperback: 272 pages

Discover what's new in Moodle 2.0, how the new features work, and how it will impact you

1. Get an insight into the new features of Moodle 2.0

2. Discover the benefits of brand new additions such as Comments and Conditional Activities

3. Master the changes in administration with Moodle 2.0

Moodle 1.9 Teaching Techniques

ISBN: 978-1-849510-06-6   Paperback: 216 pages

Creative ways to build powerful and effective online courses

1. Motivate students from all backgrounds, generations, and learning styles

2. When and how to apply the different learning solutions with workarounds, providing alternative solutions

3. Easy-to-follow, step-by-step instructions with screenshots and examples for Moodle's powerful features

Please check **www.PacktPub.com** for information on our titles

Lightning Source UK Ltd.
Milton Keynes UK
175740UK00003BA/26/P

9 781849 514200